How to Create
101
Fun Things

Sanjoli Mahajan

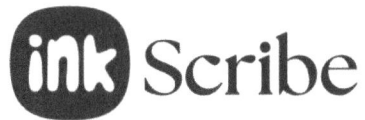

How to Create 101 Fun Things

Copyright © 2025 Sanjoli Mahajan

Publisher: Inkscribe Media Pvt. Ltd
ISBN Number: 978-1-966421-20-7

ABOUT THE BOOK

How to Create 101 Fun Things is a charming and beginner-friendly drawing guide that brings cuteness to life, one doodle at a time. Designed for aspiring artists, stationery lovers, and anyone who enjoys playful creativity, this book teaches you how to draw 101 unique and adorable things—from smiling fruits and cozy animals to tiny everyday objects

With clear step-by-step instructions and plenty of space to practice, each page is crafted to make drawing feel fun, stress-free, and totally doable—even if you think you "can't draw." The illustrations are designed in a kawaii-inspired style, making it perfect for bullet journals, planners, greeting cards, or just to brighten your day.

Whether you're picking up a pen for the first time or looking to refresh your sketchbook with fresh ideas, How to Create 101 Cute Things will help you unlock your creativity and fill your world with Fun.

HELLO, LITTLE
EXPLORER

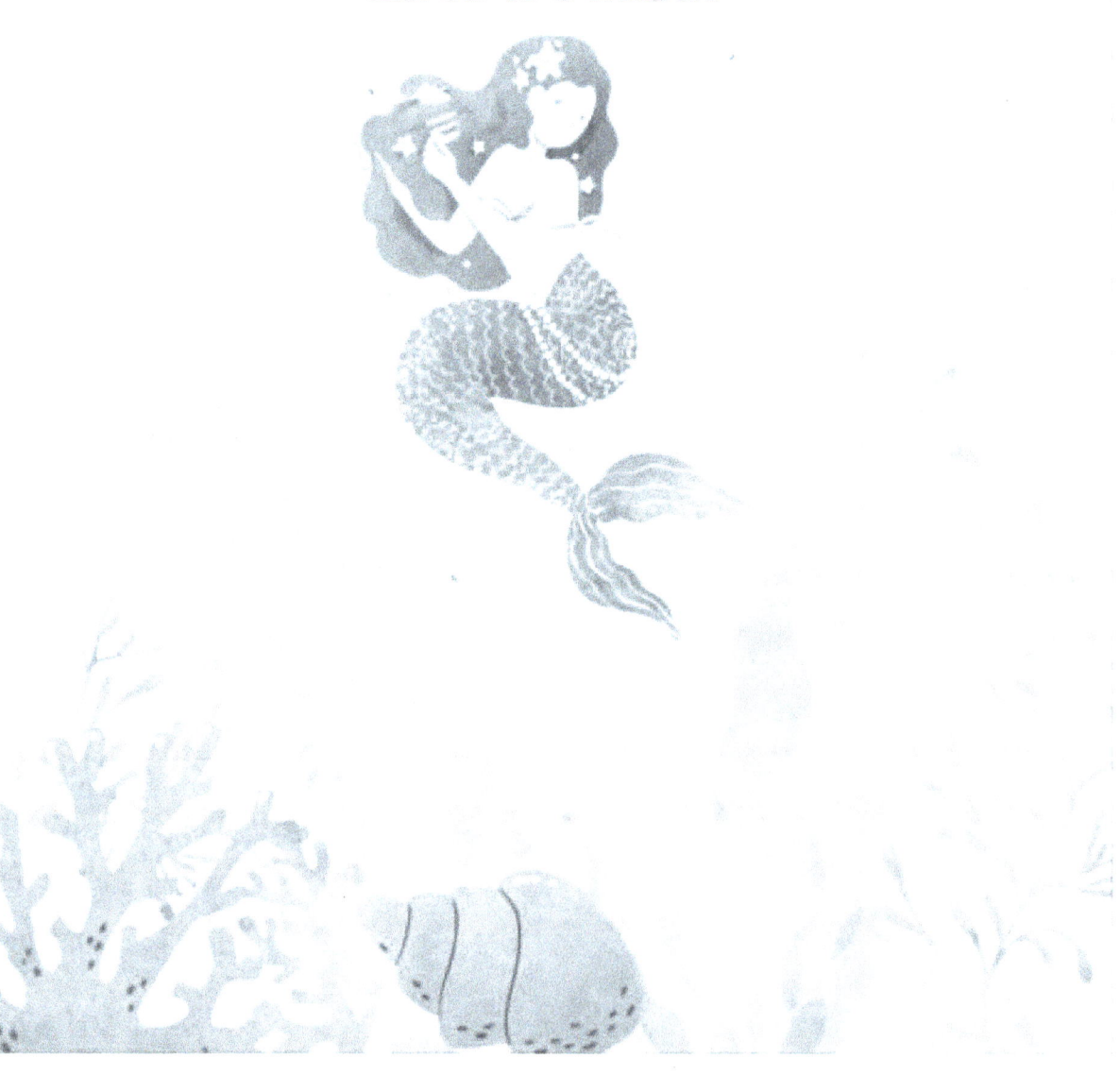

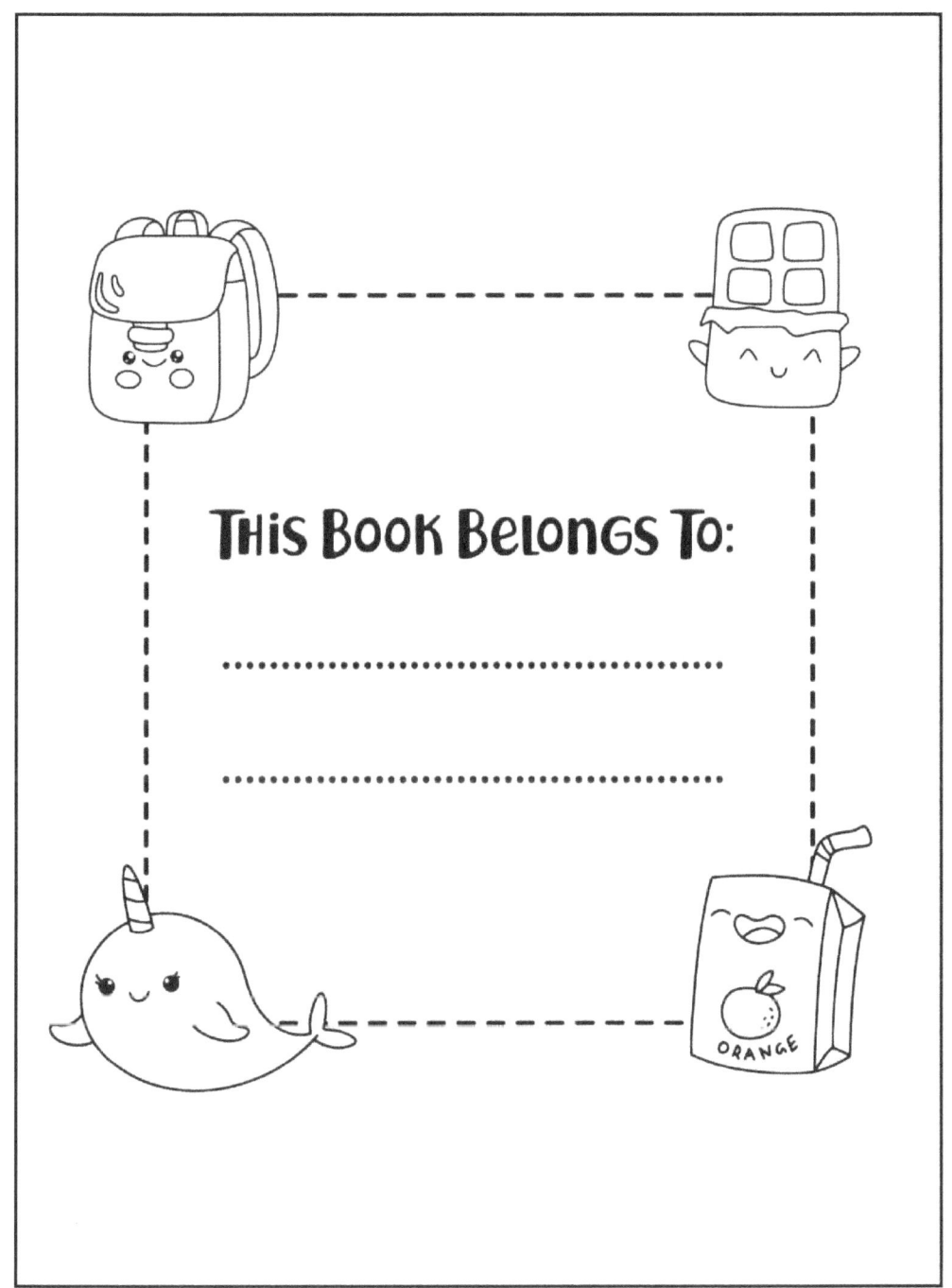

This Book Belongs To:

....

....

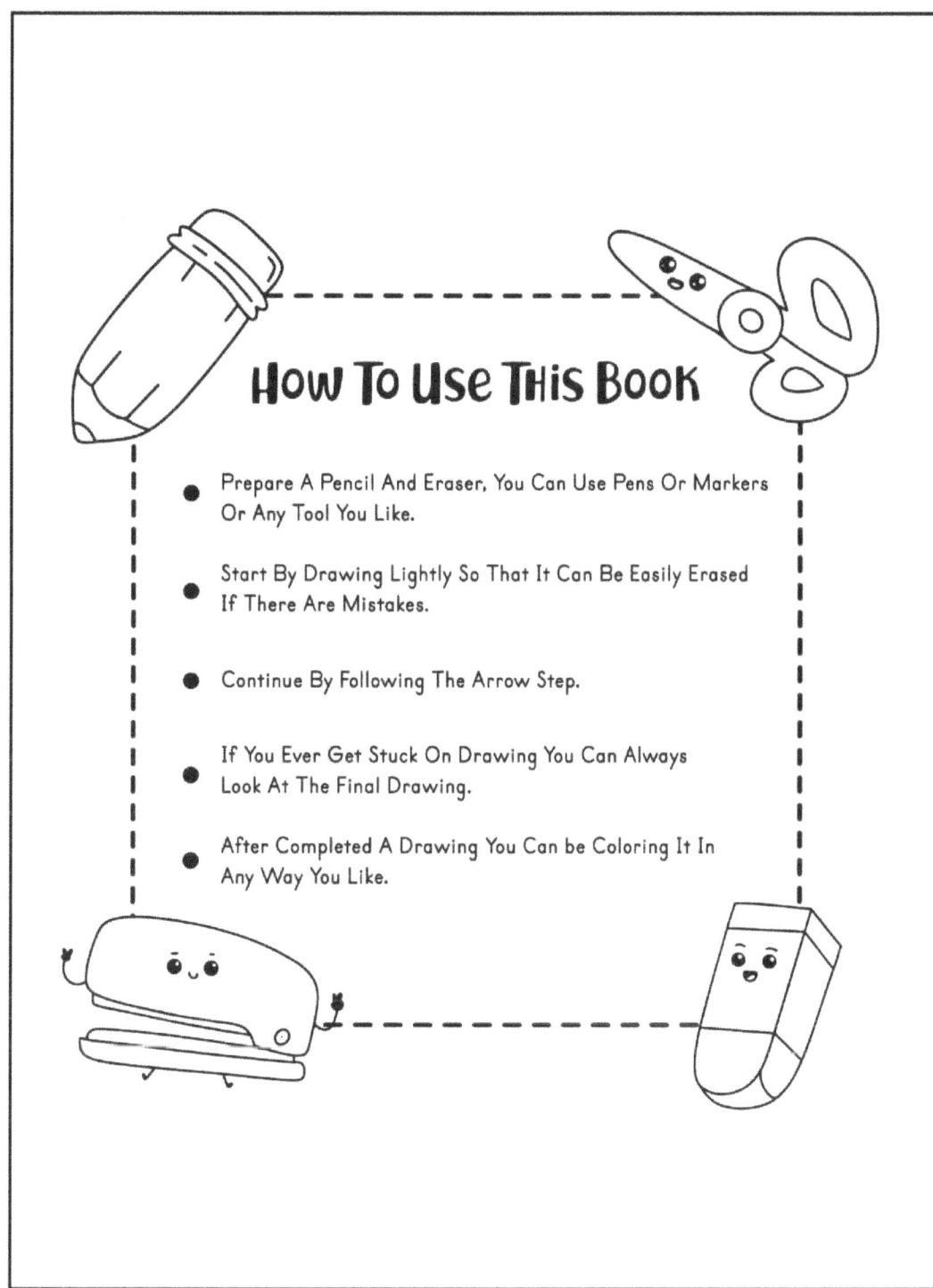

How To Use This Book

- Prepare A Pencil And Eraser, You Can Use Pens Or Markers Or Any Tool You Like.

- Start By Drawing Lightly So That It Can Be Easily Erased If There Are Mistakes.

- Continue By Following The Arrow Step.

- If You Ever Get Stuck On Drawing You Can Always Look At The Final Drawing.

- After Completed A Drawing You Can be Coloring It In Any Way You Like.

WHAT'S INSIDE

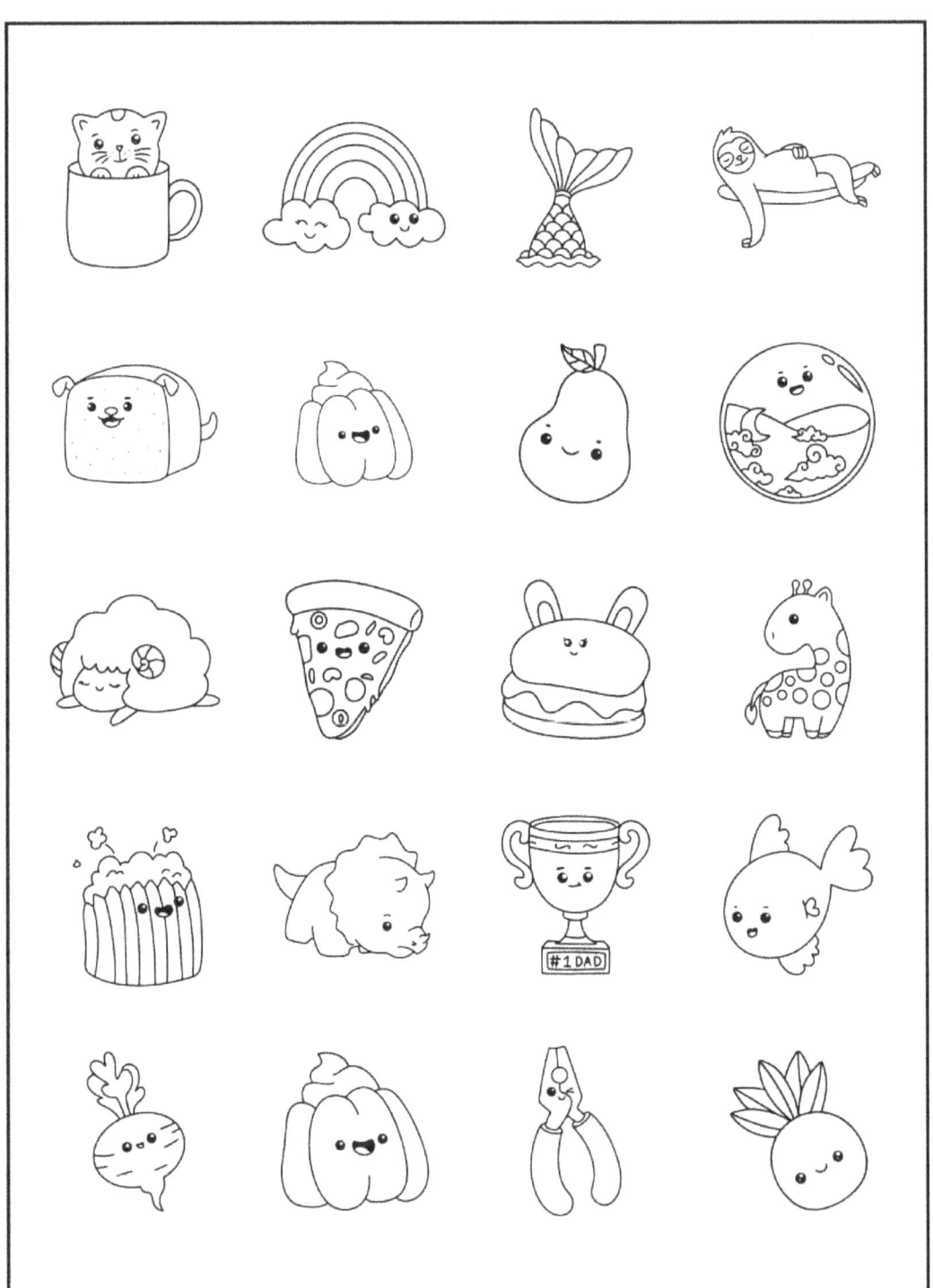

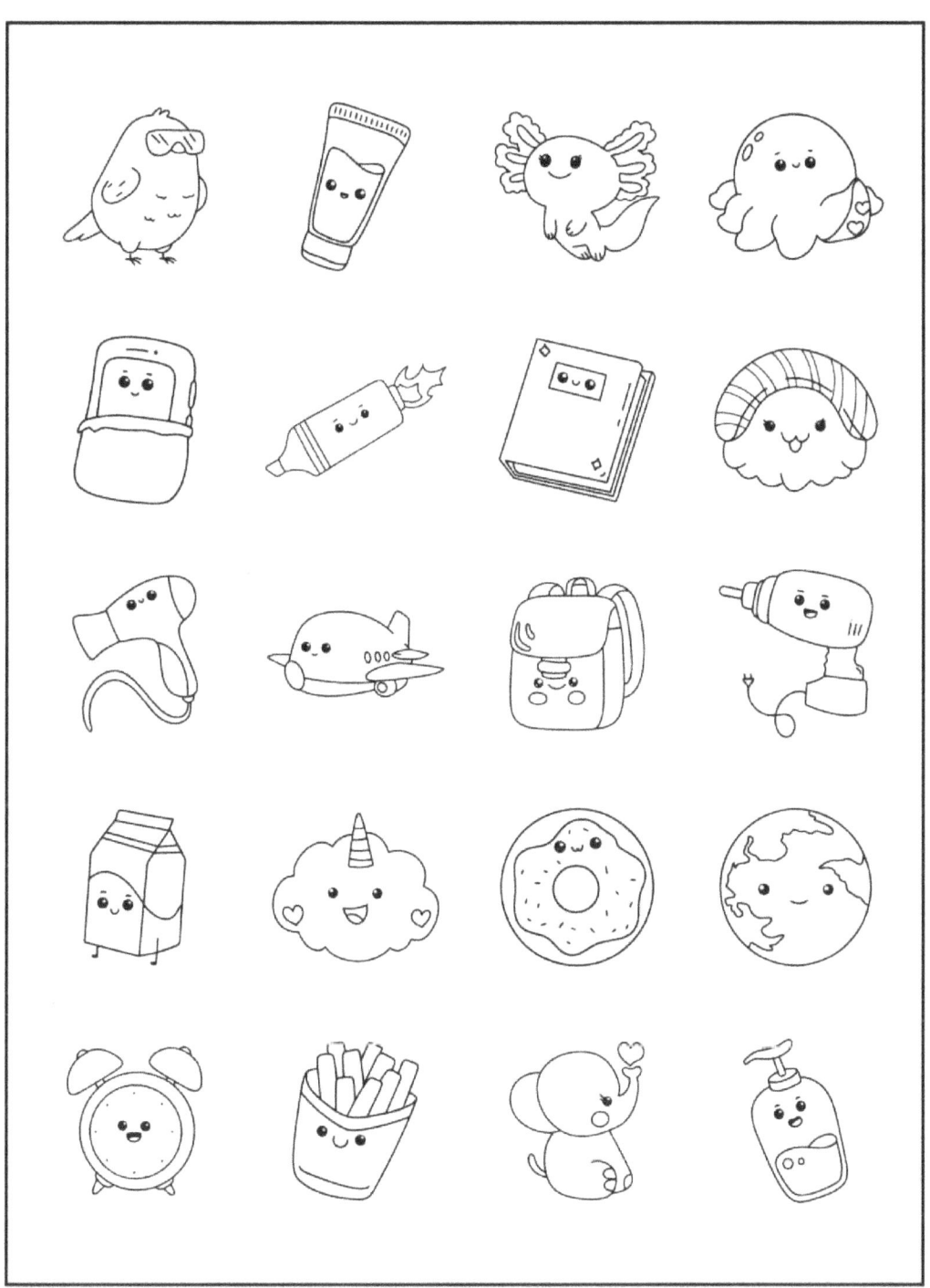

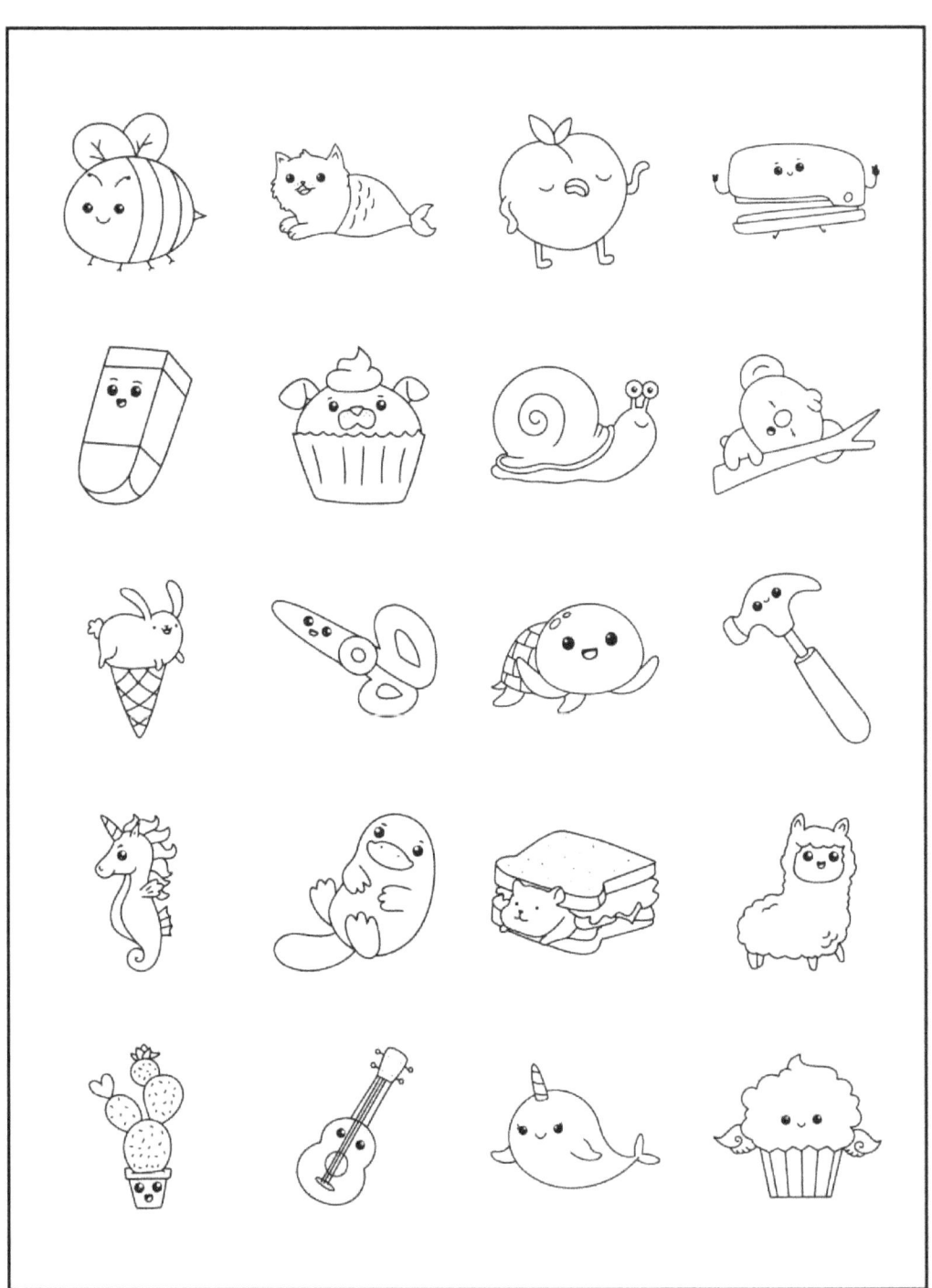

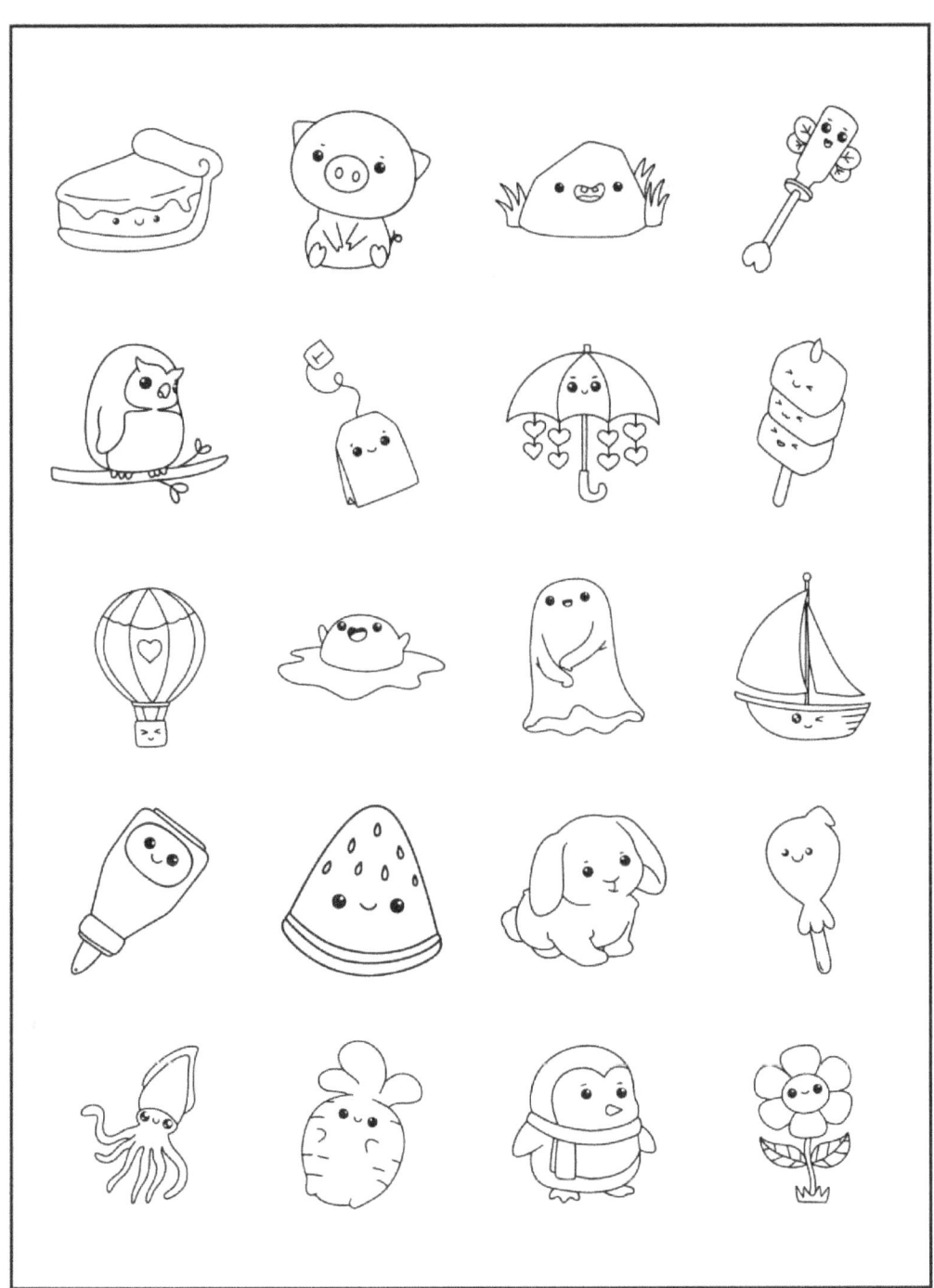

ELEPHANT

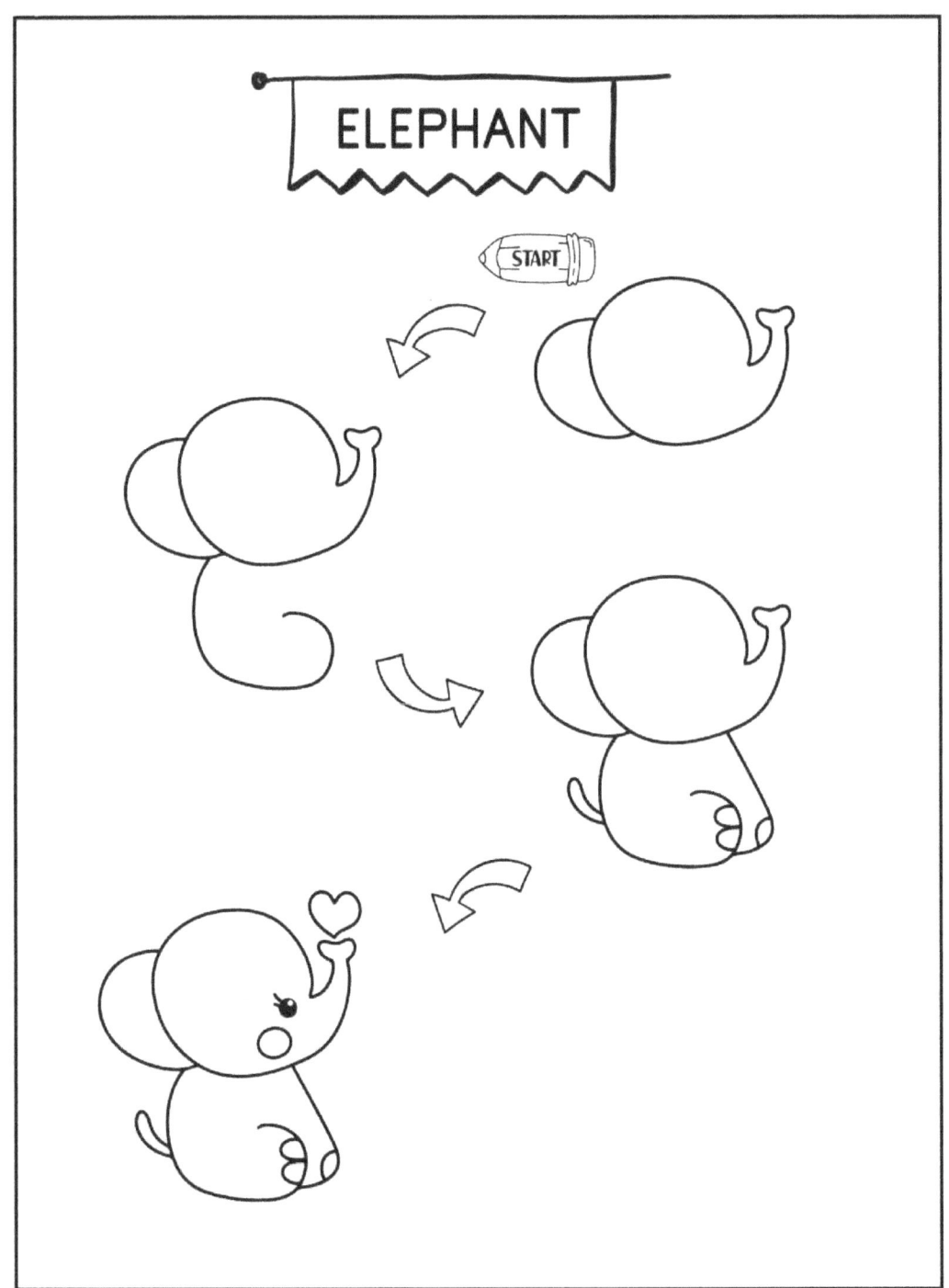

CUPCAKE

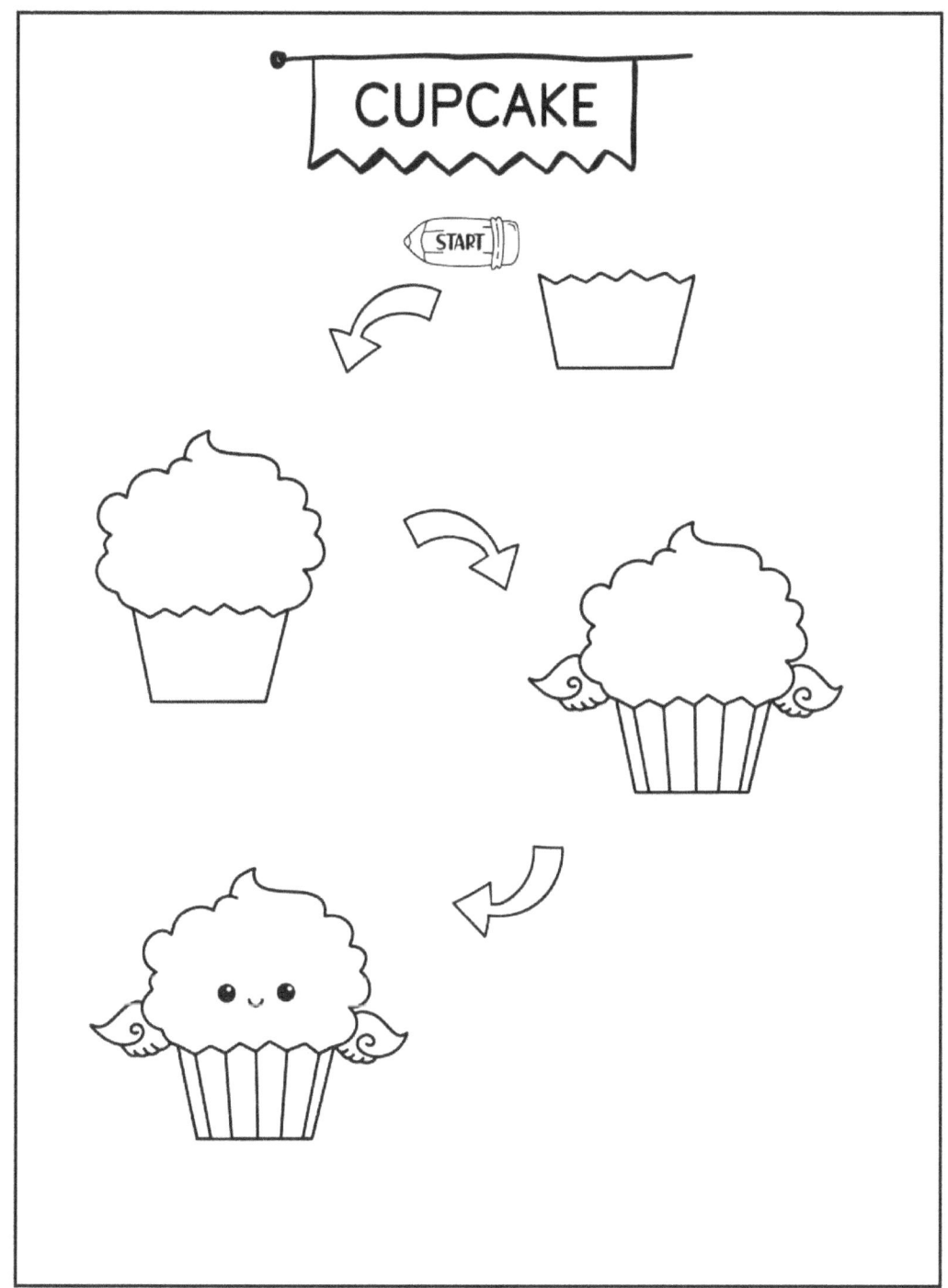

AXOLOTL

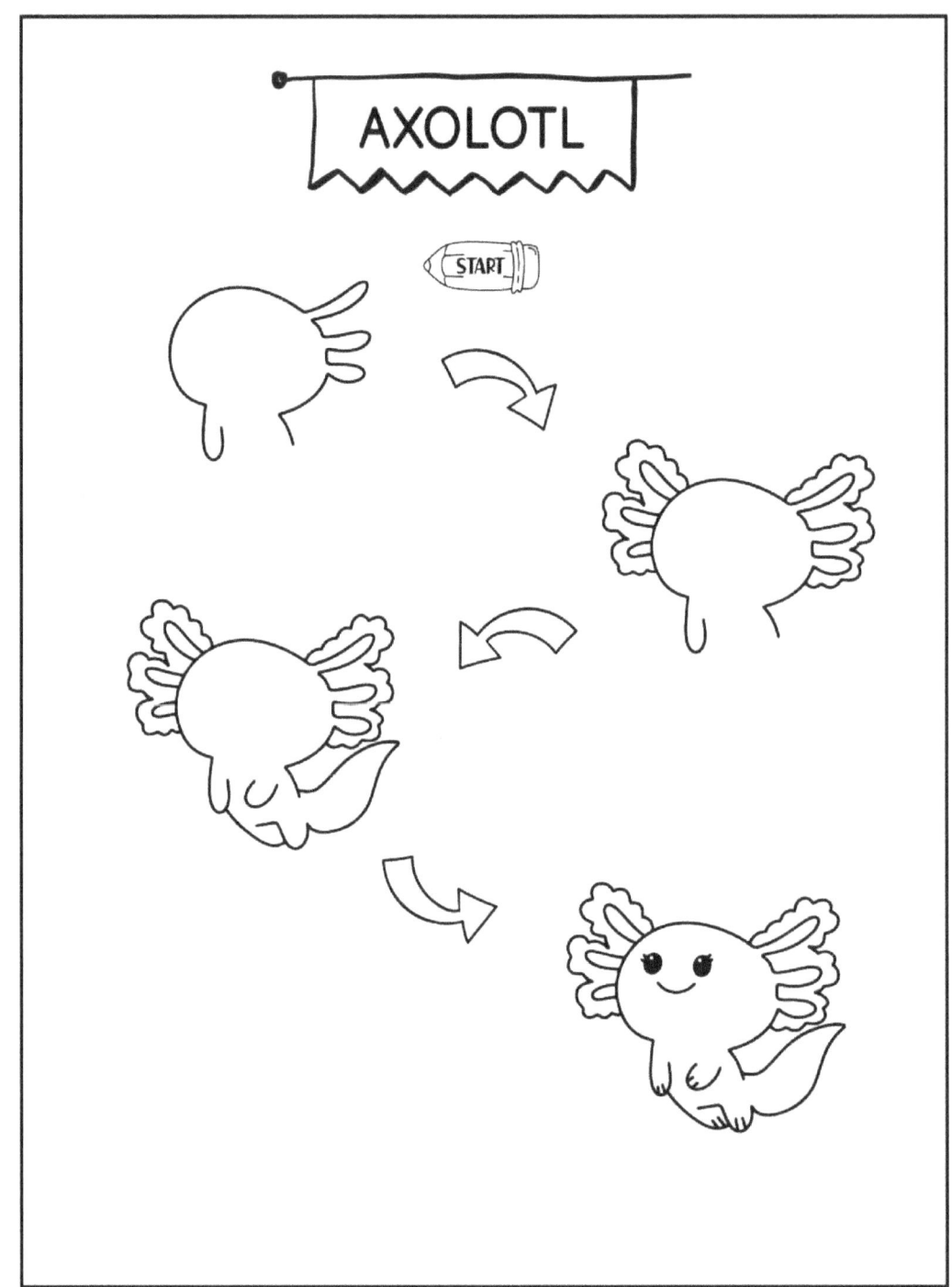

START

AVOCADO

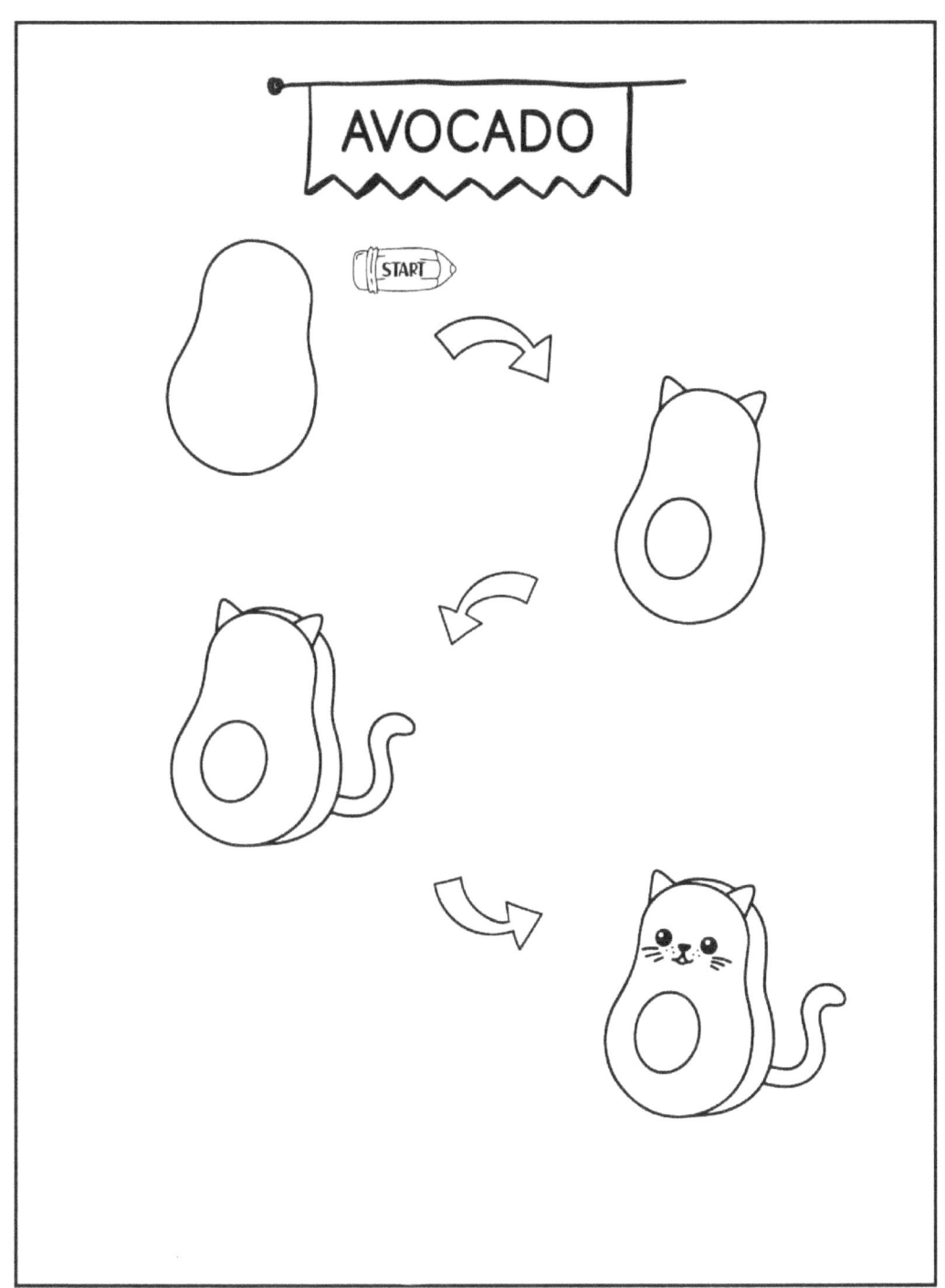

BUTTERFLY

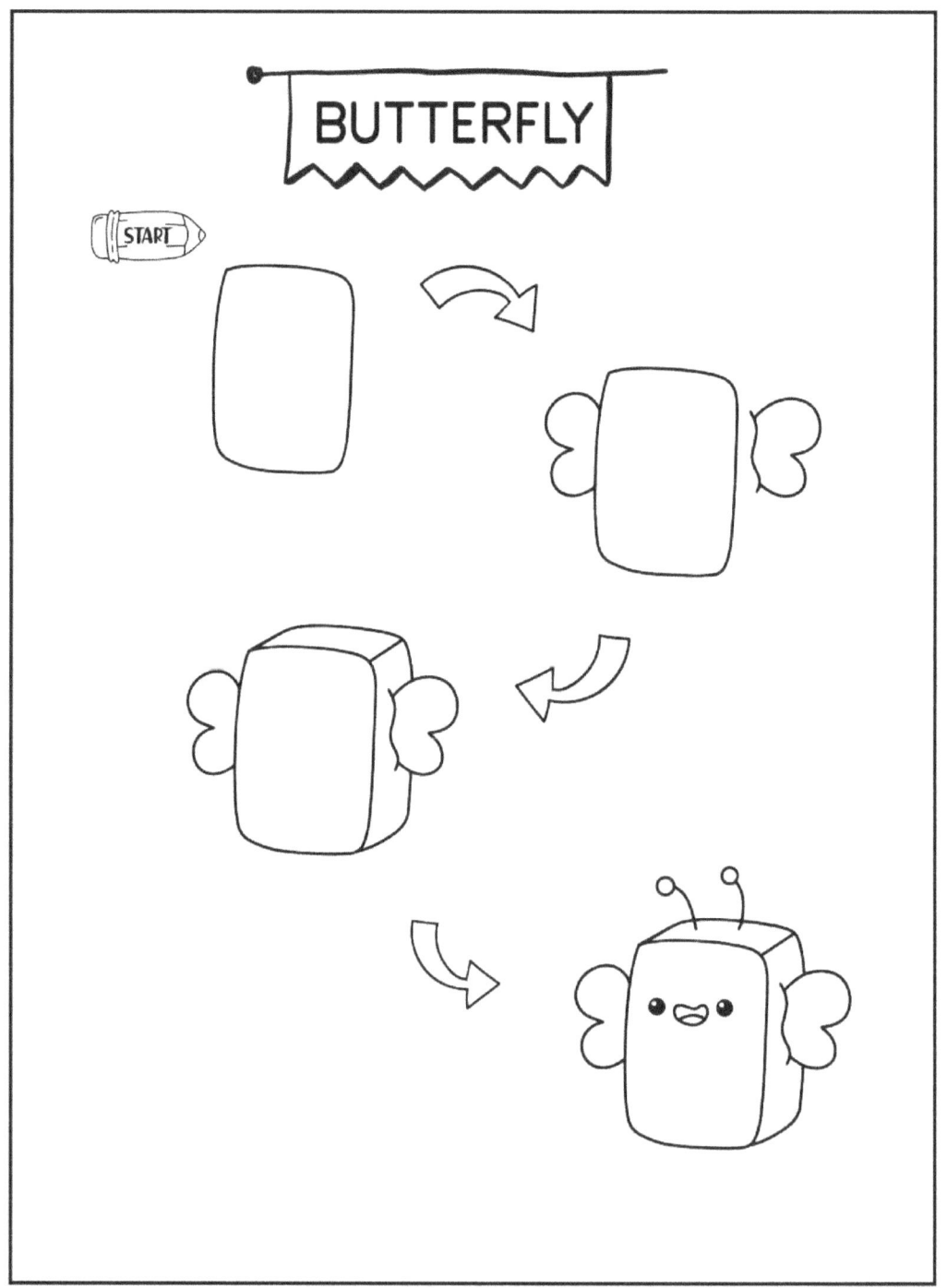

ALOE VERA

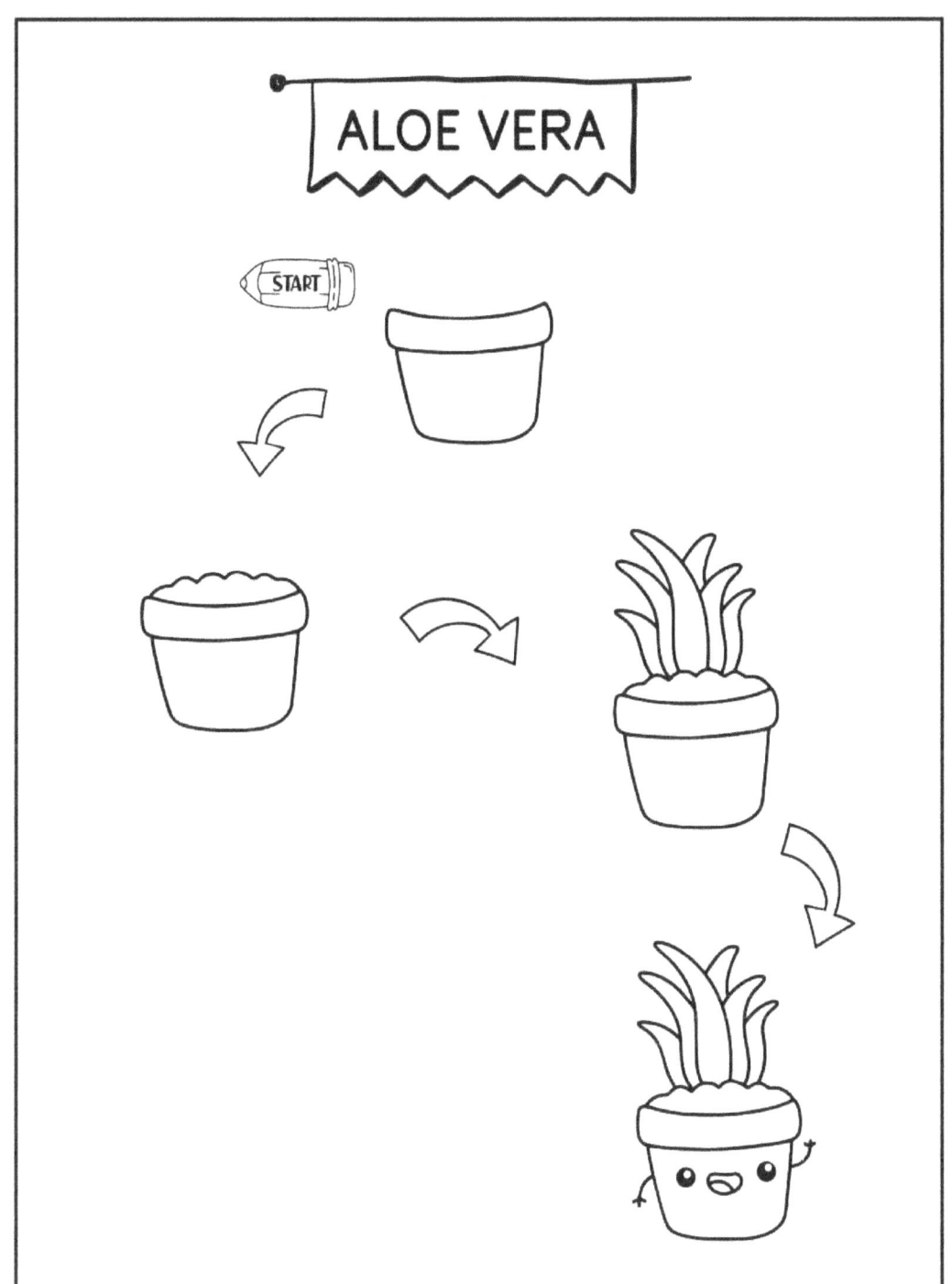

DINOSAUR

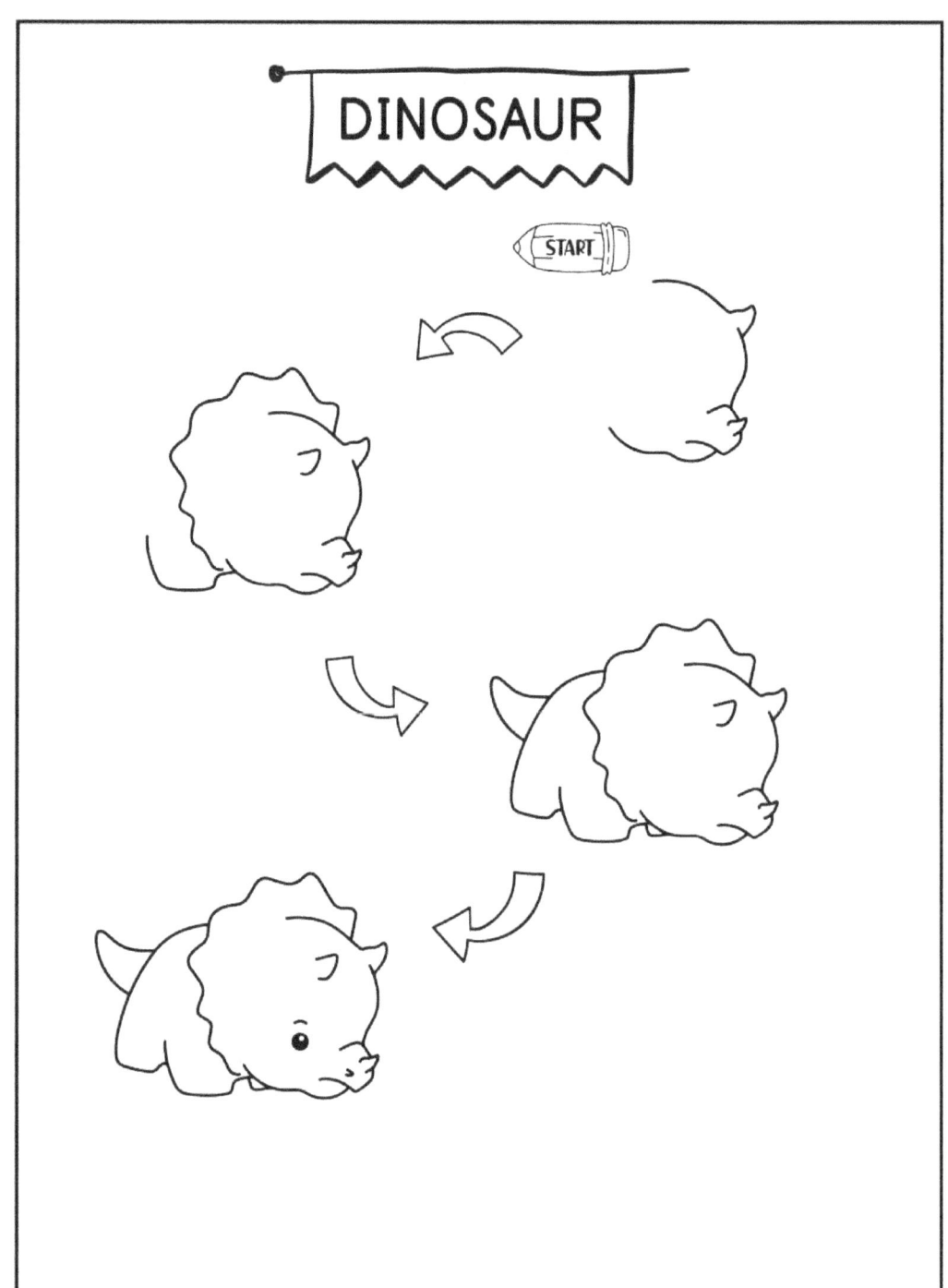

BANANA

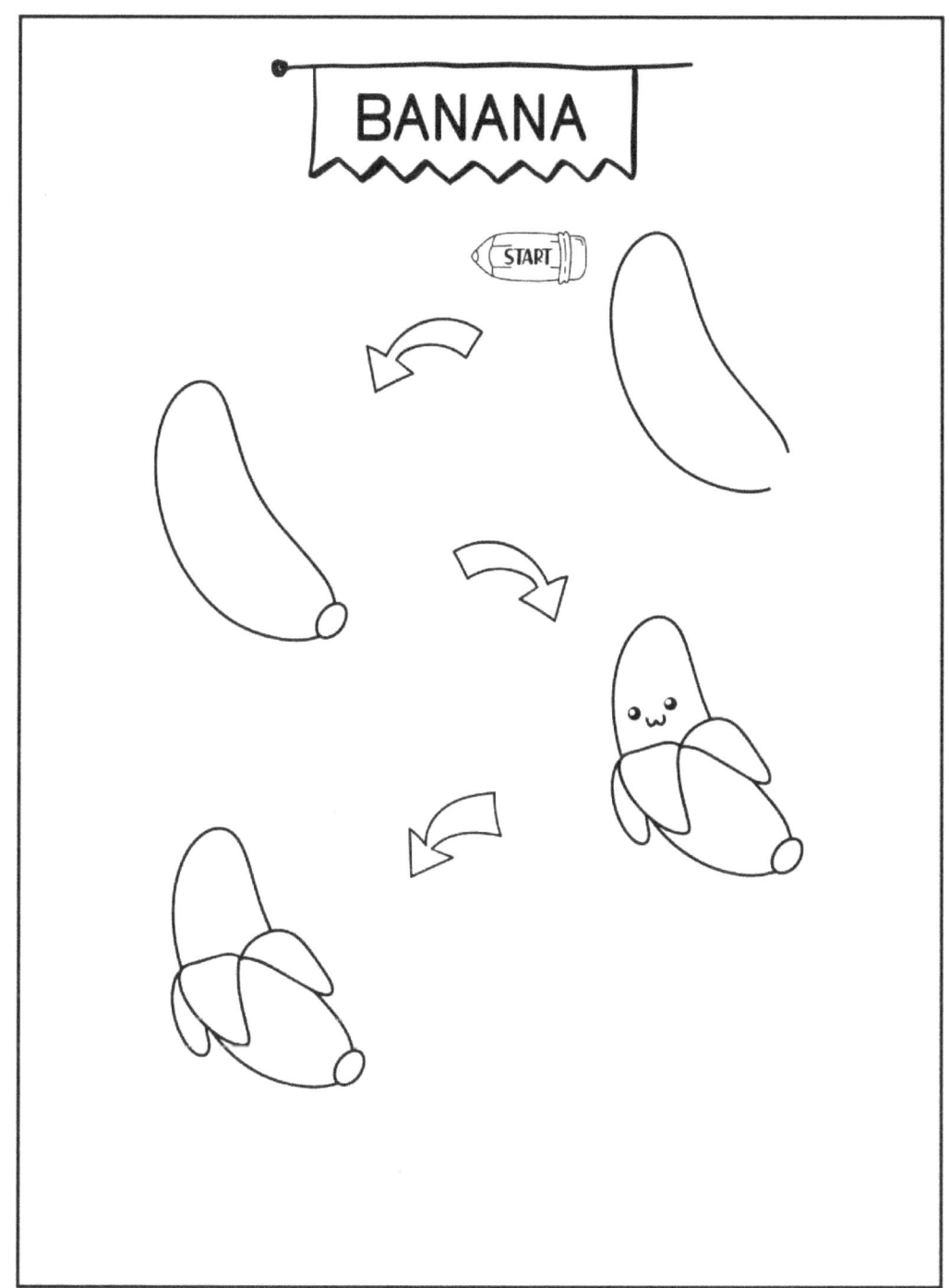

NARWHAL

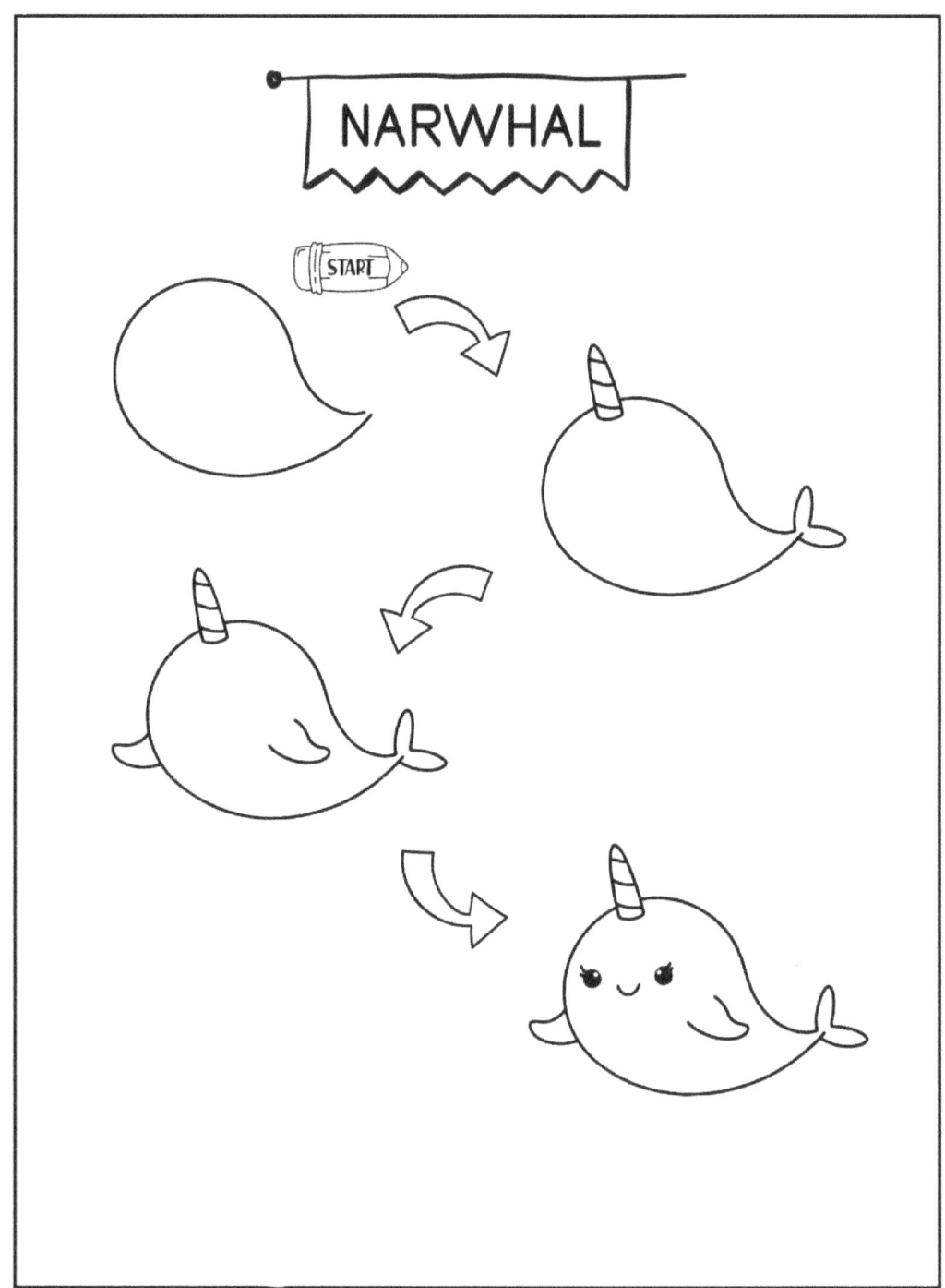

POPCORN

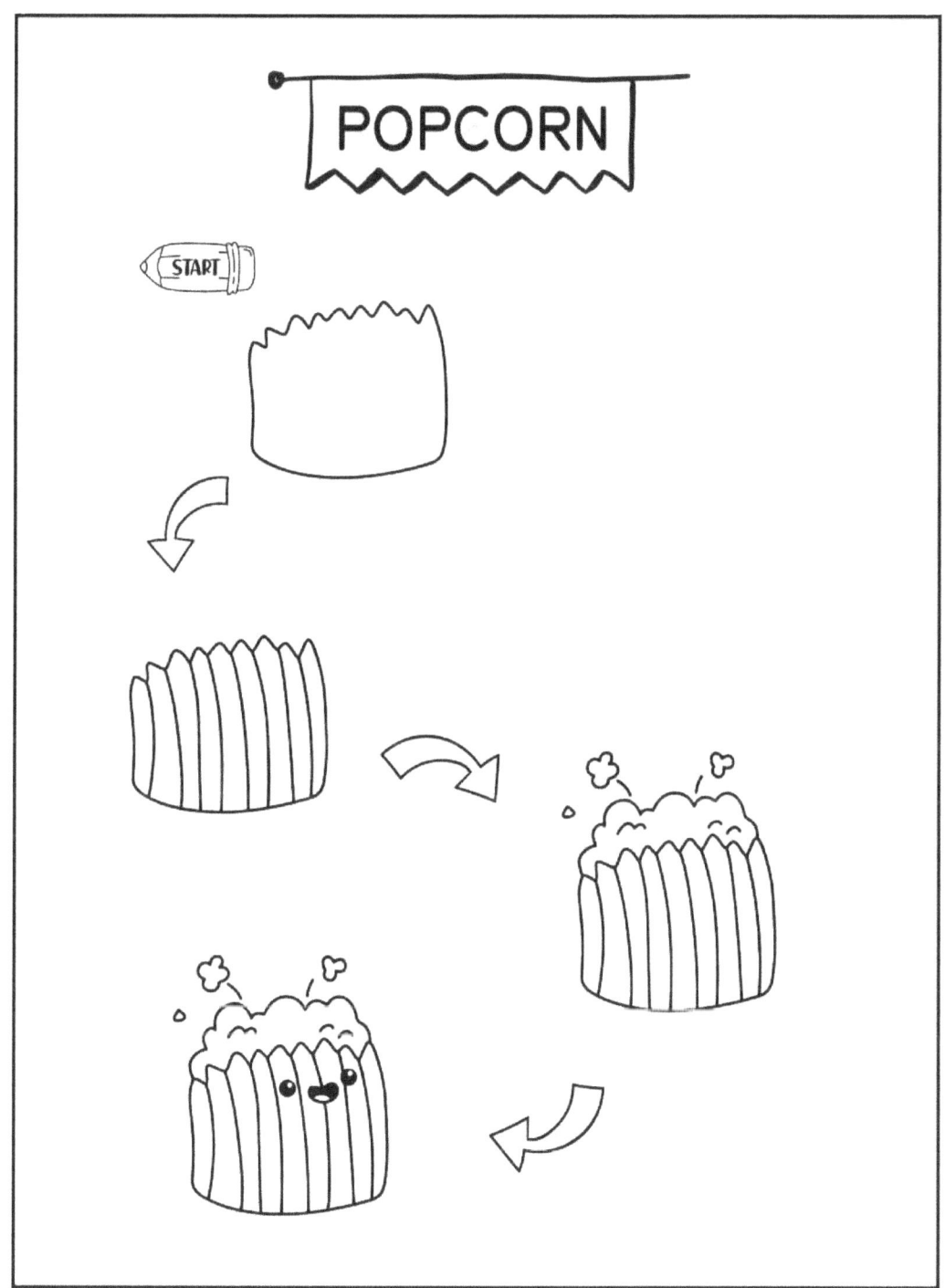

UMBRELLA

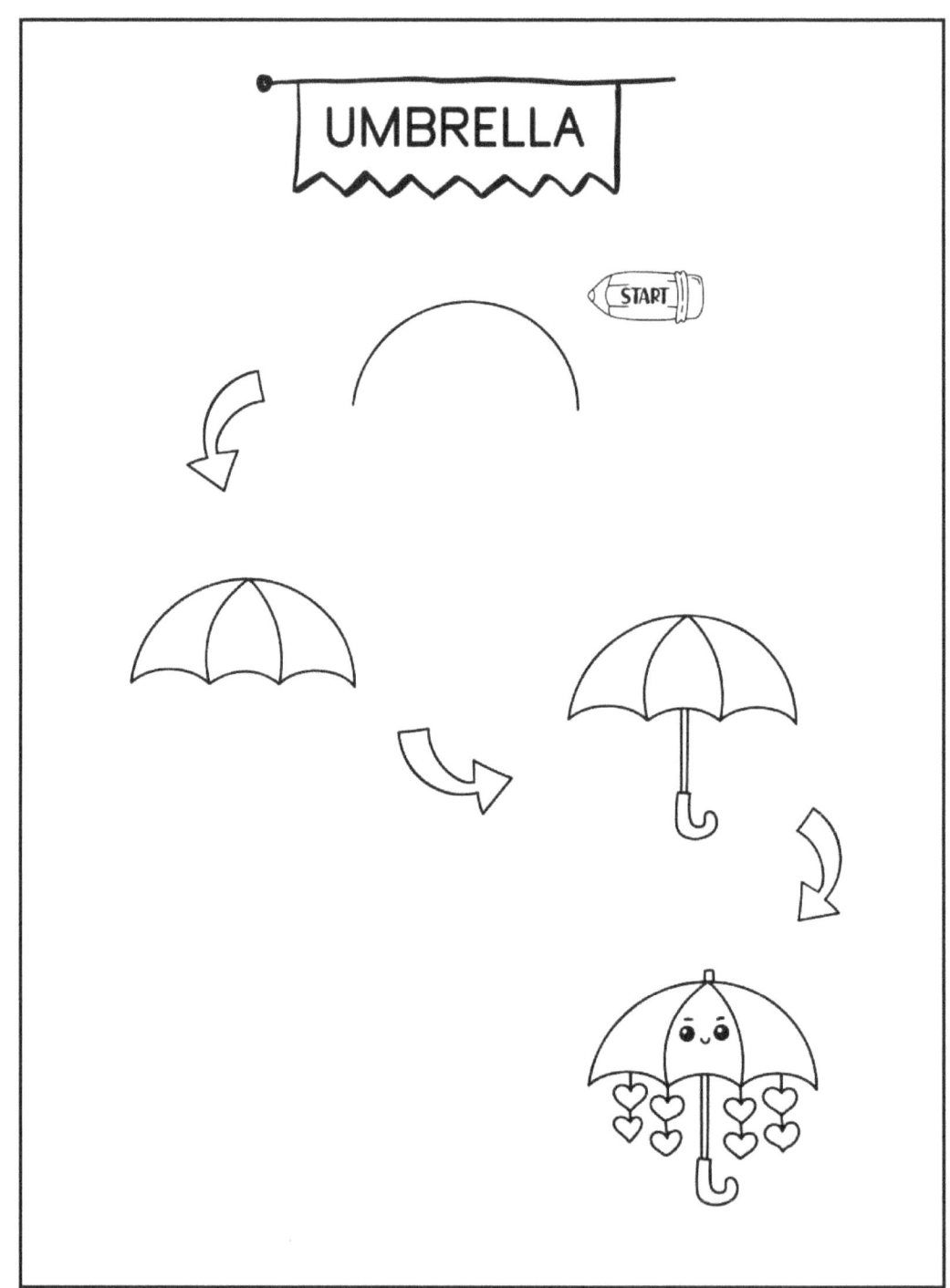

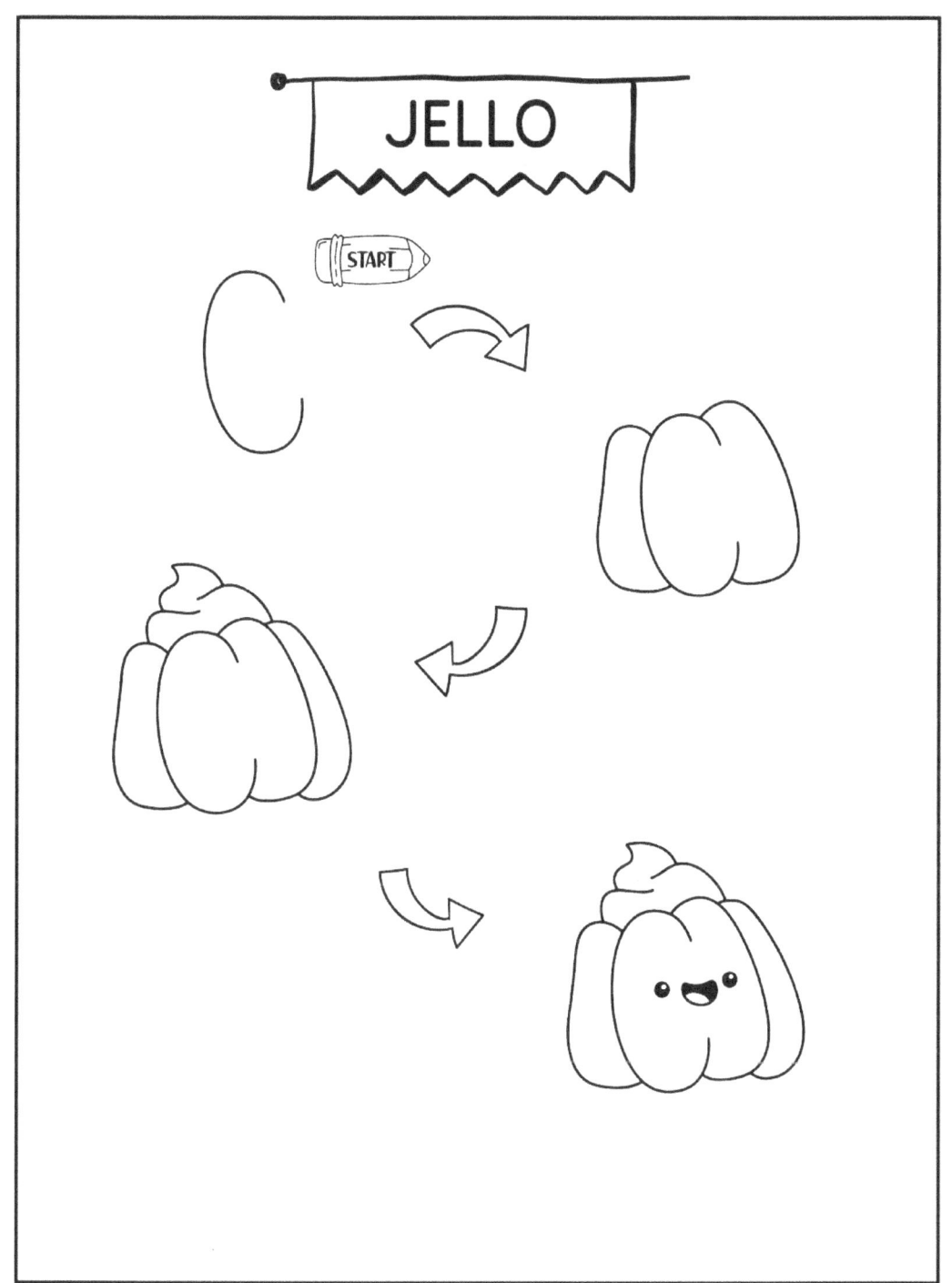

HAMSTER

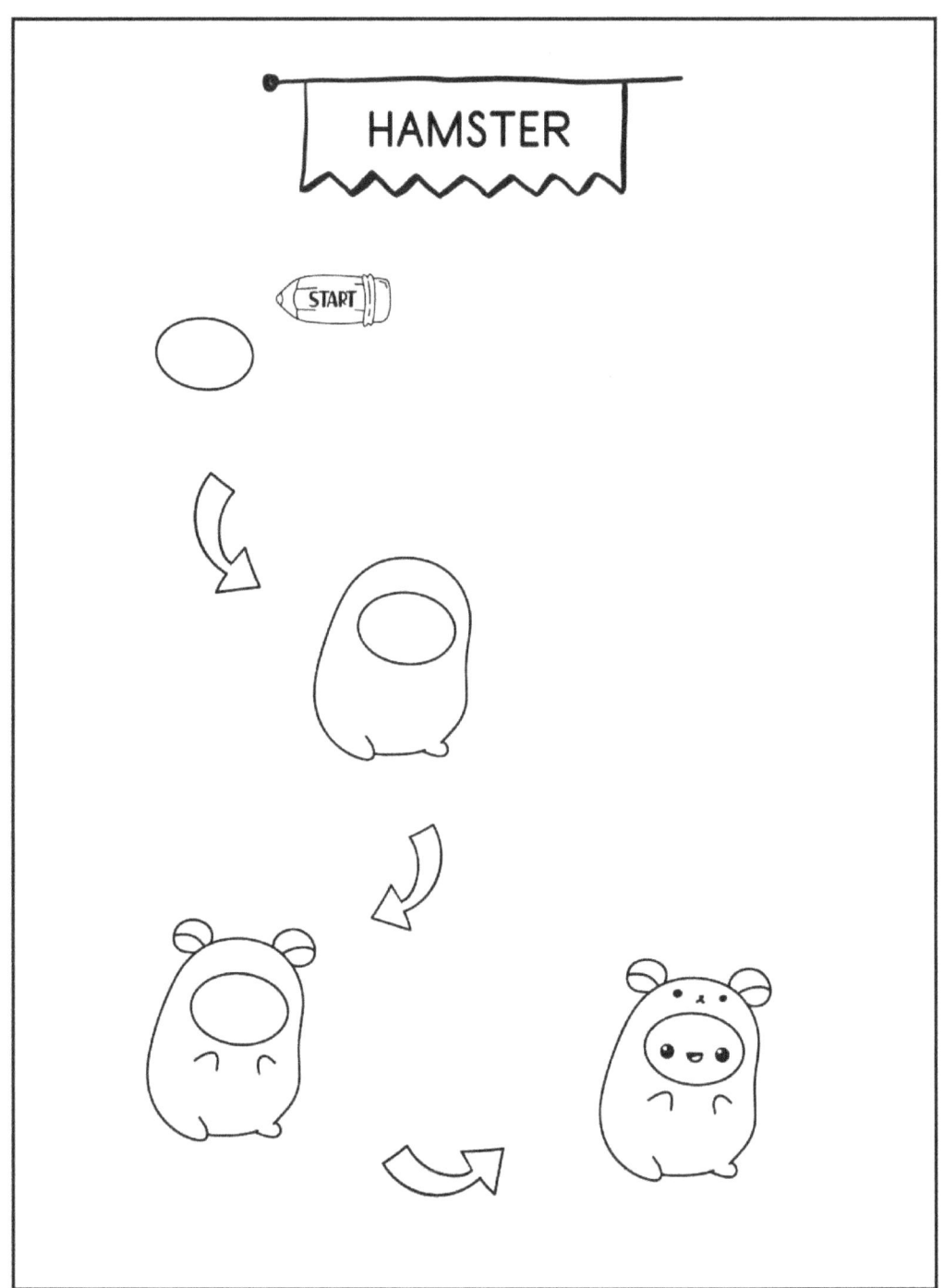

CHERRY

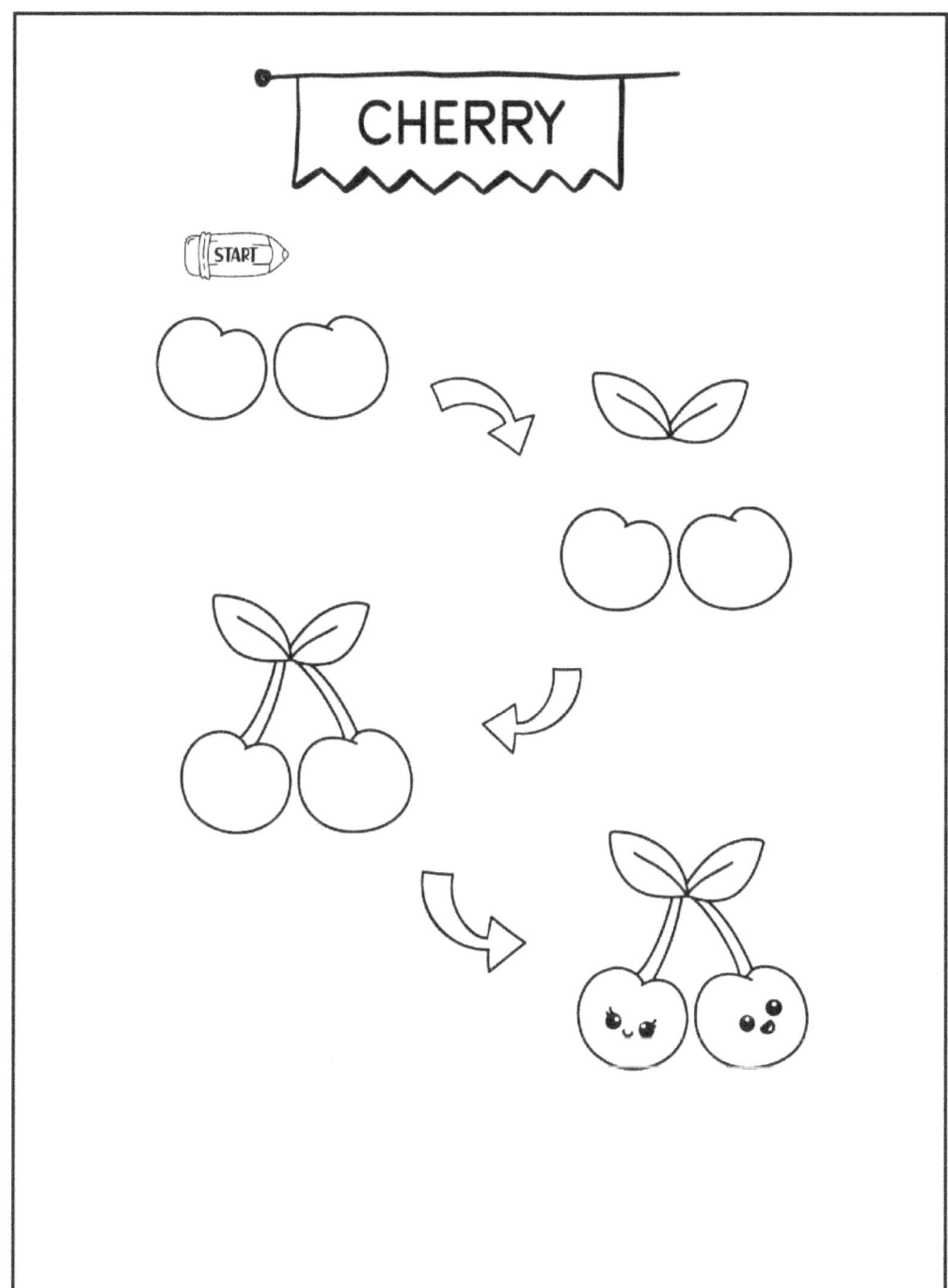

SUSHI

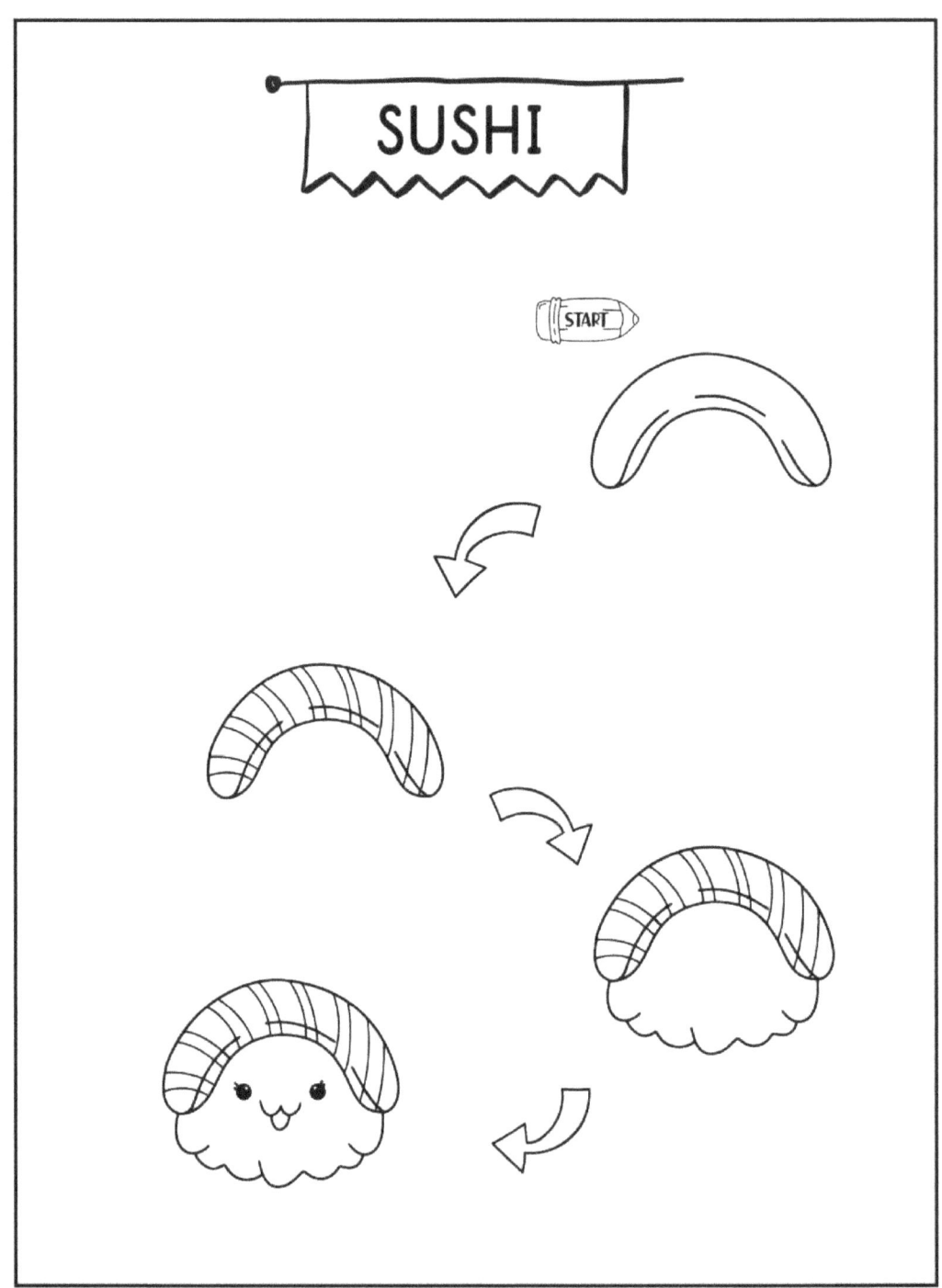

28

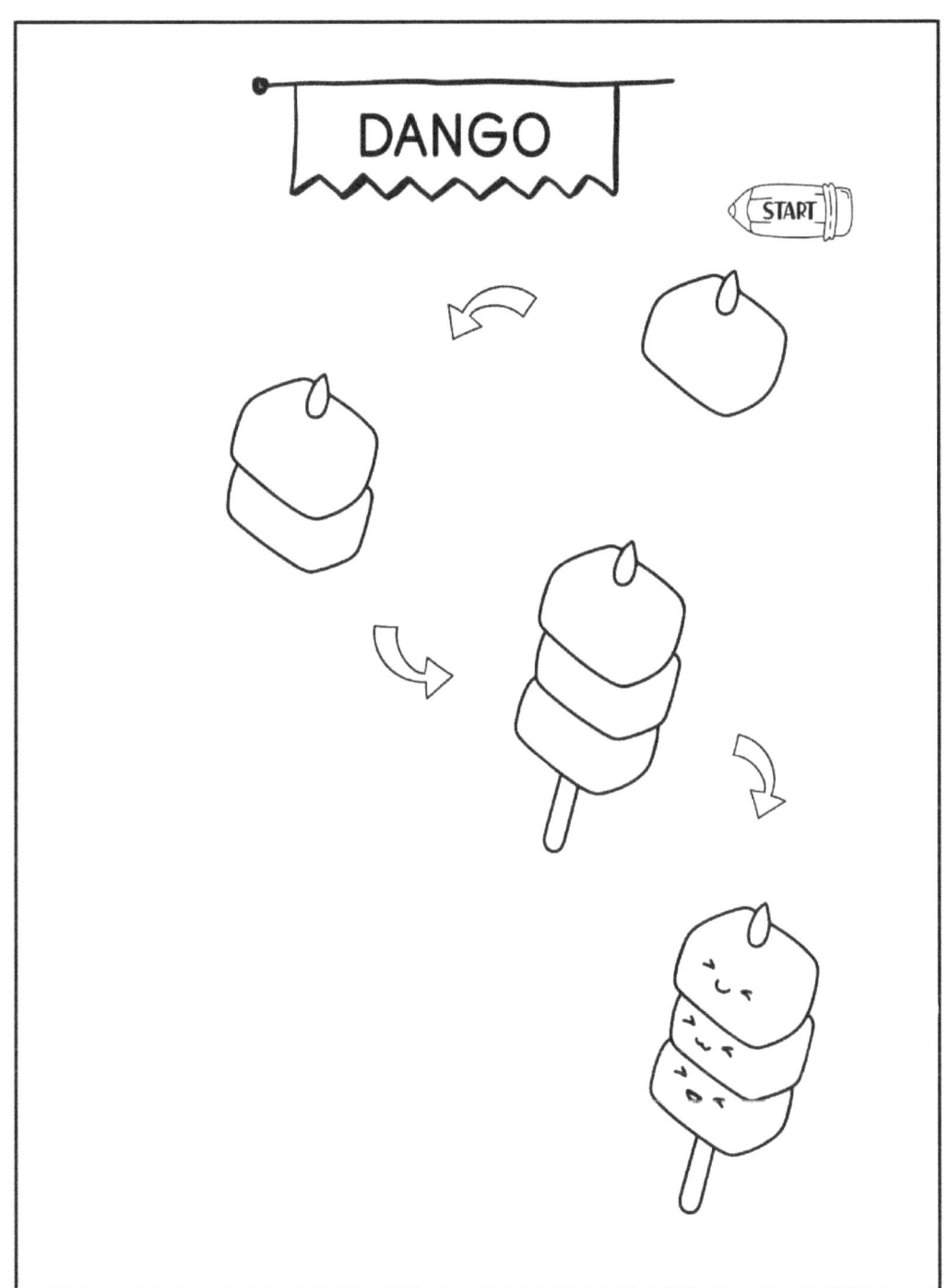

WATERMELON

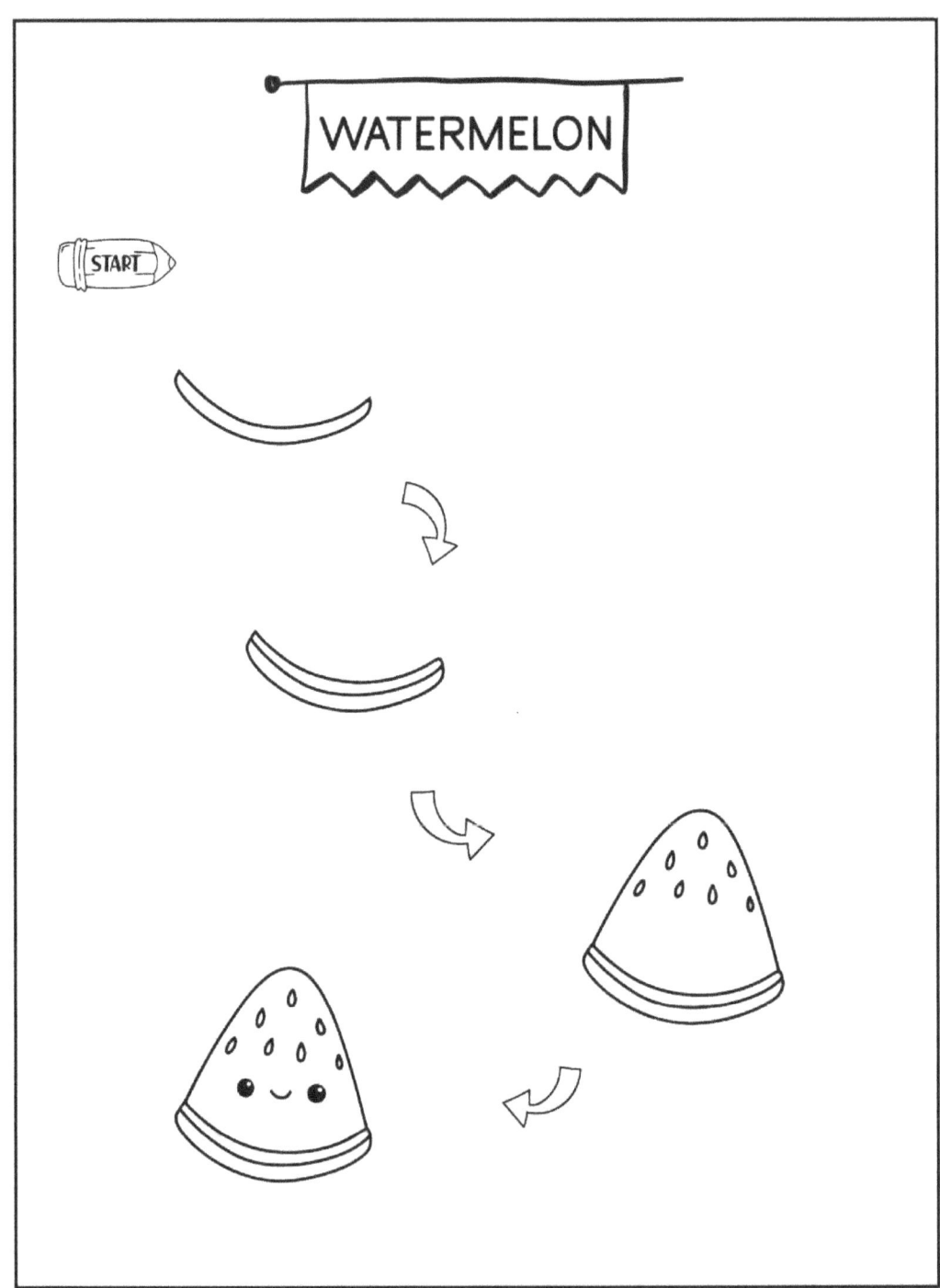

BOAT

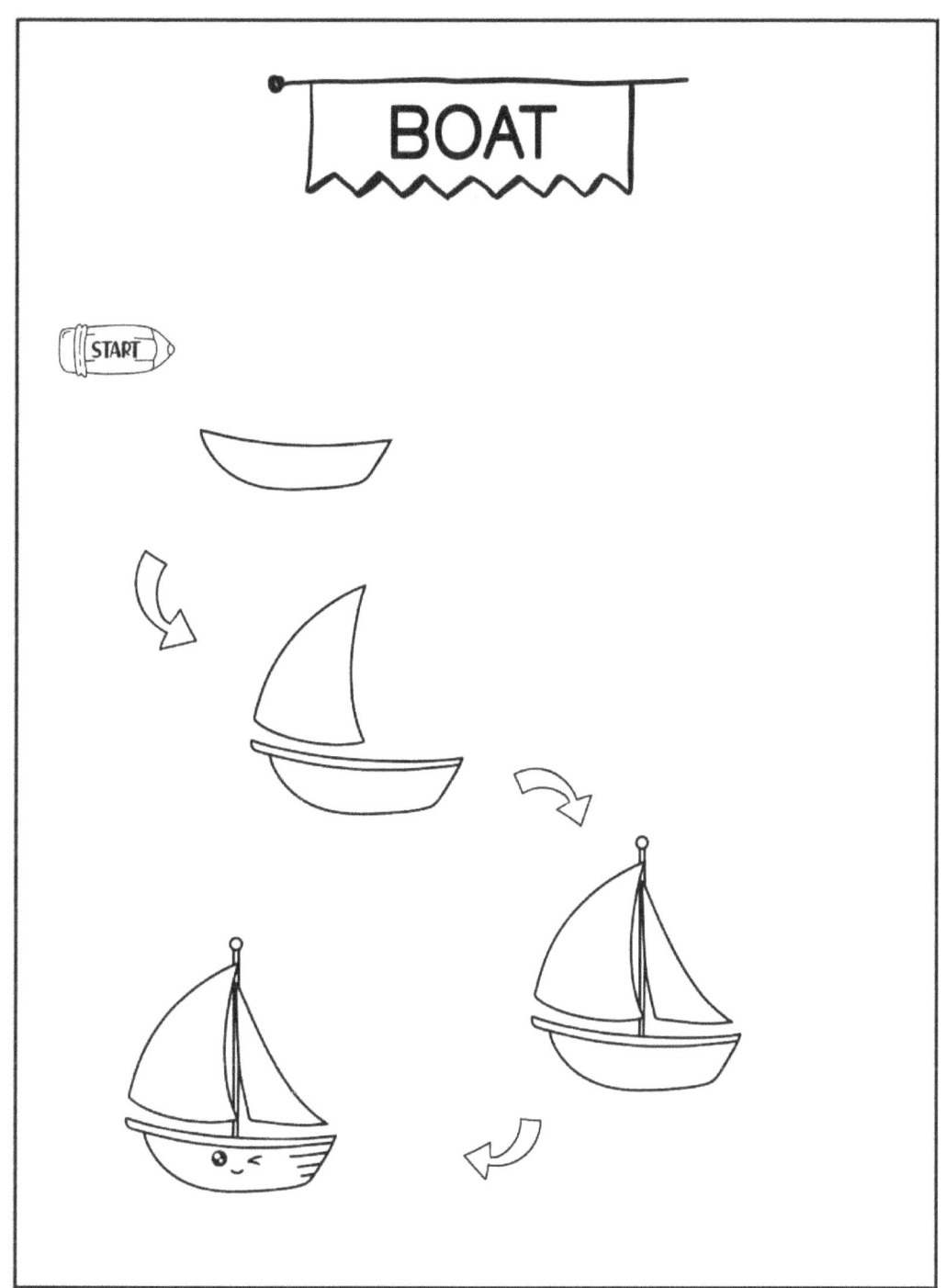

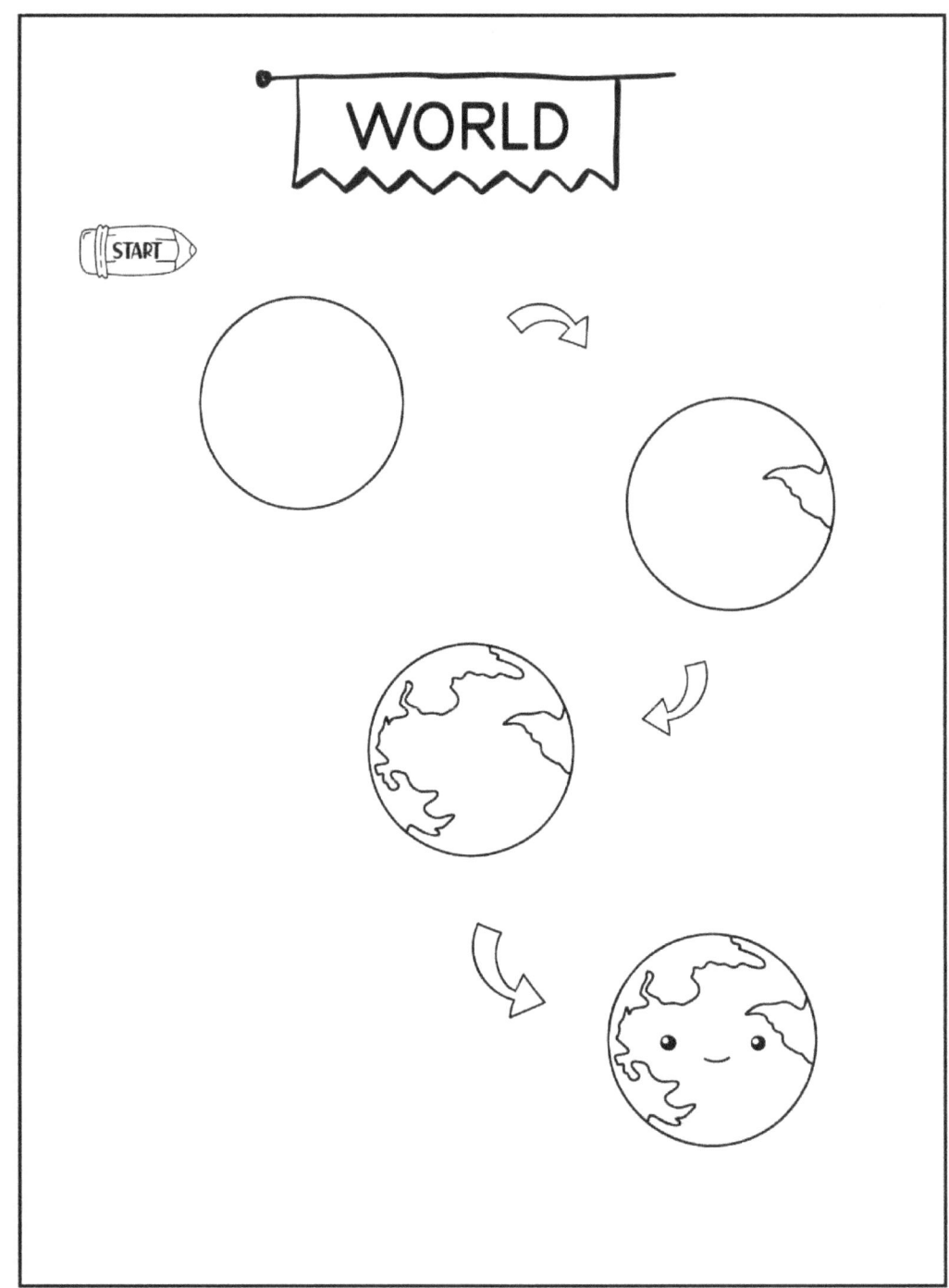

WORLD

START

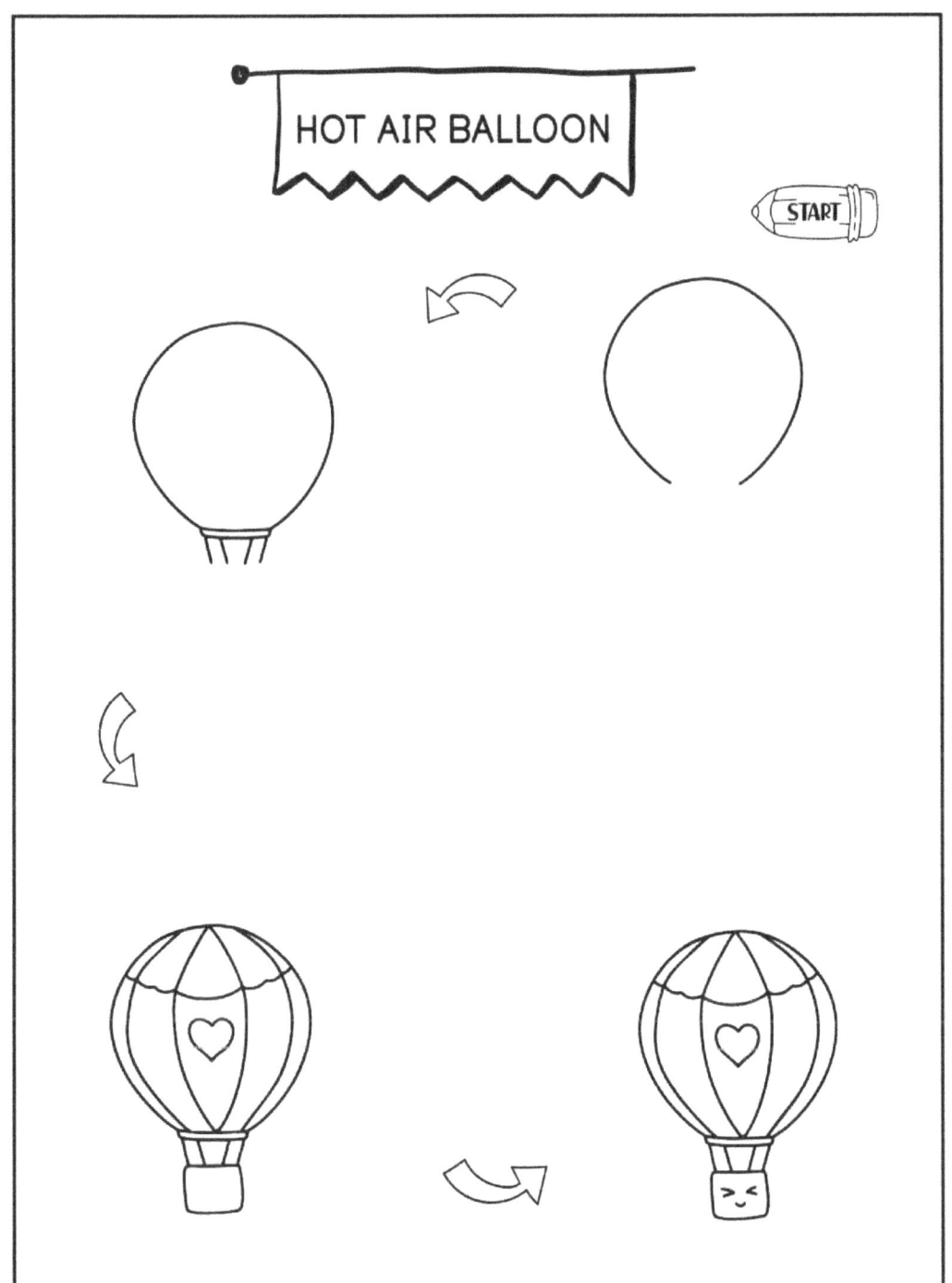

HOT AIR BALLOON

START

PHONE

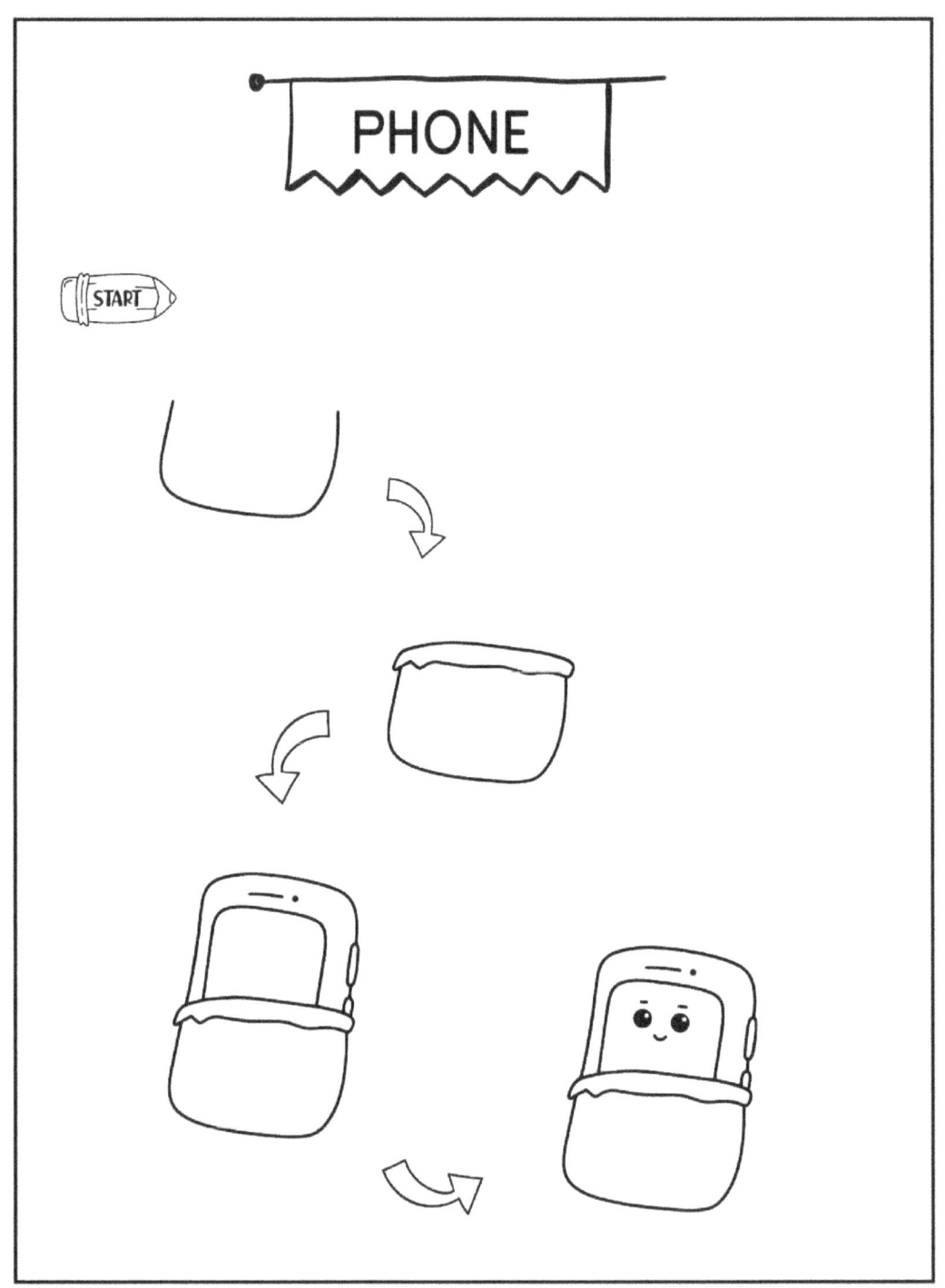

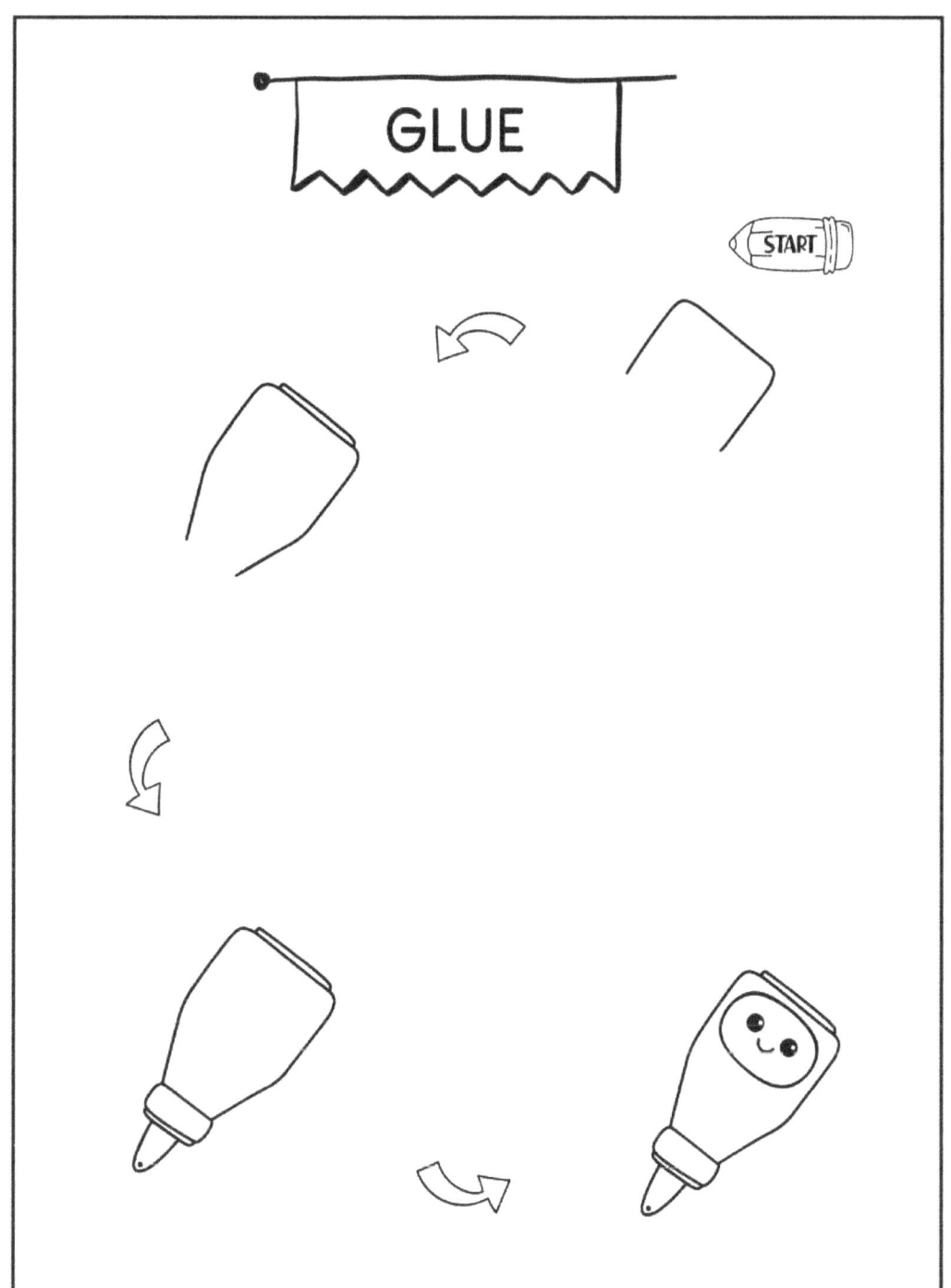

MARKER

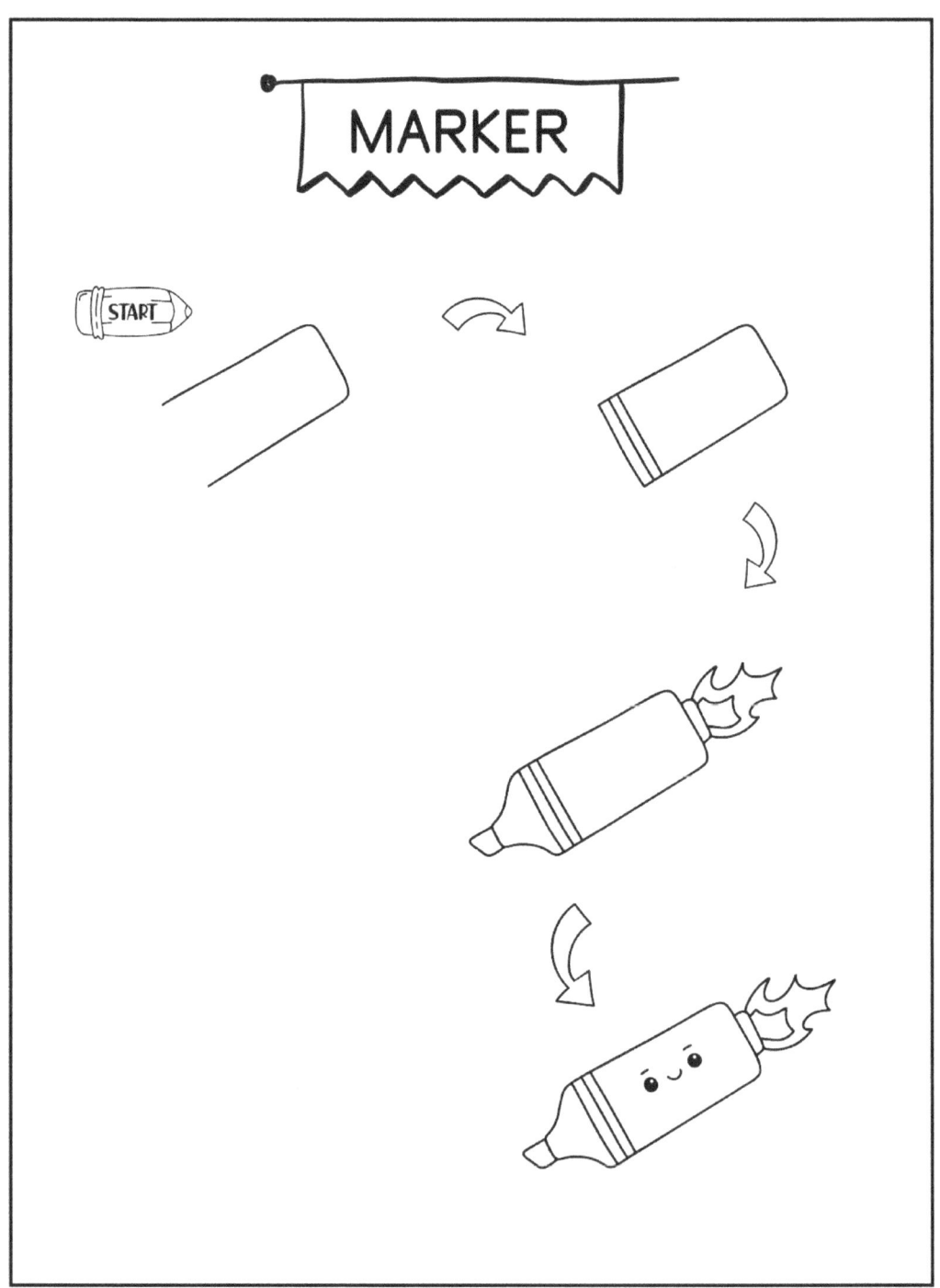

FIRE

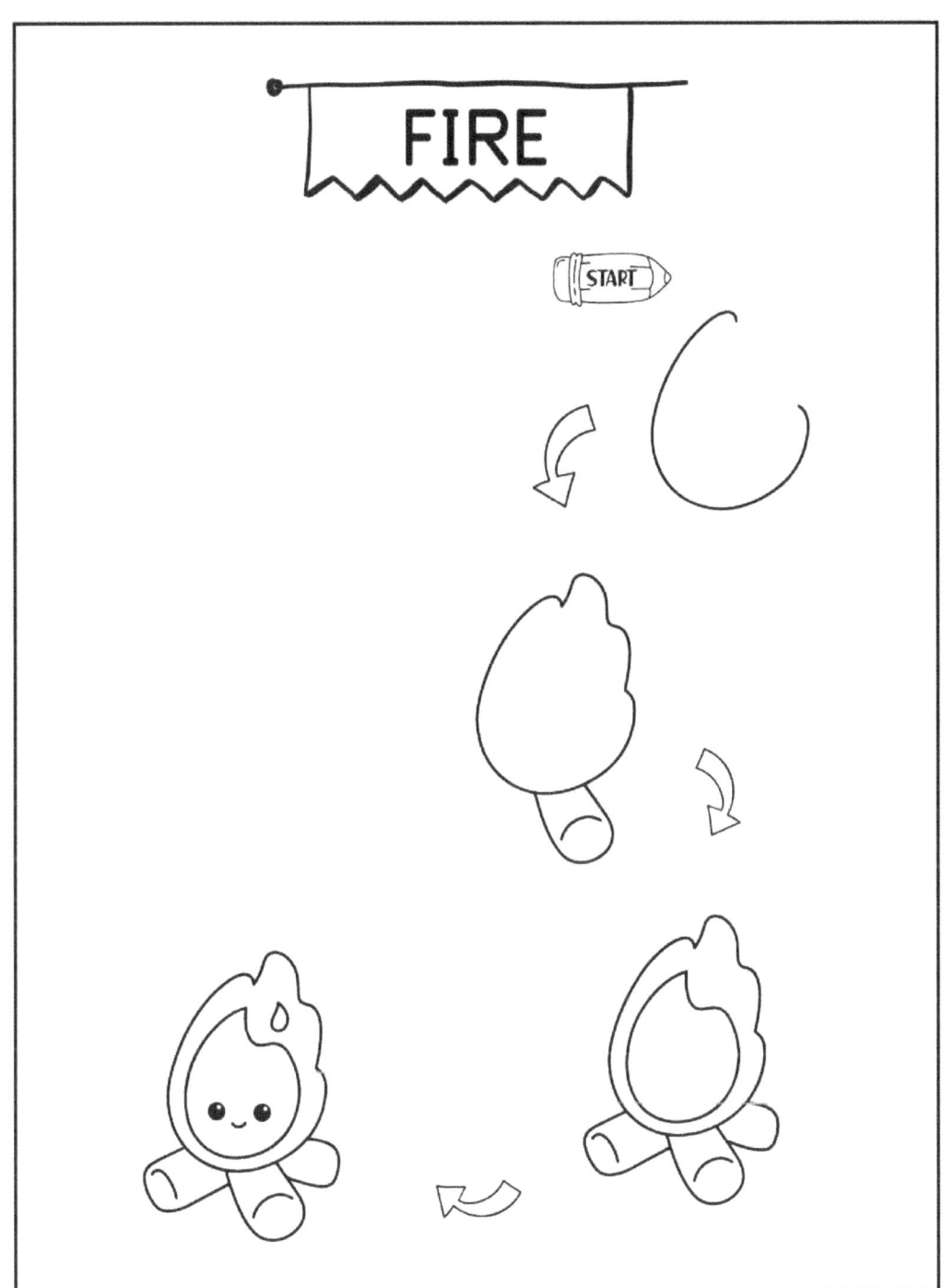

CLOCK

START

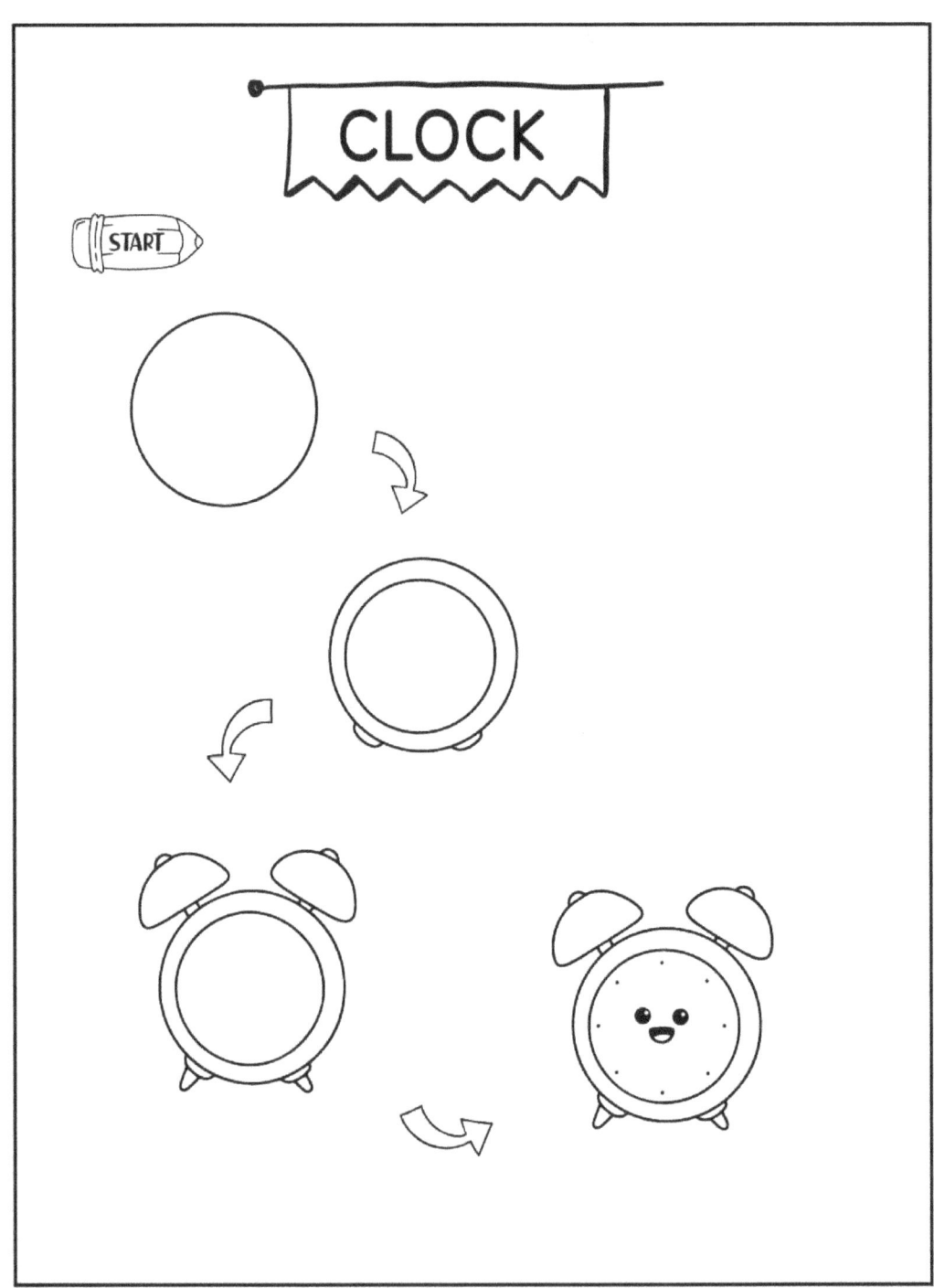

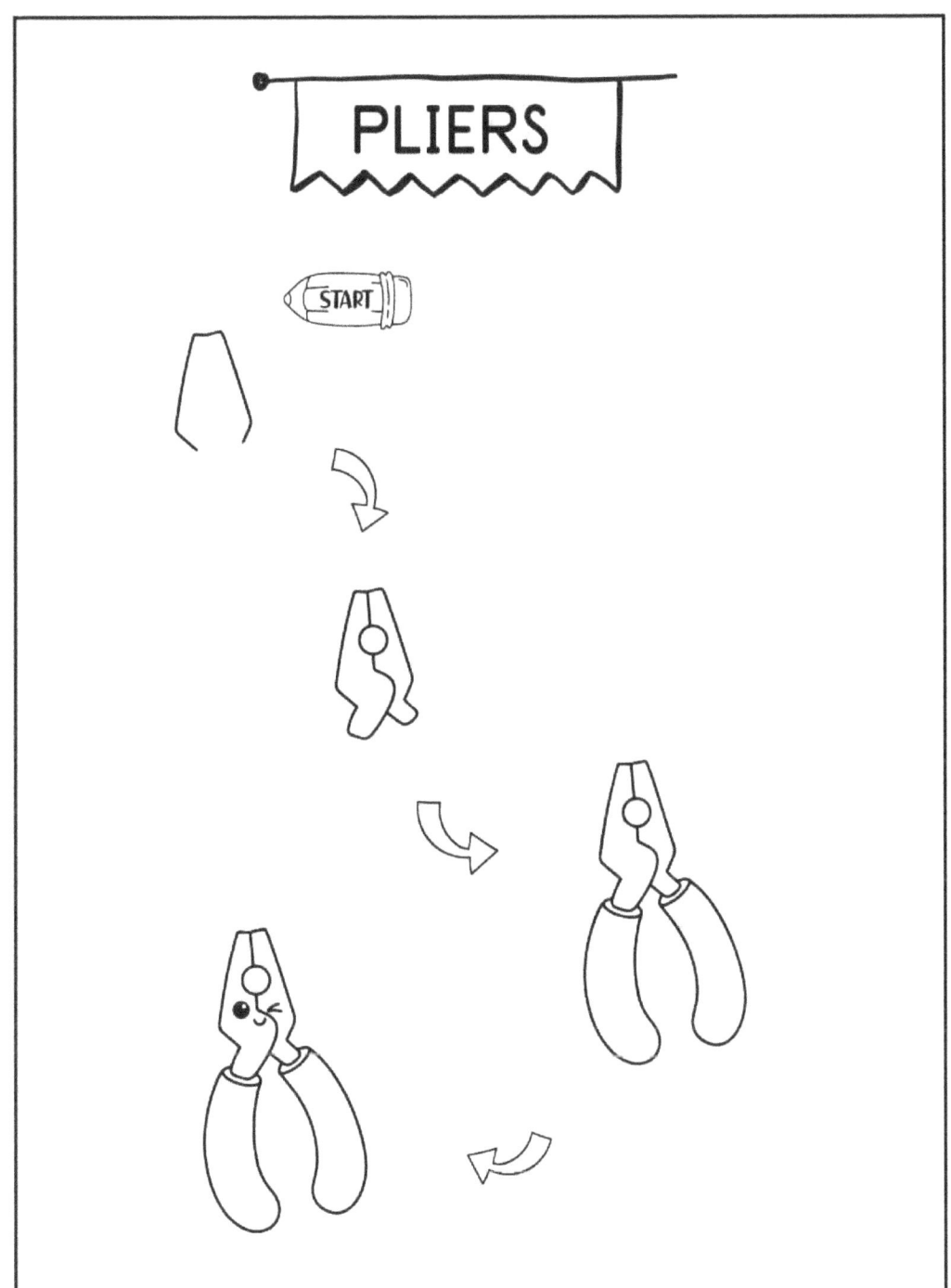

PLIERS

START

OWL

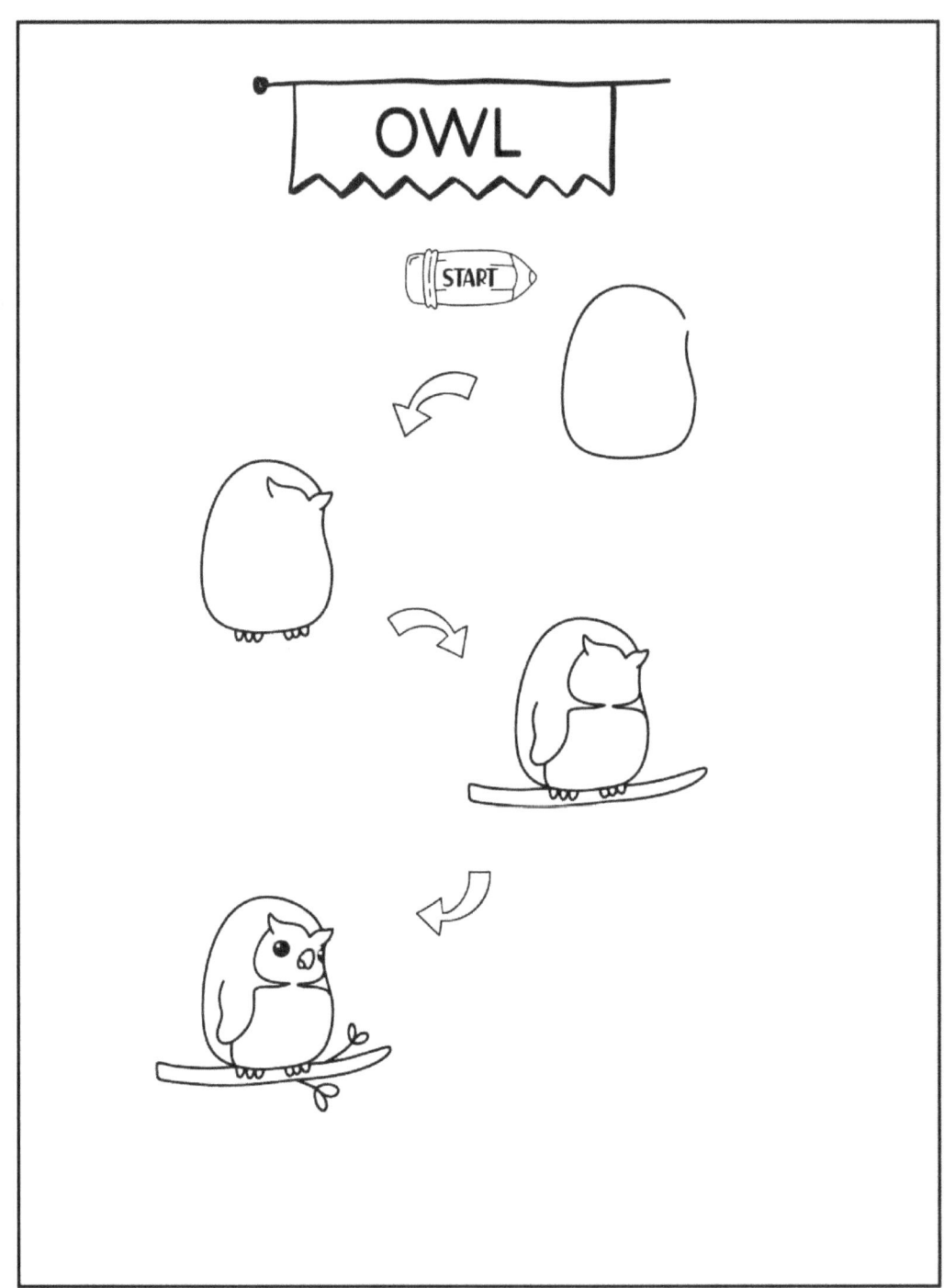

START

SCREWDRIVER

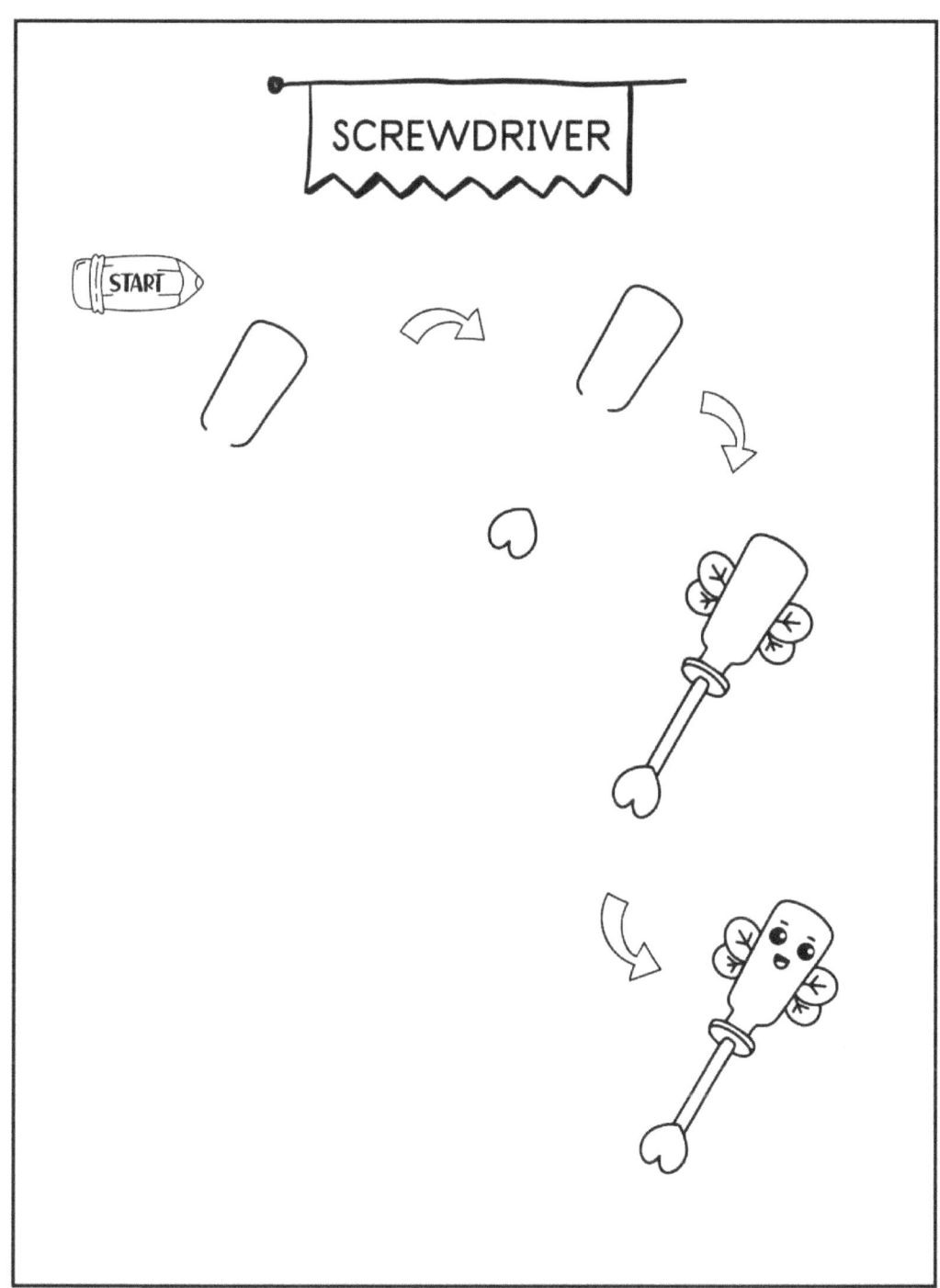

START

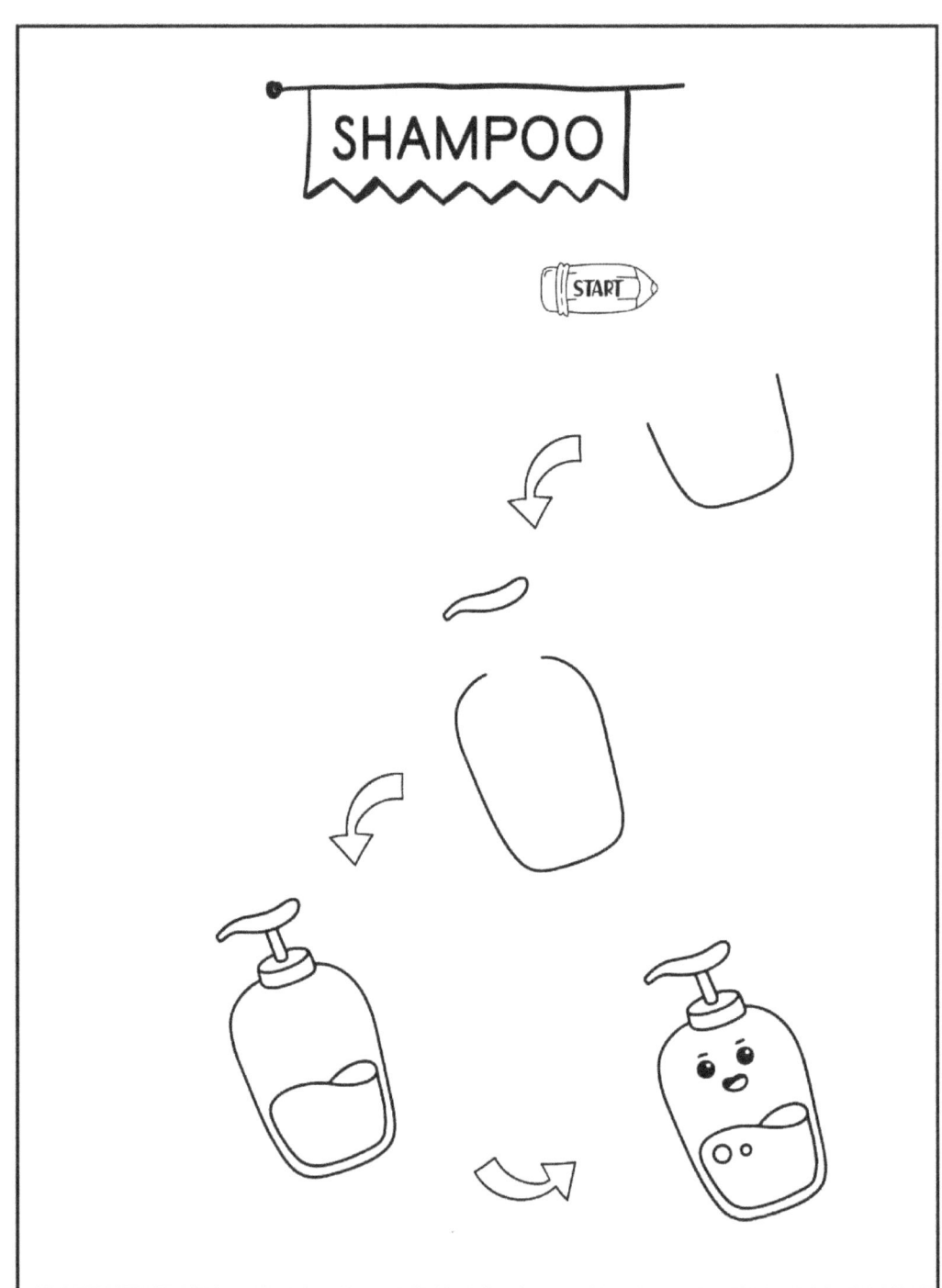

HAMMER

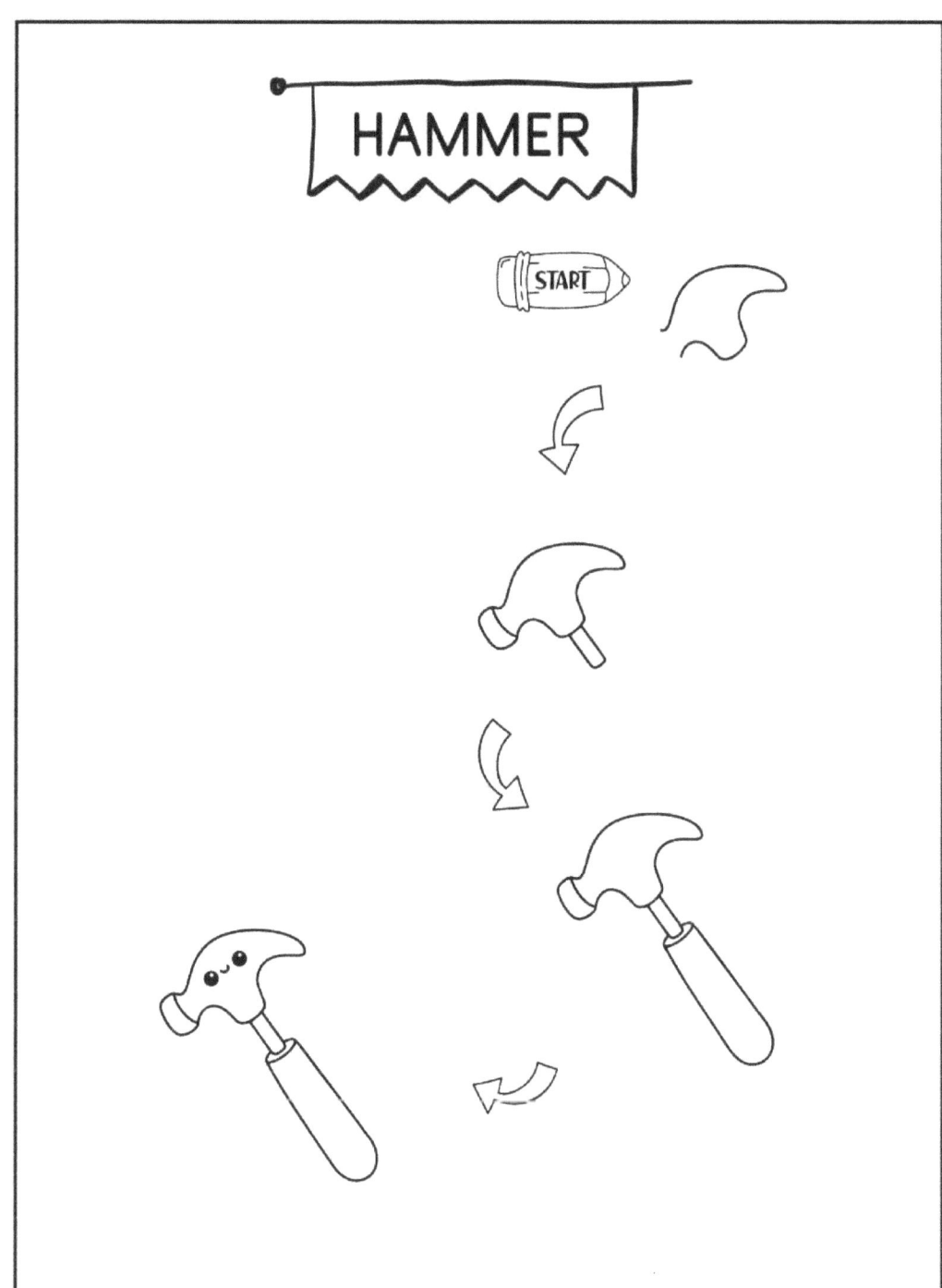

START

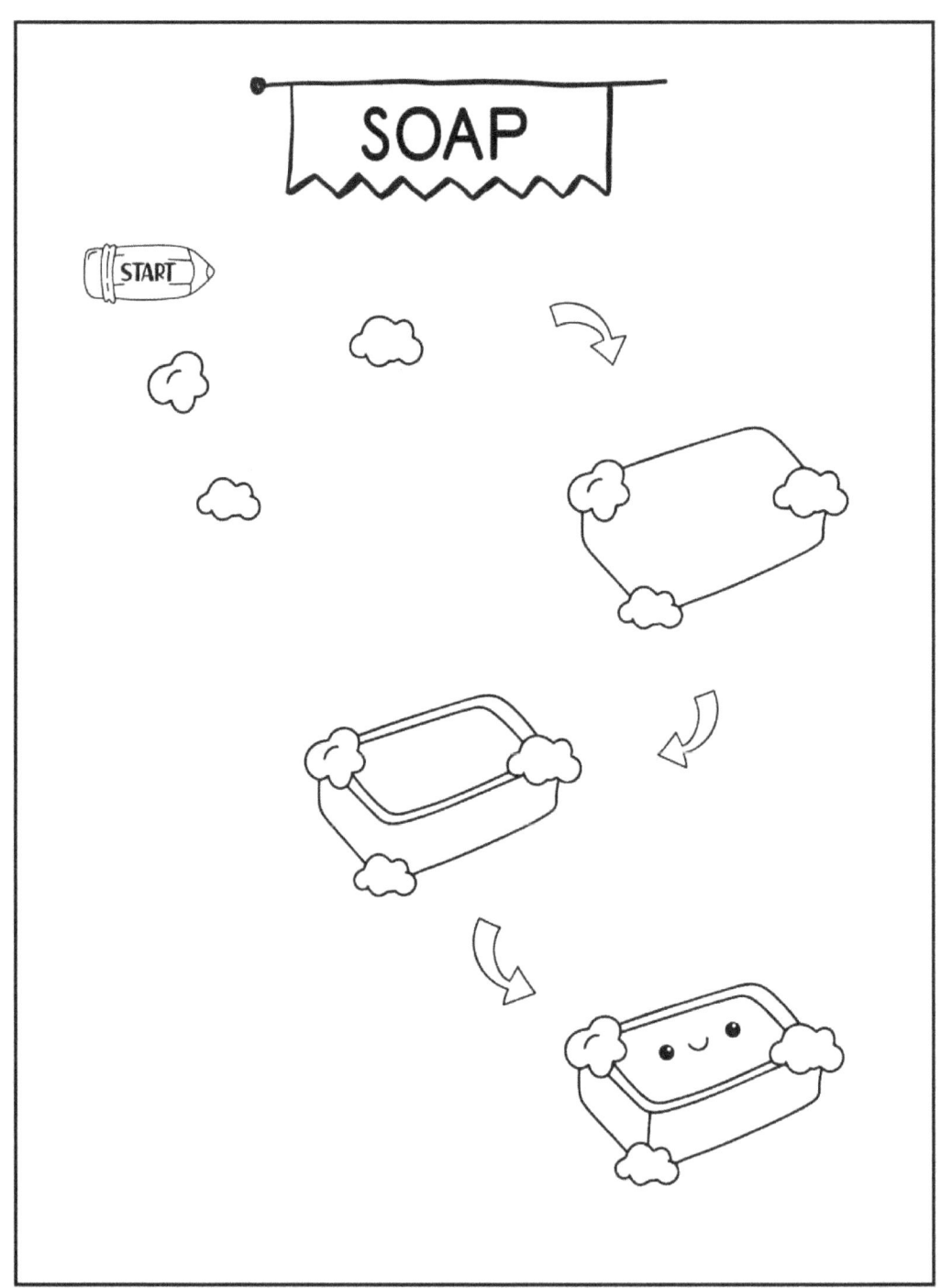

PLANE

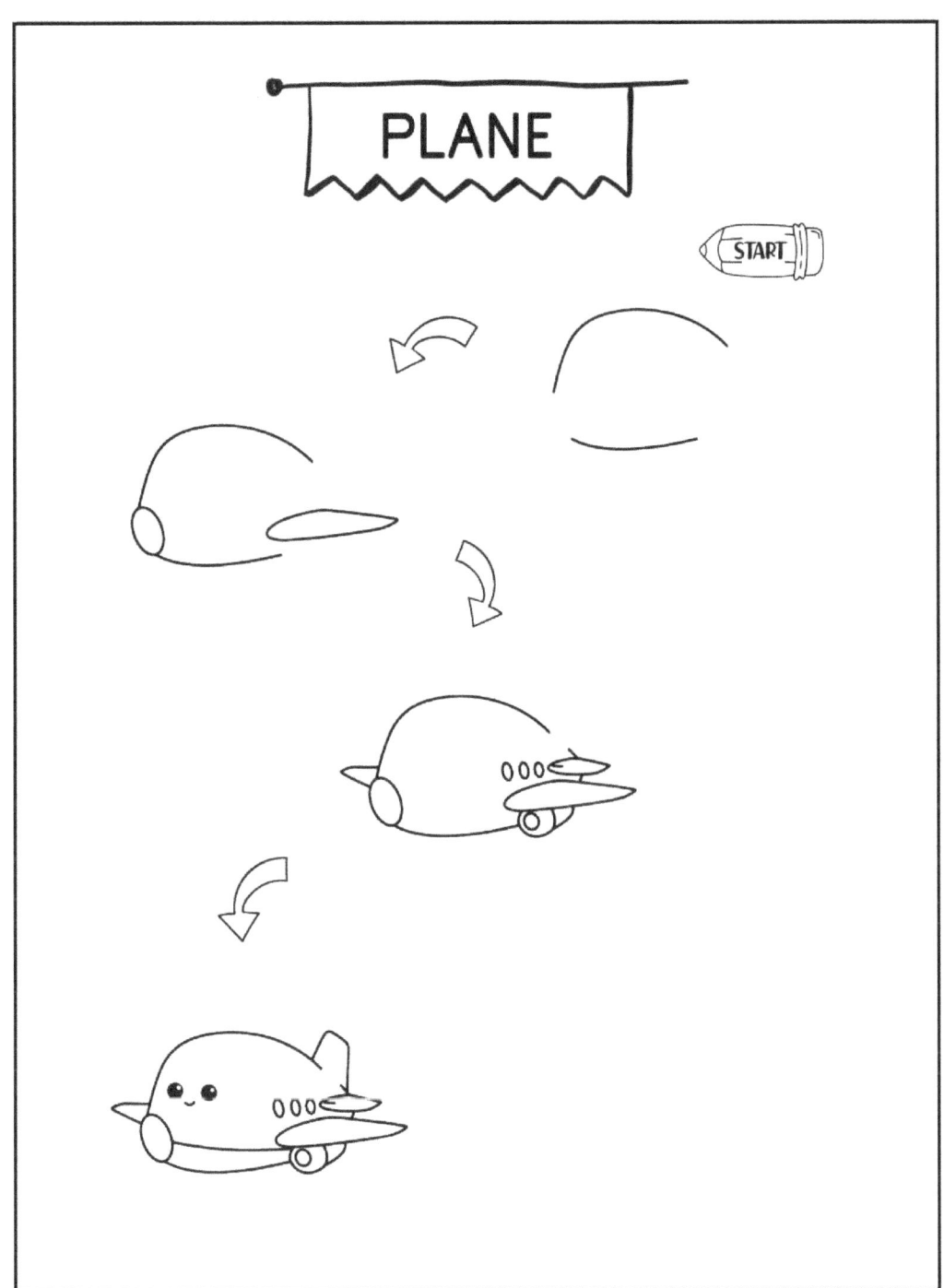

FISH

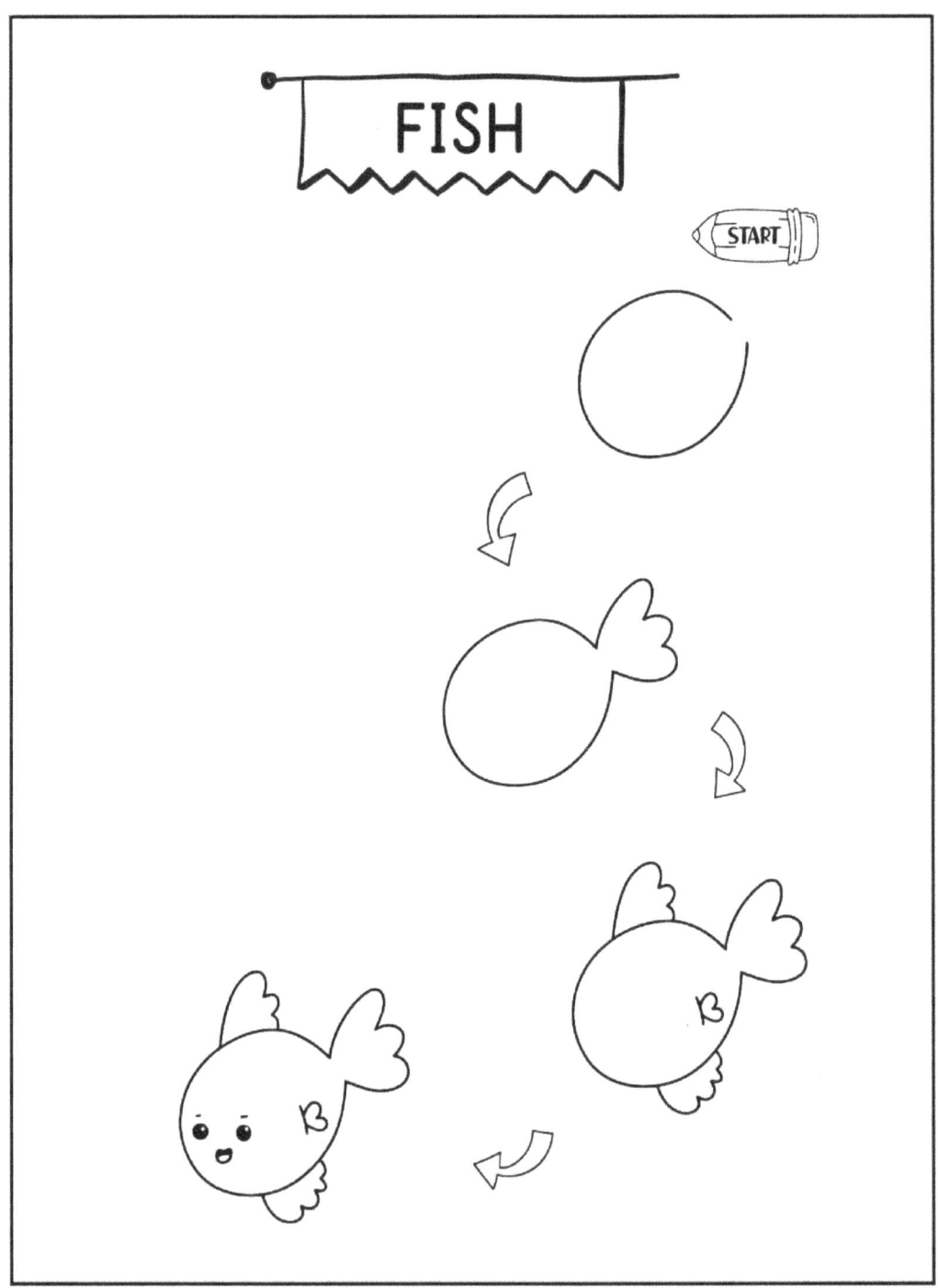

DRILL

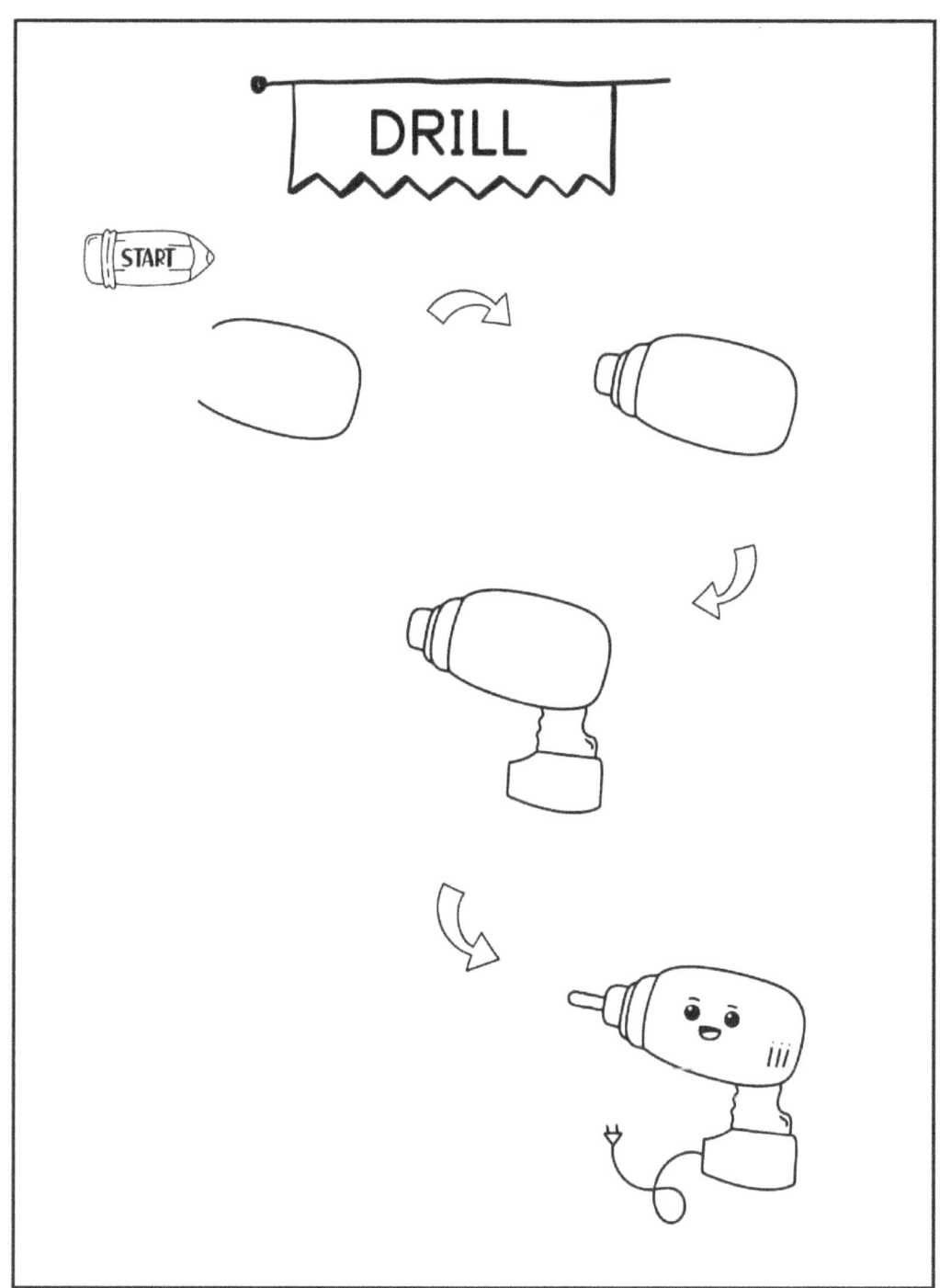

GIRAFFE

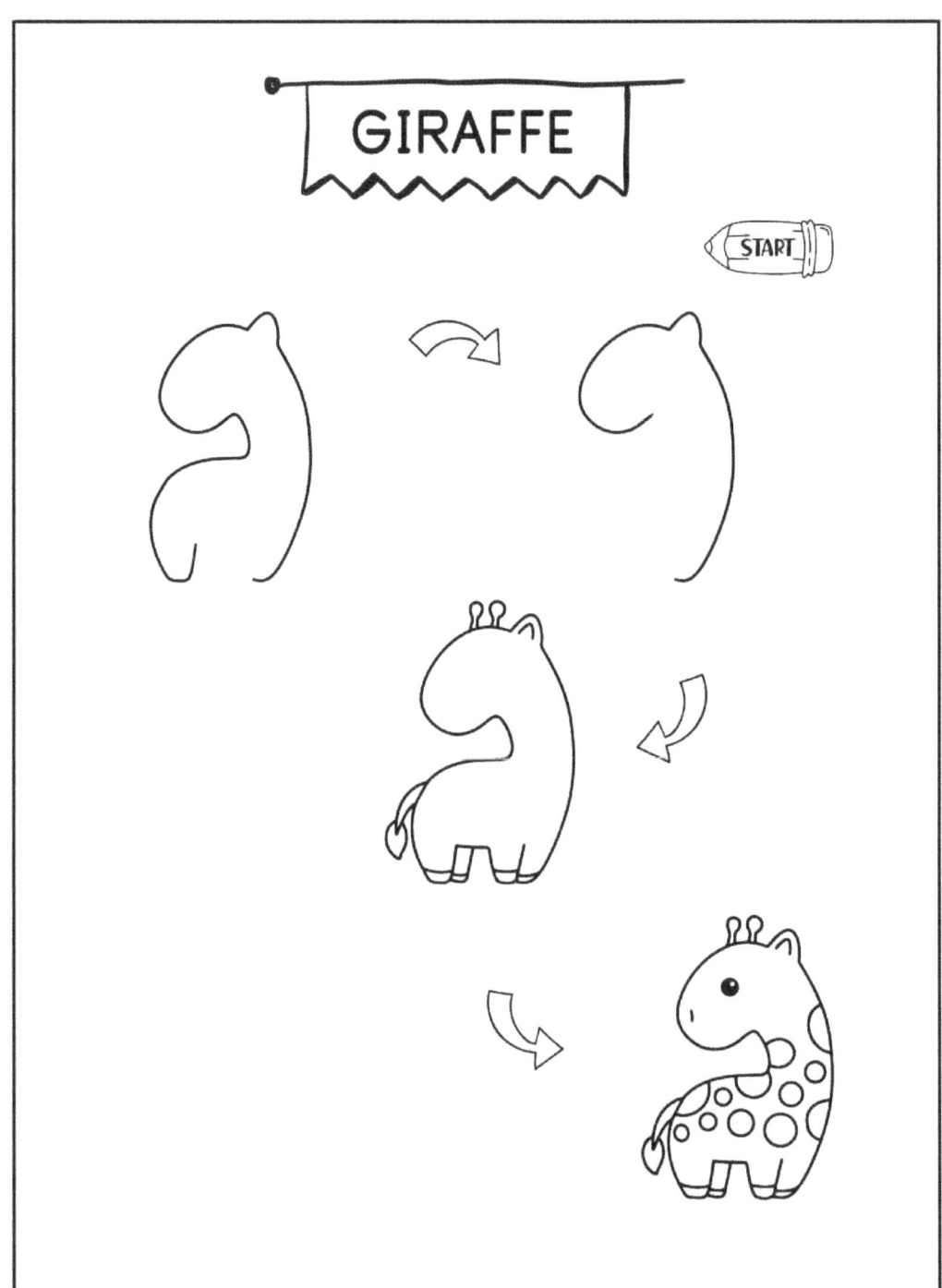

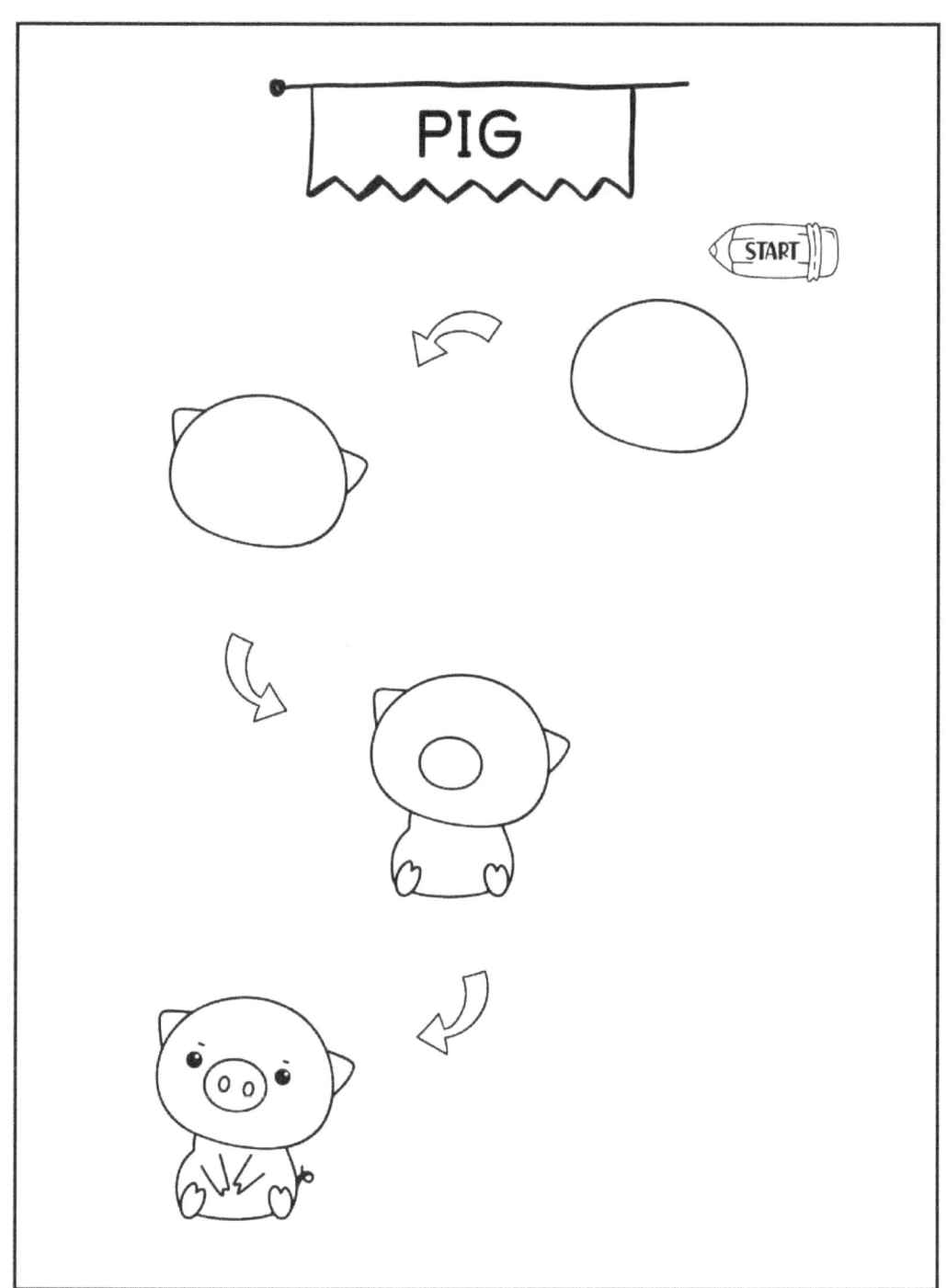

BUBBLE

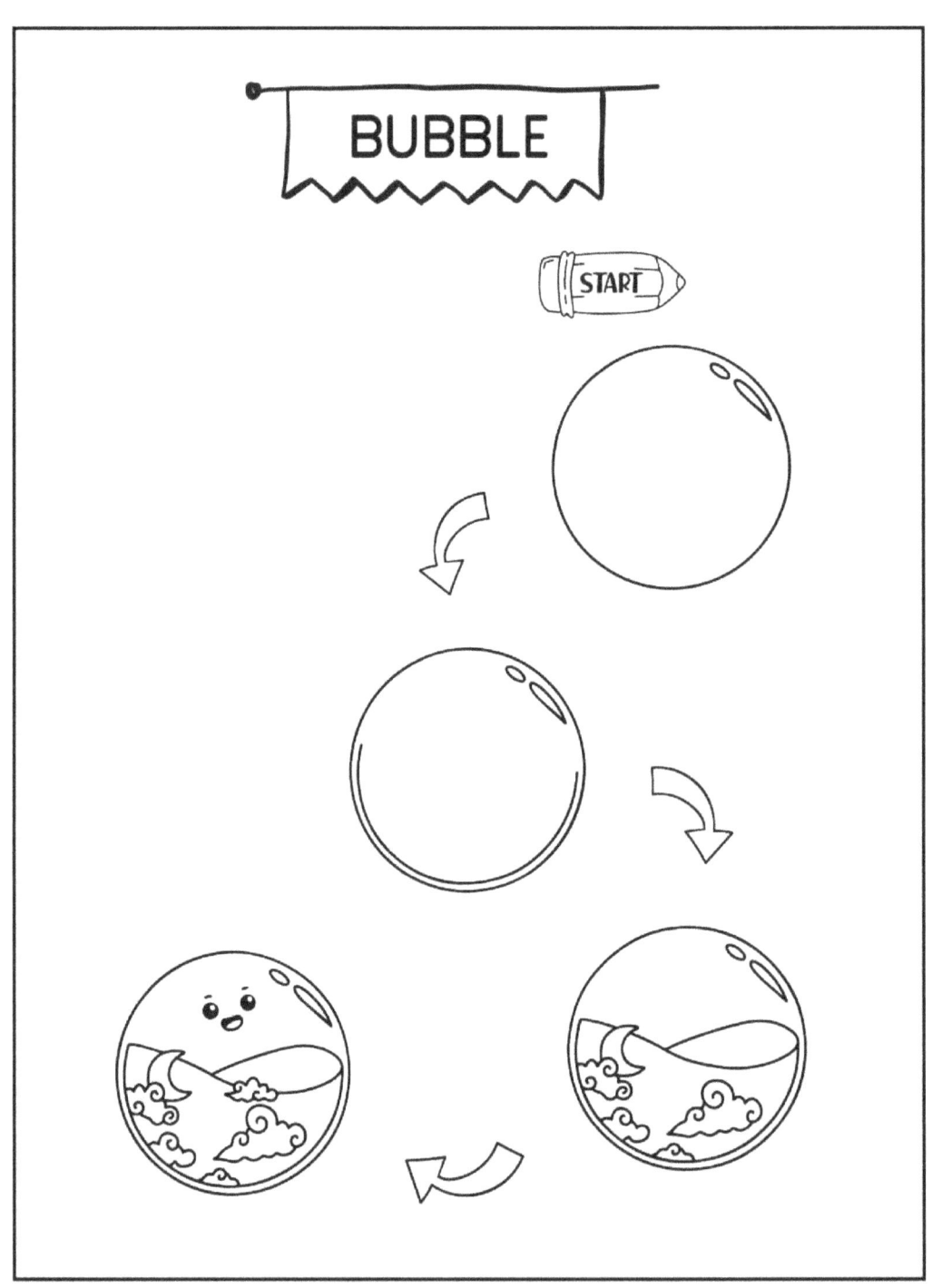

RABBIT

START

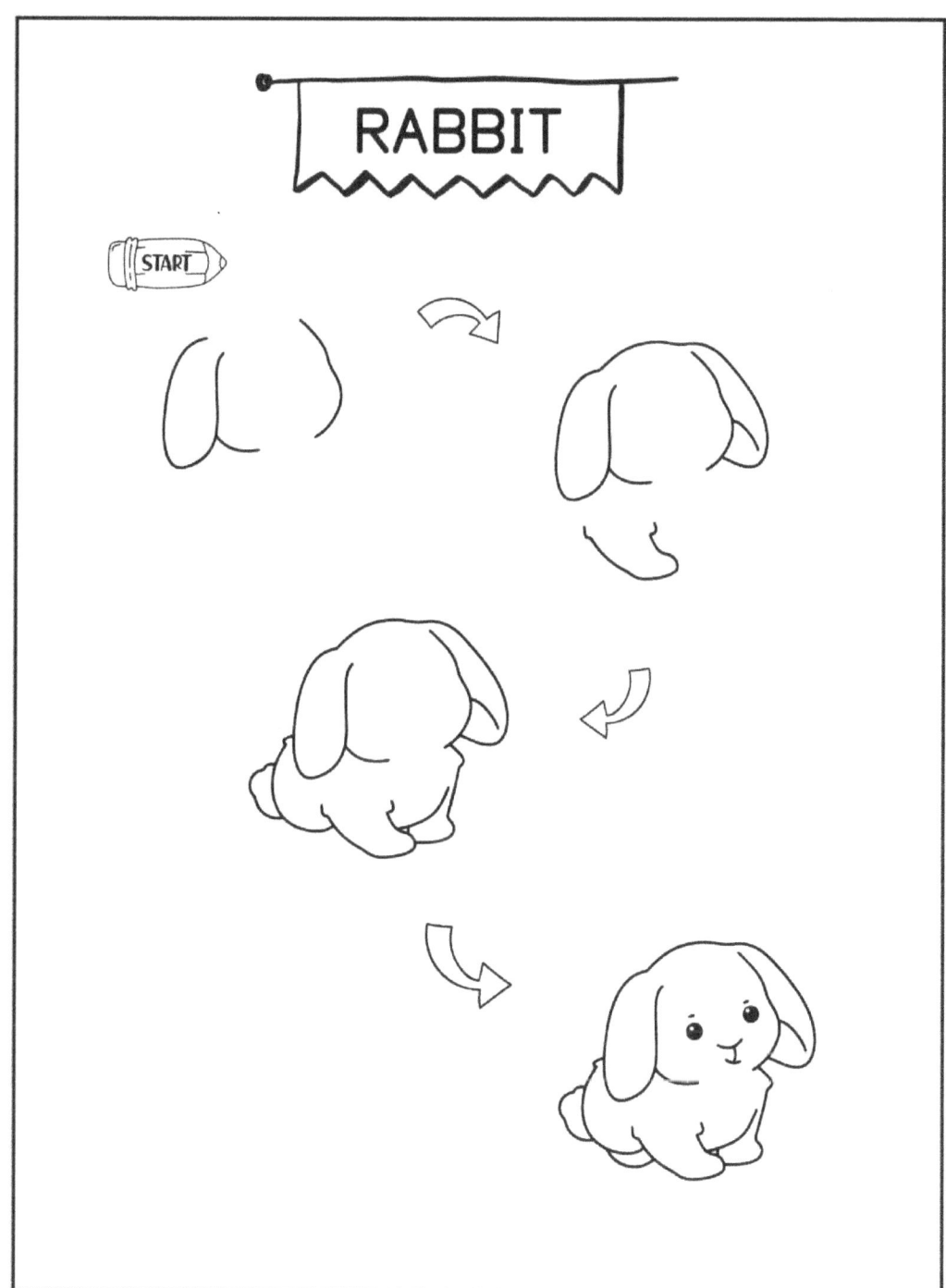

51

CHICKS

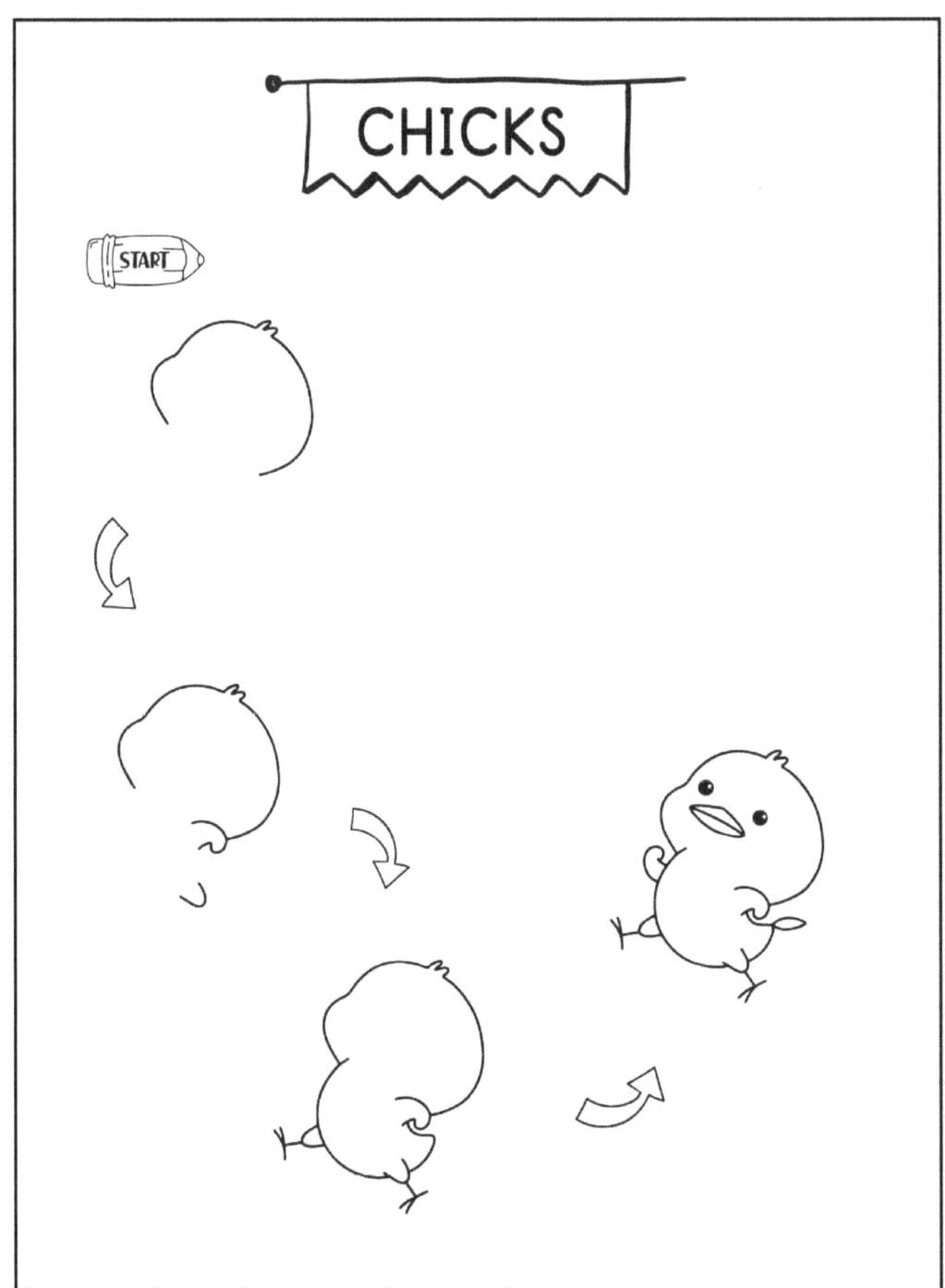

START

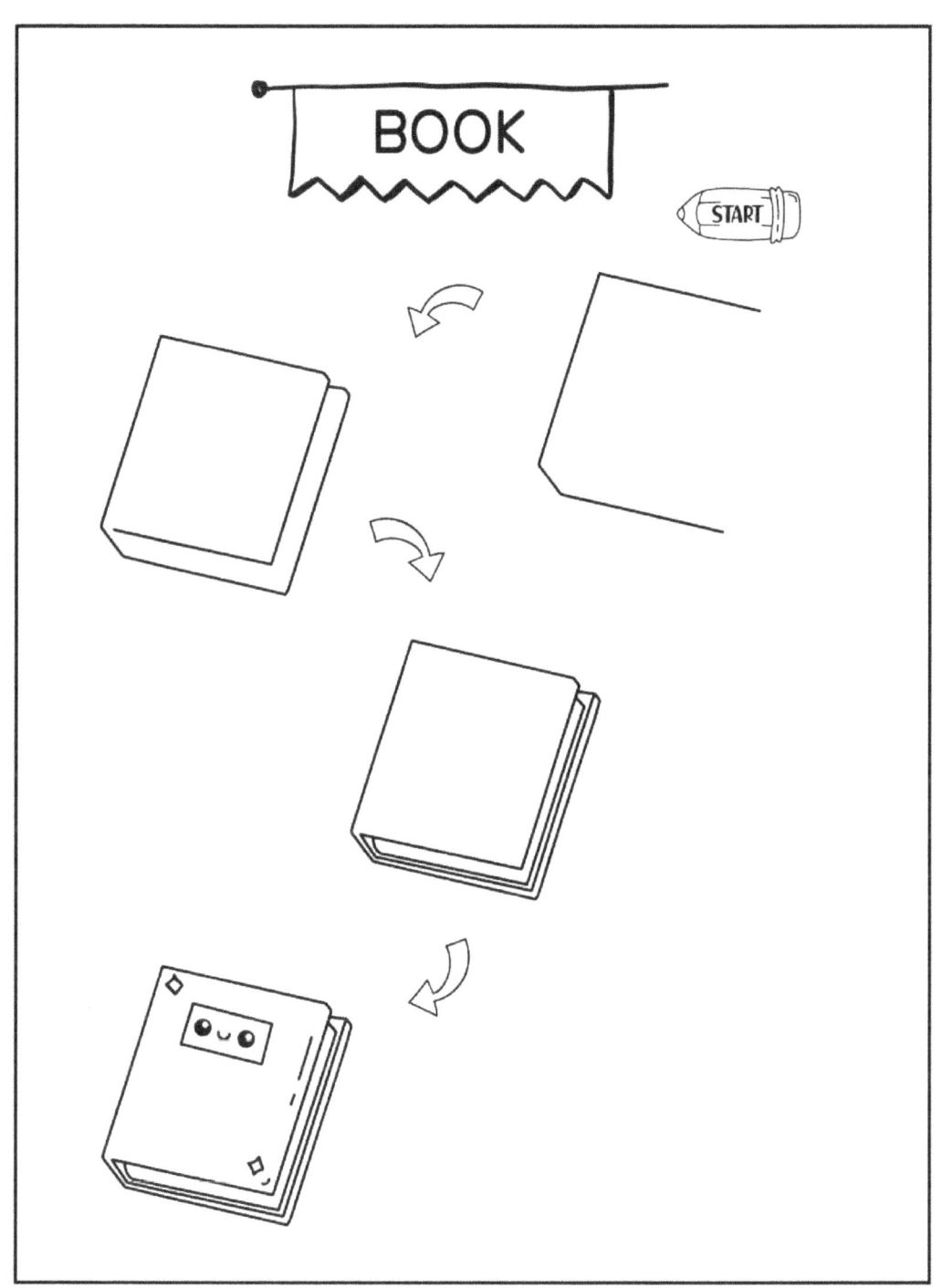

BOOK

START

LIPSTICK

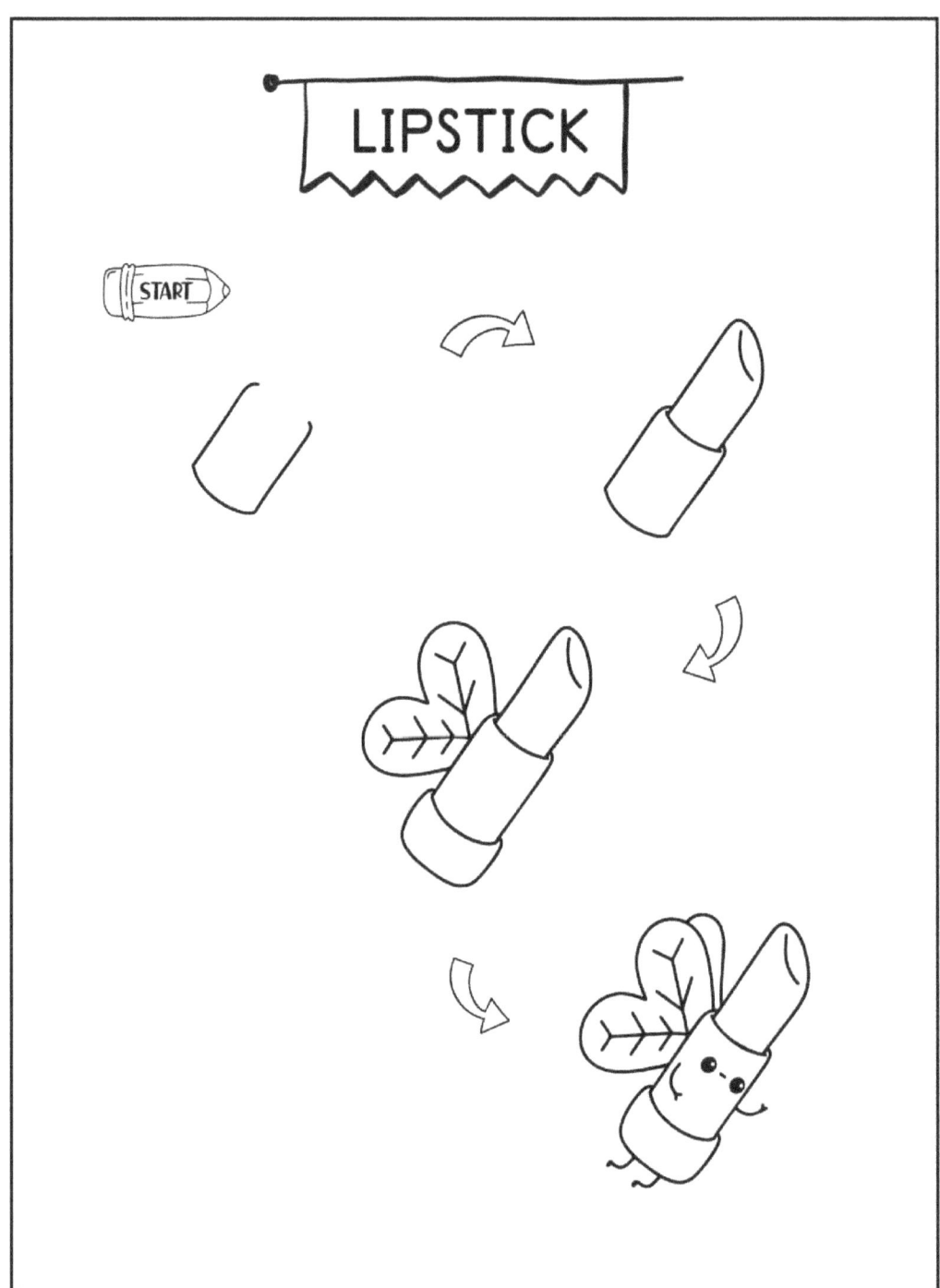

FACE WASH

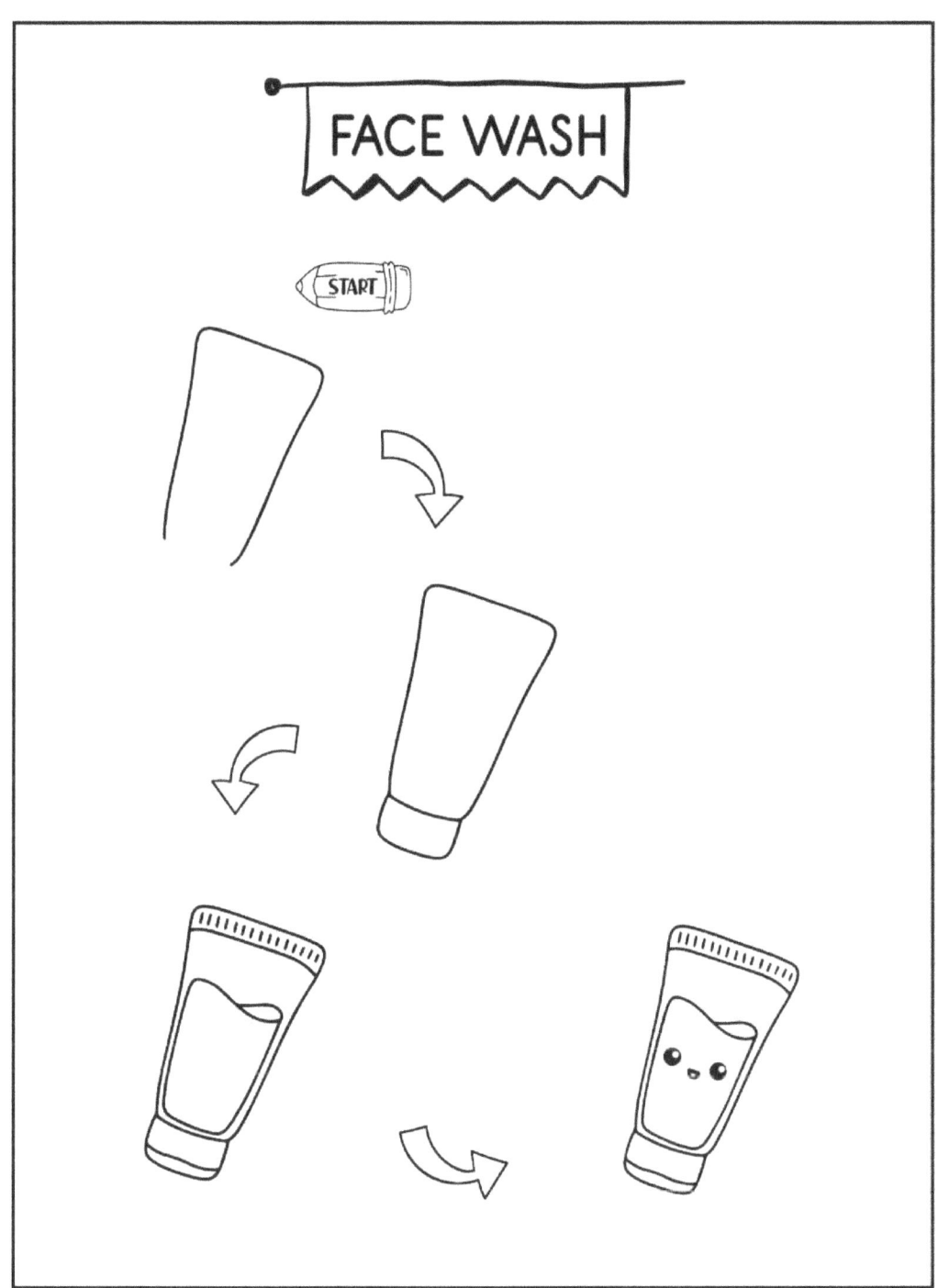

CARROT

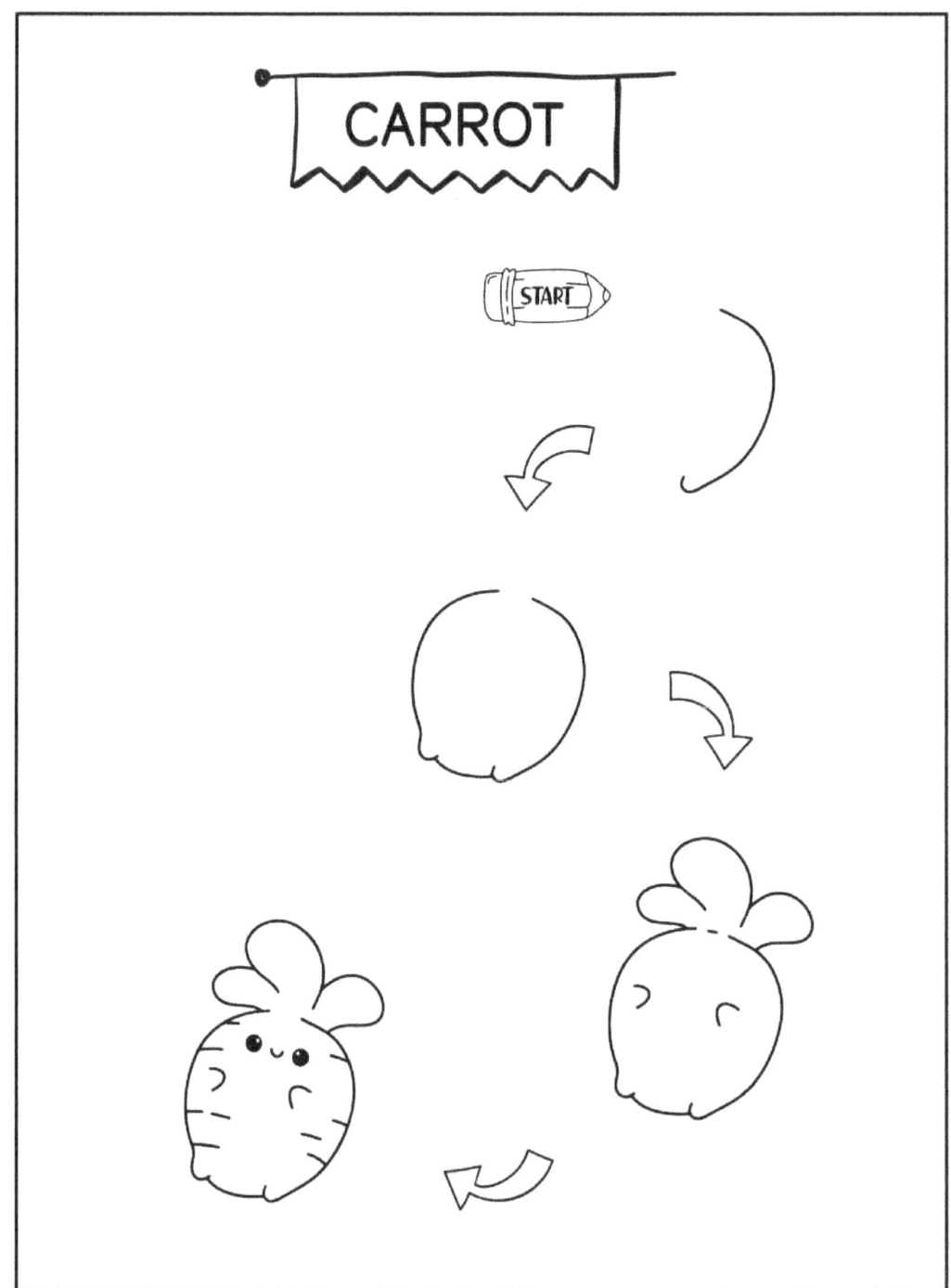

SHEEP

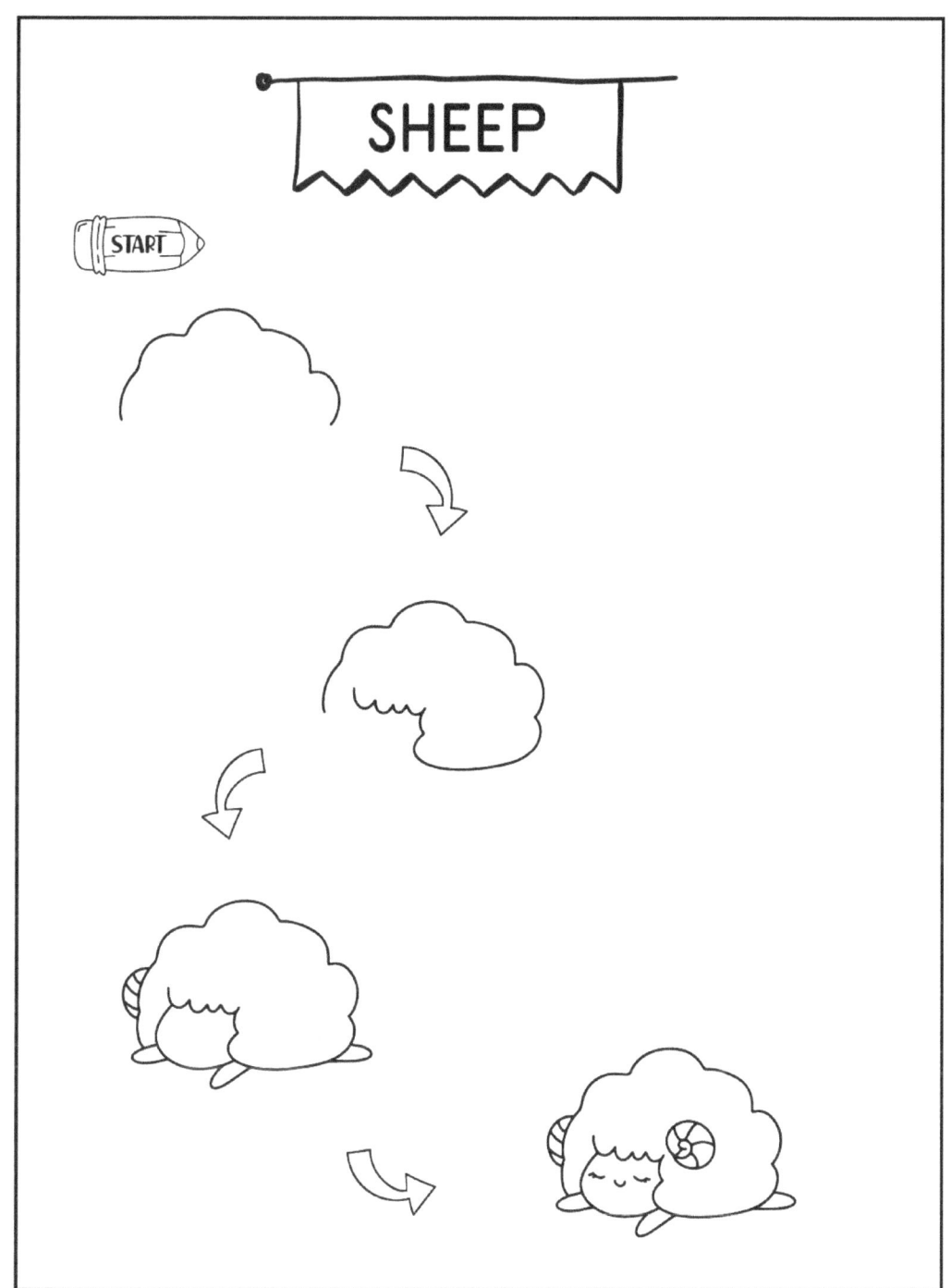

TEA BAG

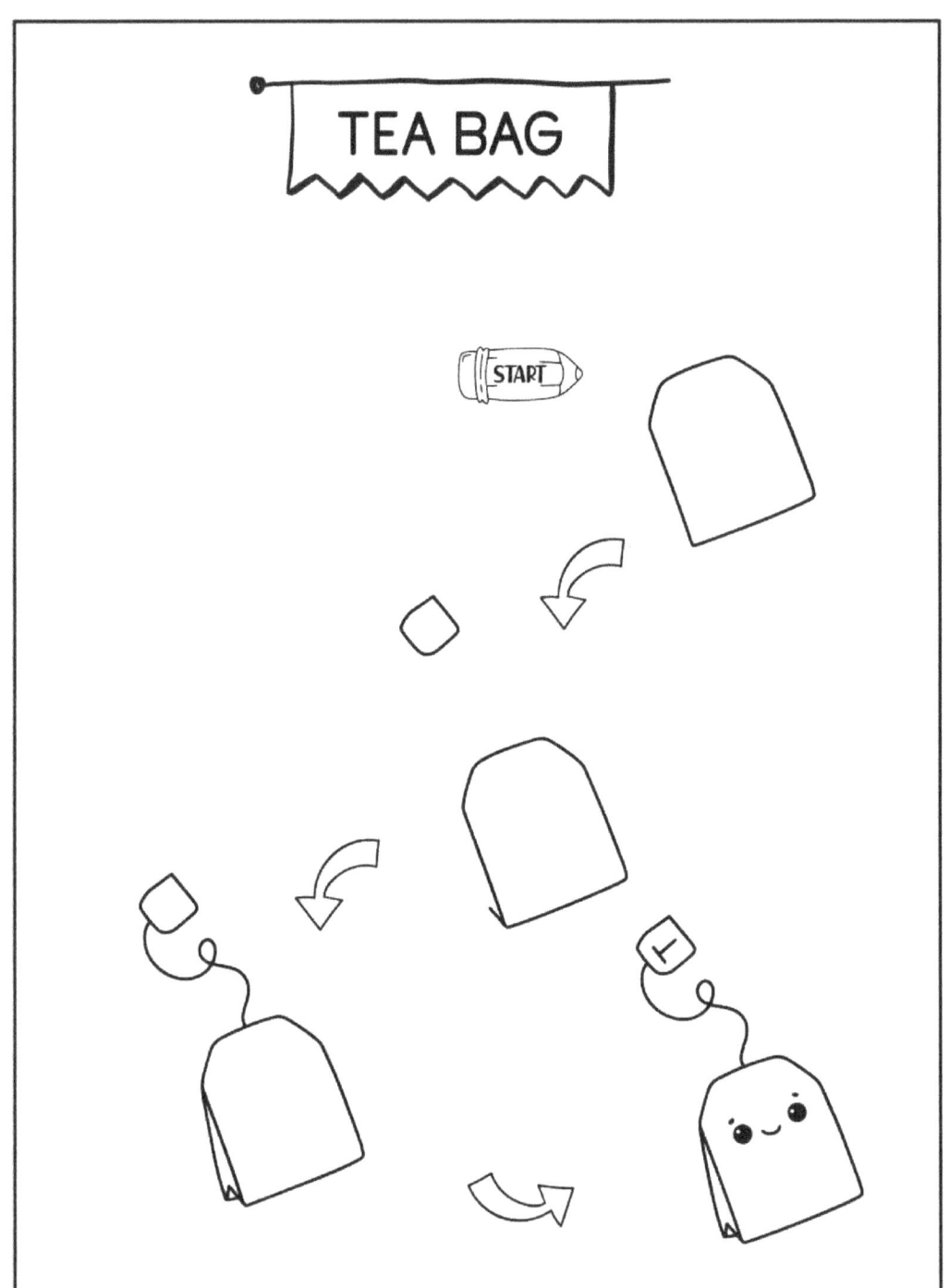

SPACESHIP

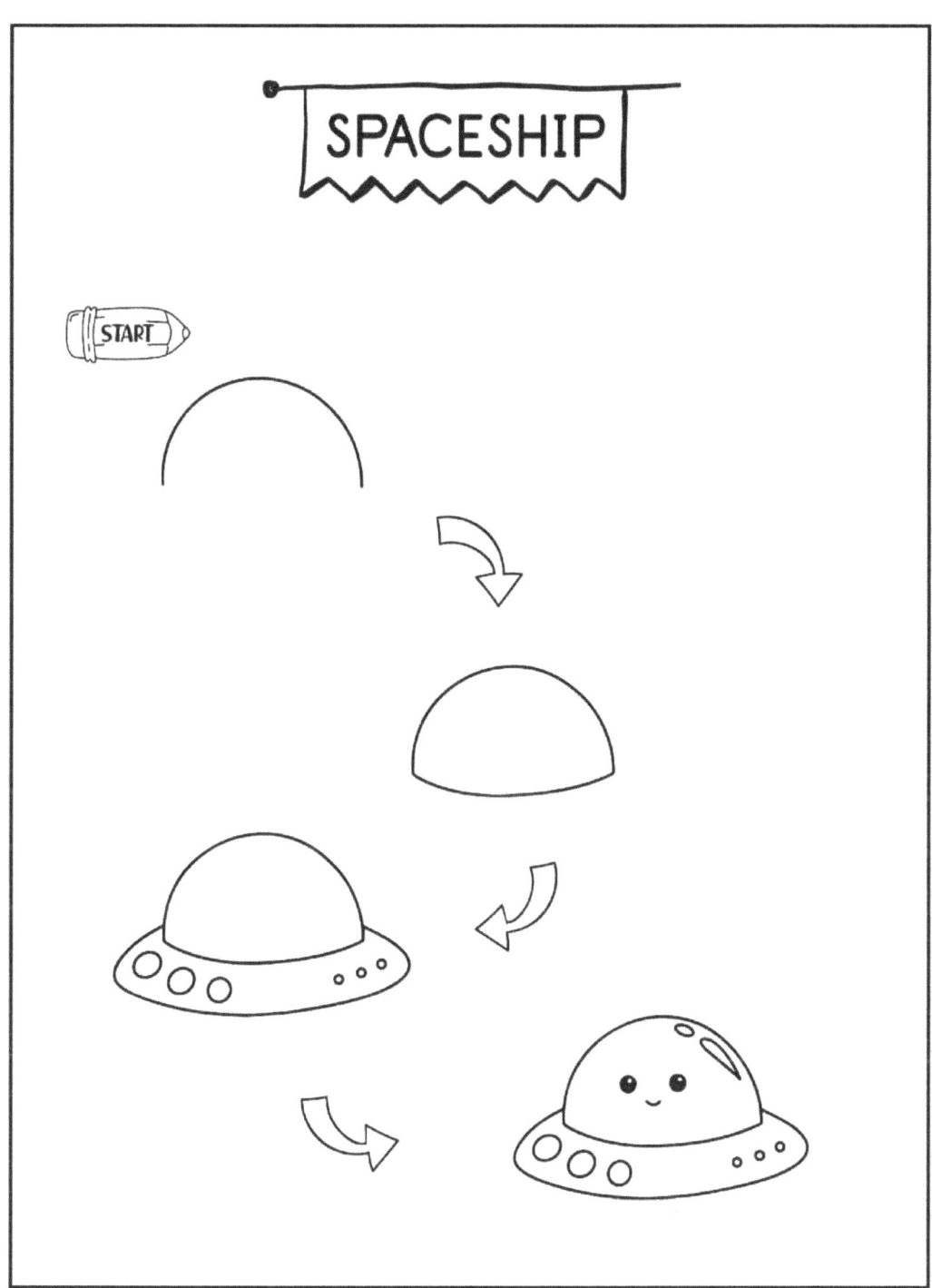

CACTUS

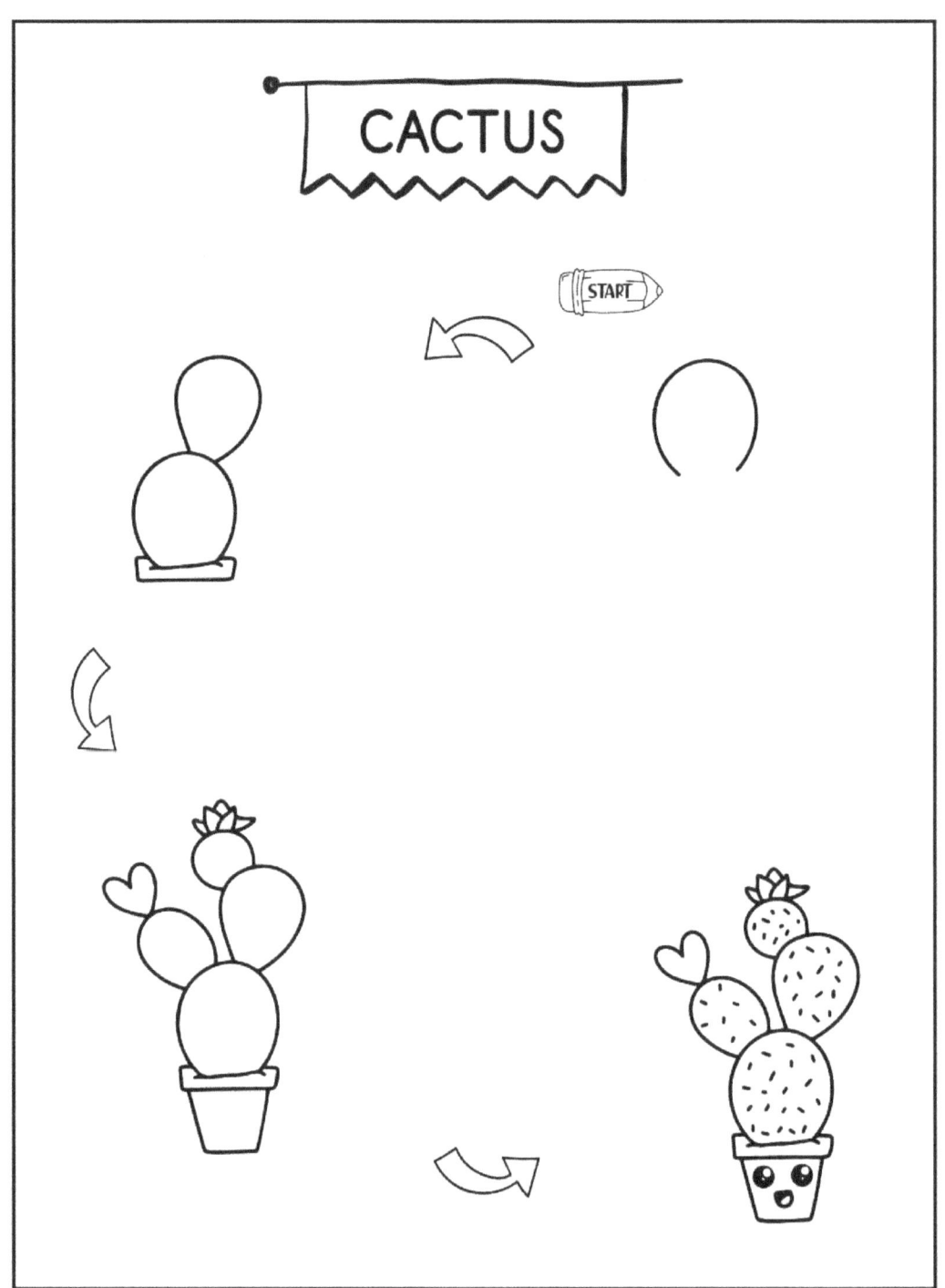

OCTOPUS

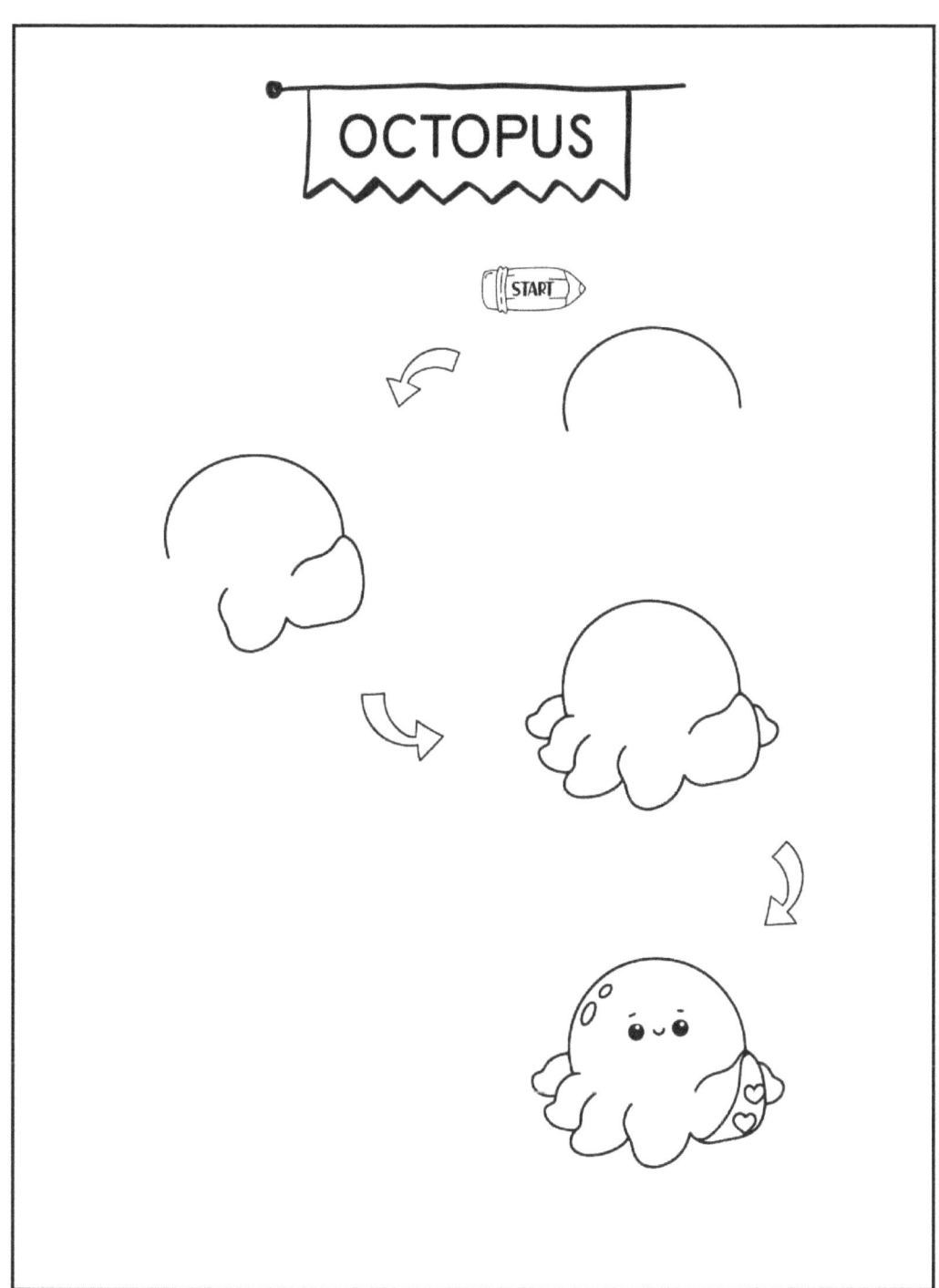

PENGUIN

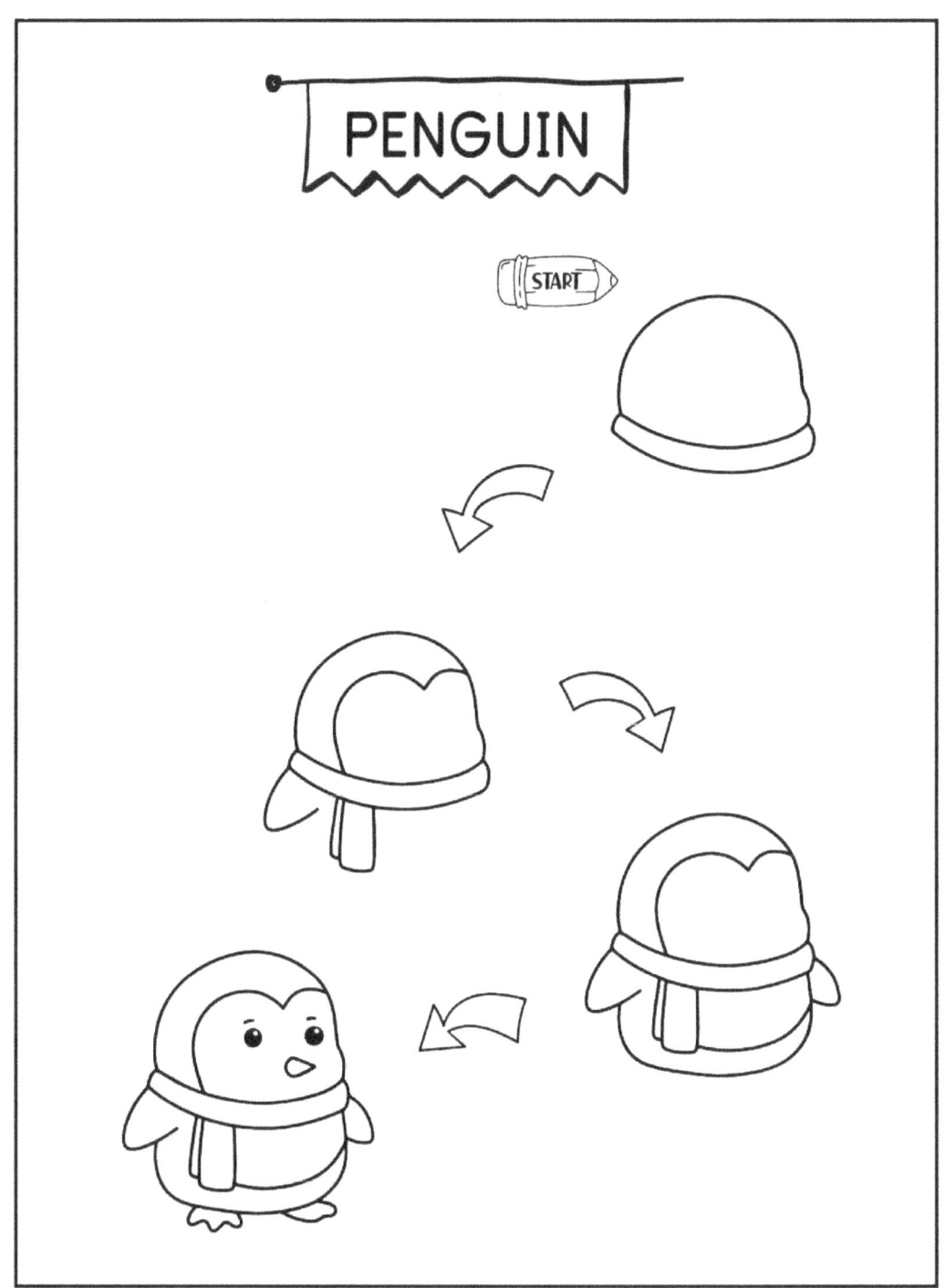

START

KOALA

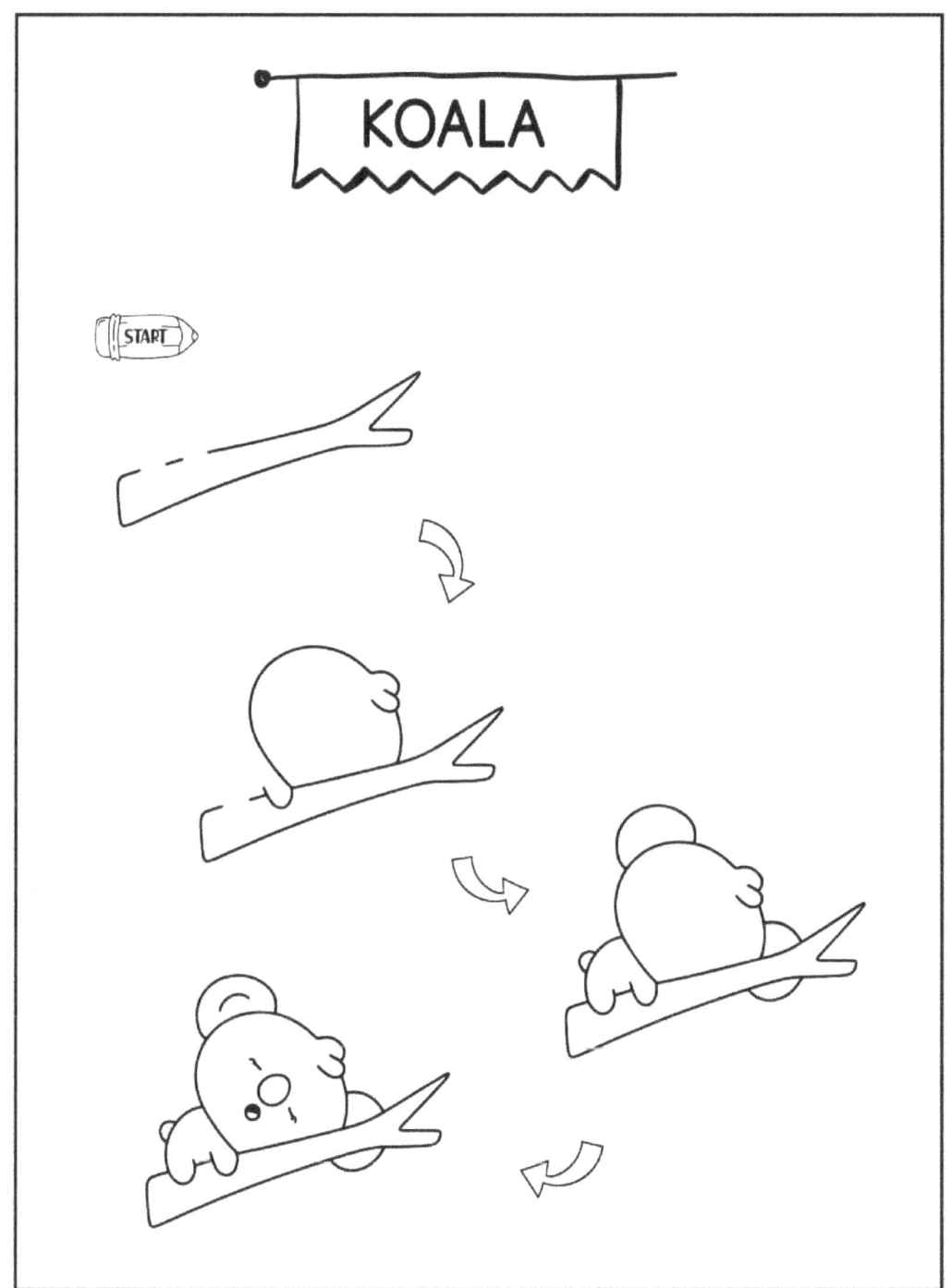

START

63

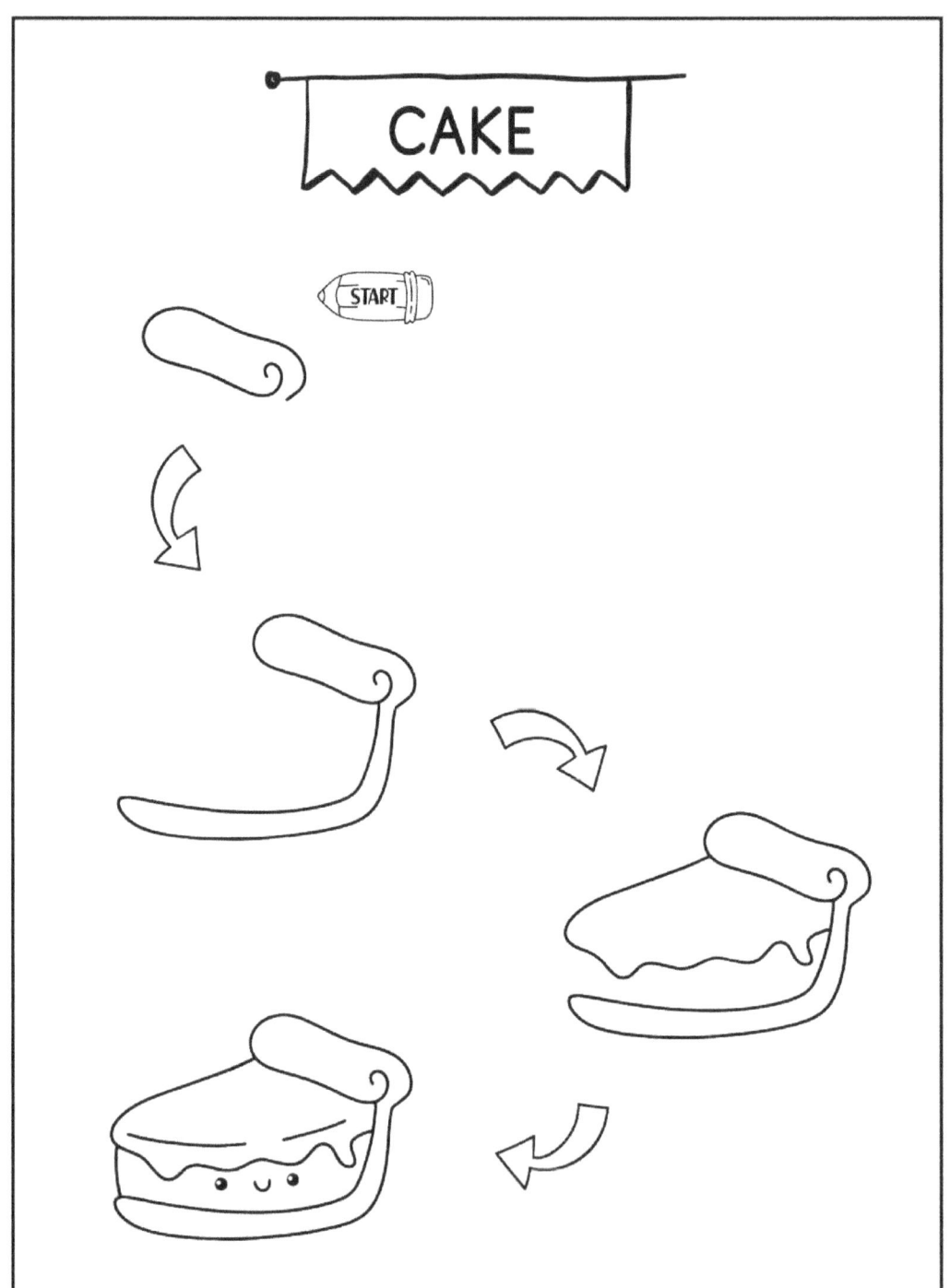

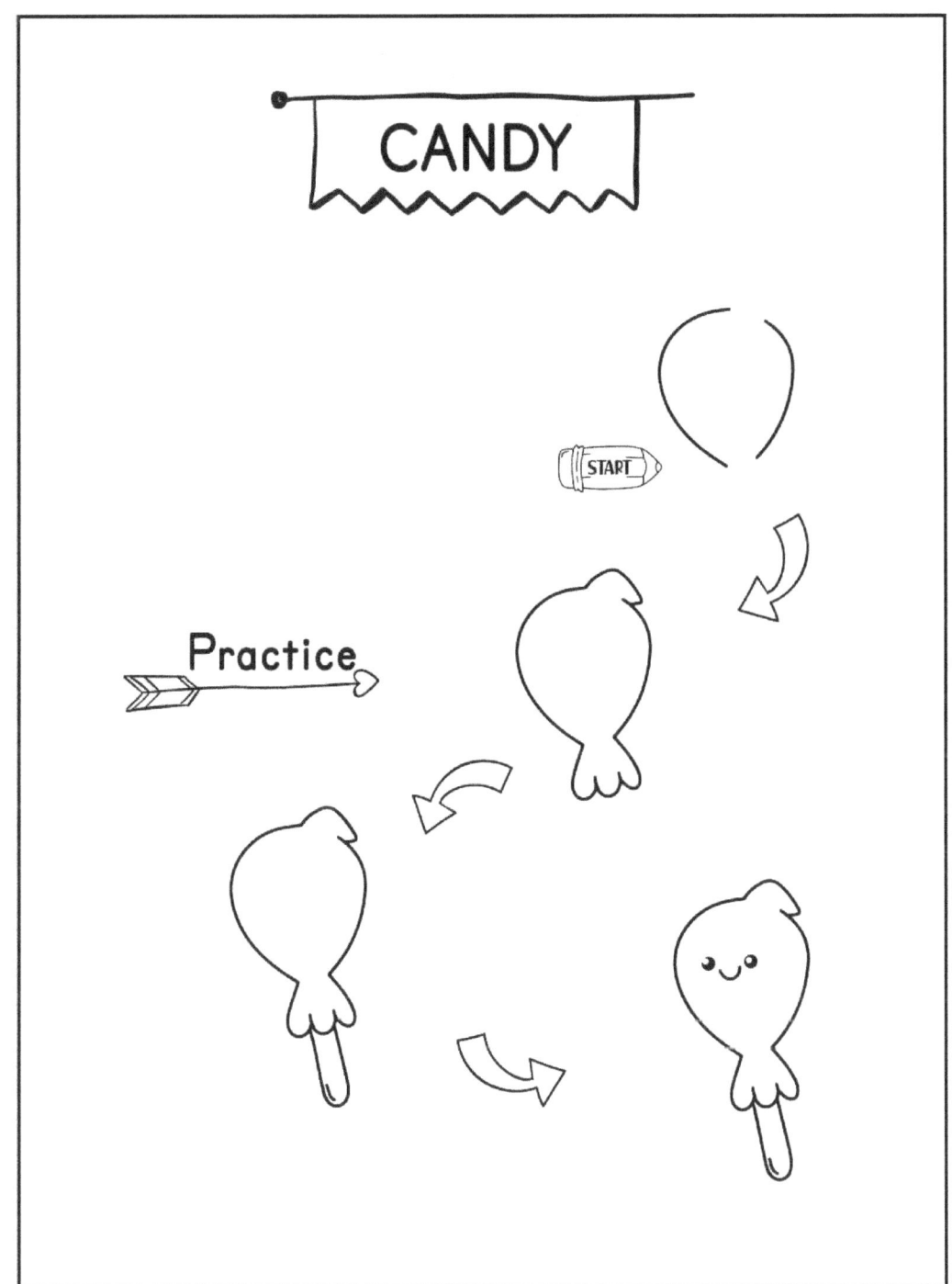

CANDY

START

Practice

ERASER

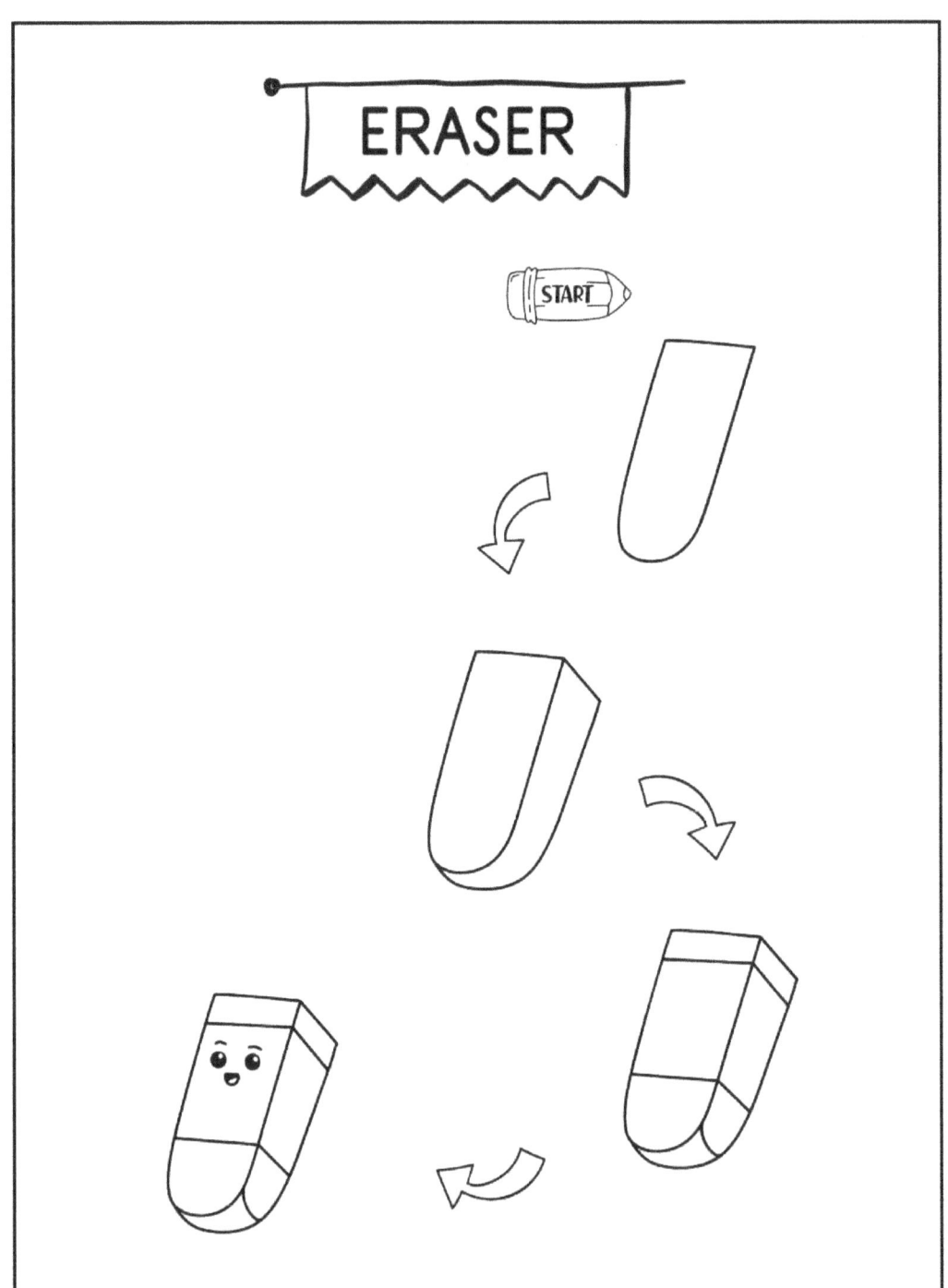

PLATYPUS

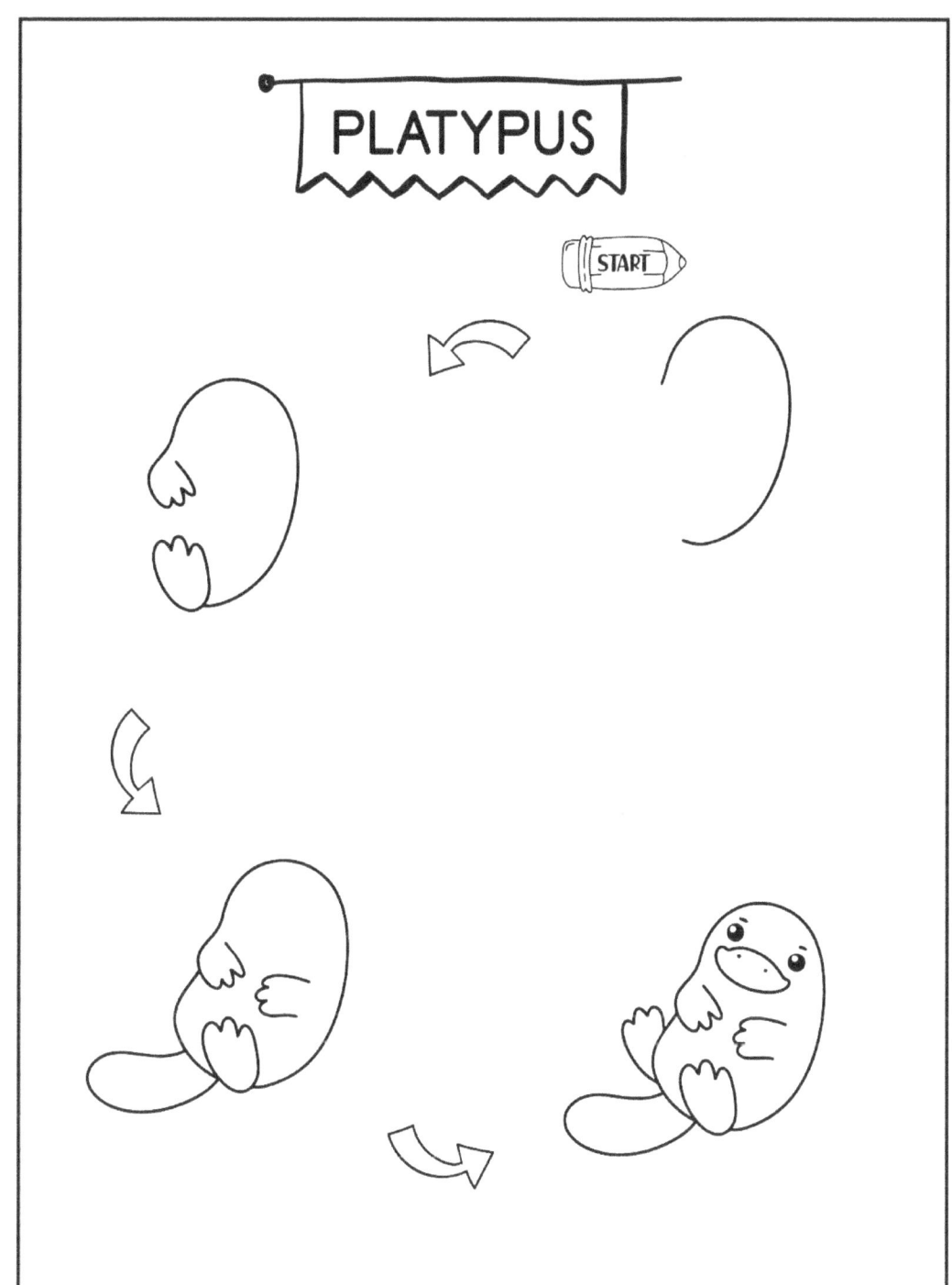

RAINBOW

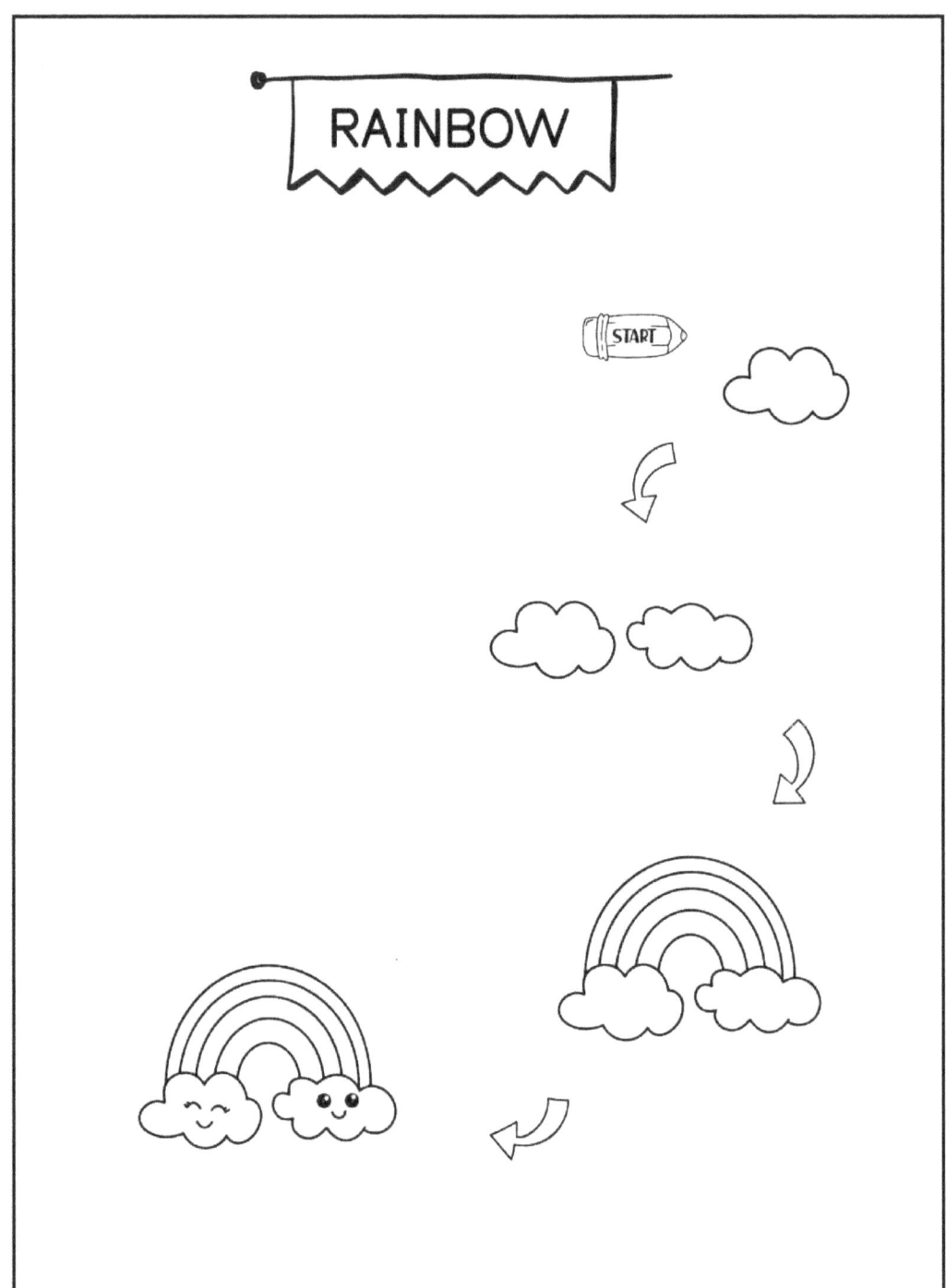

MILK BOX

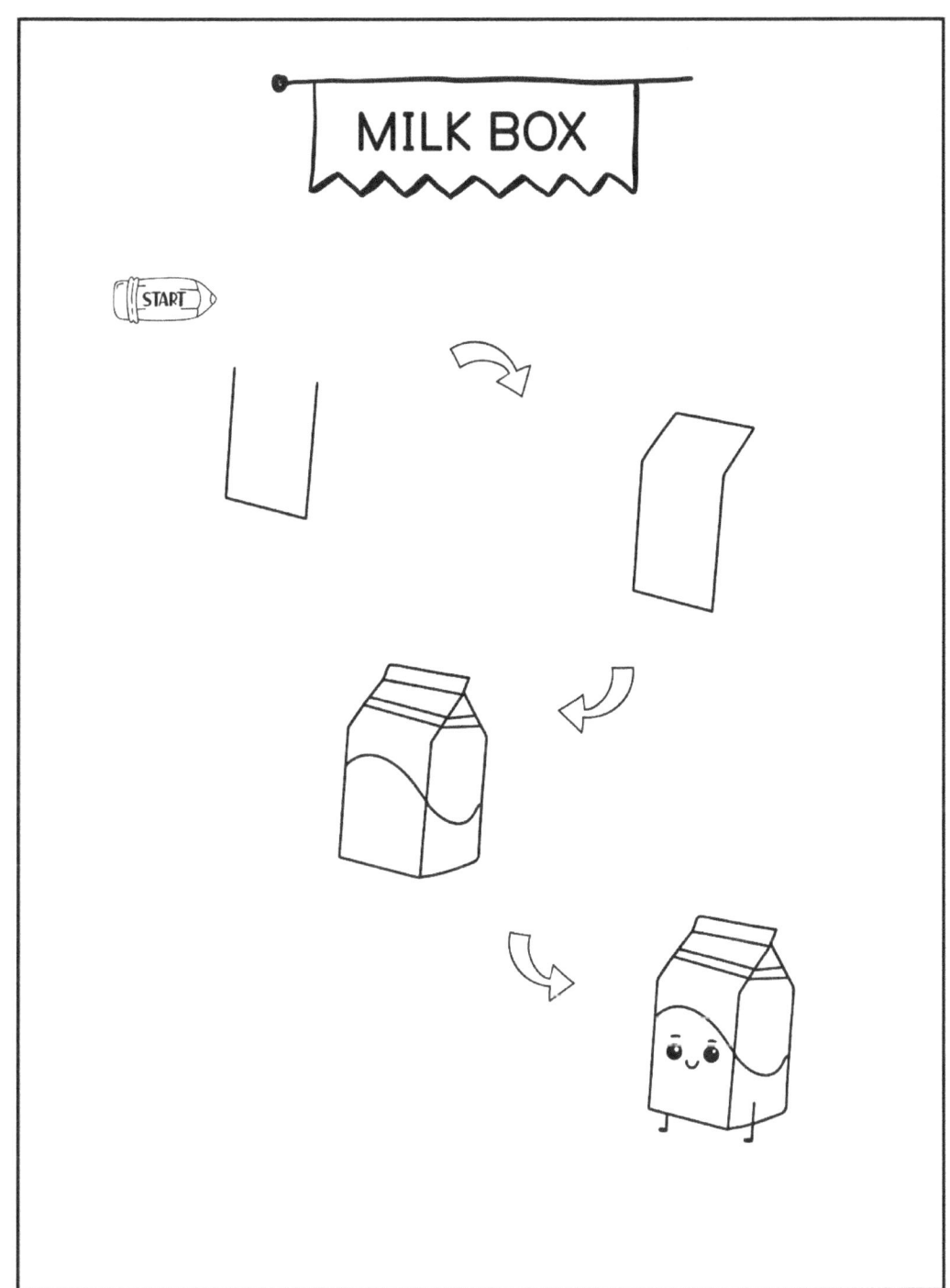

POTION BOTTLES

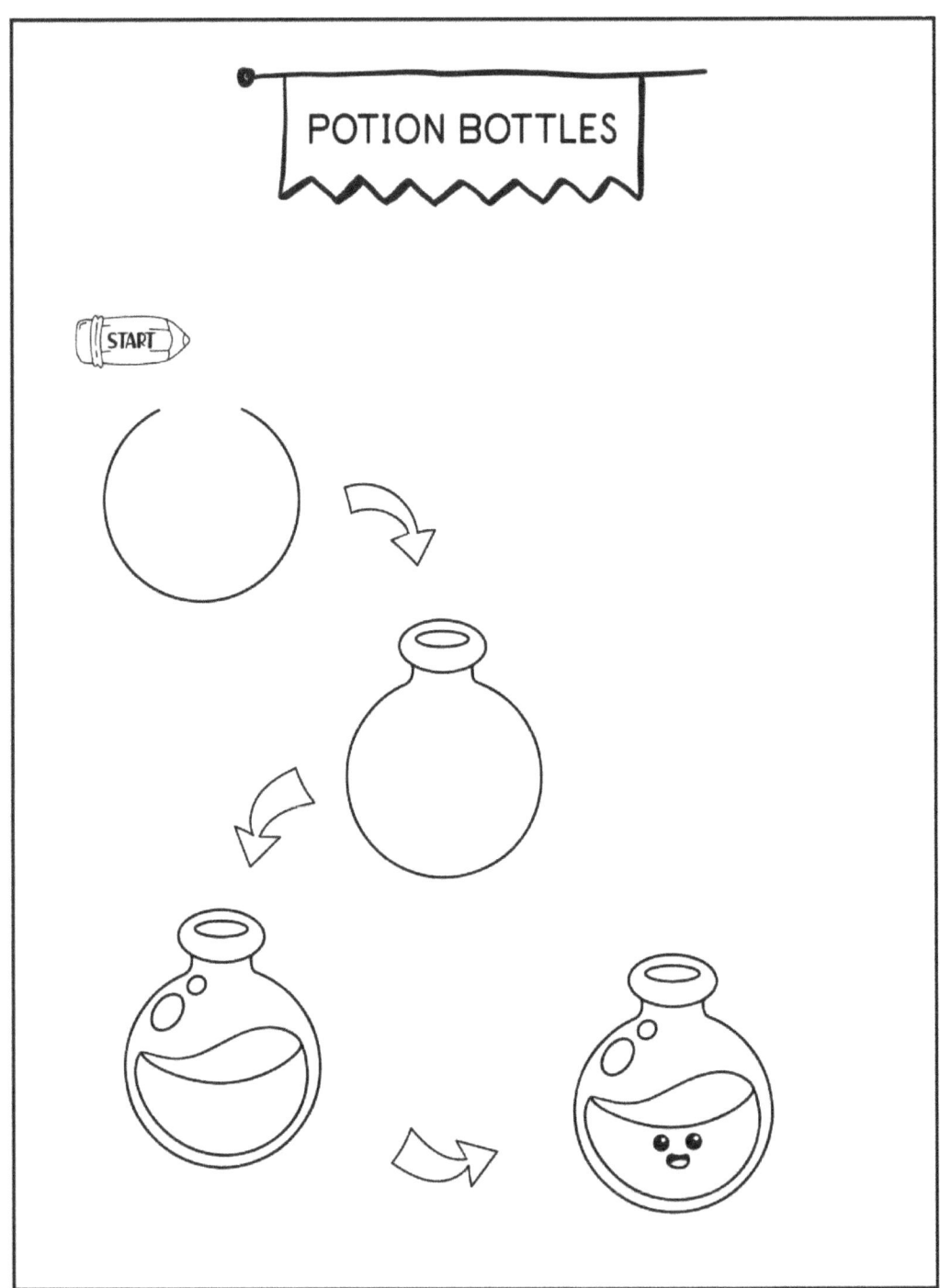

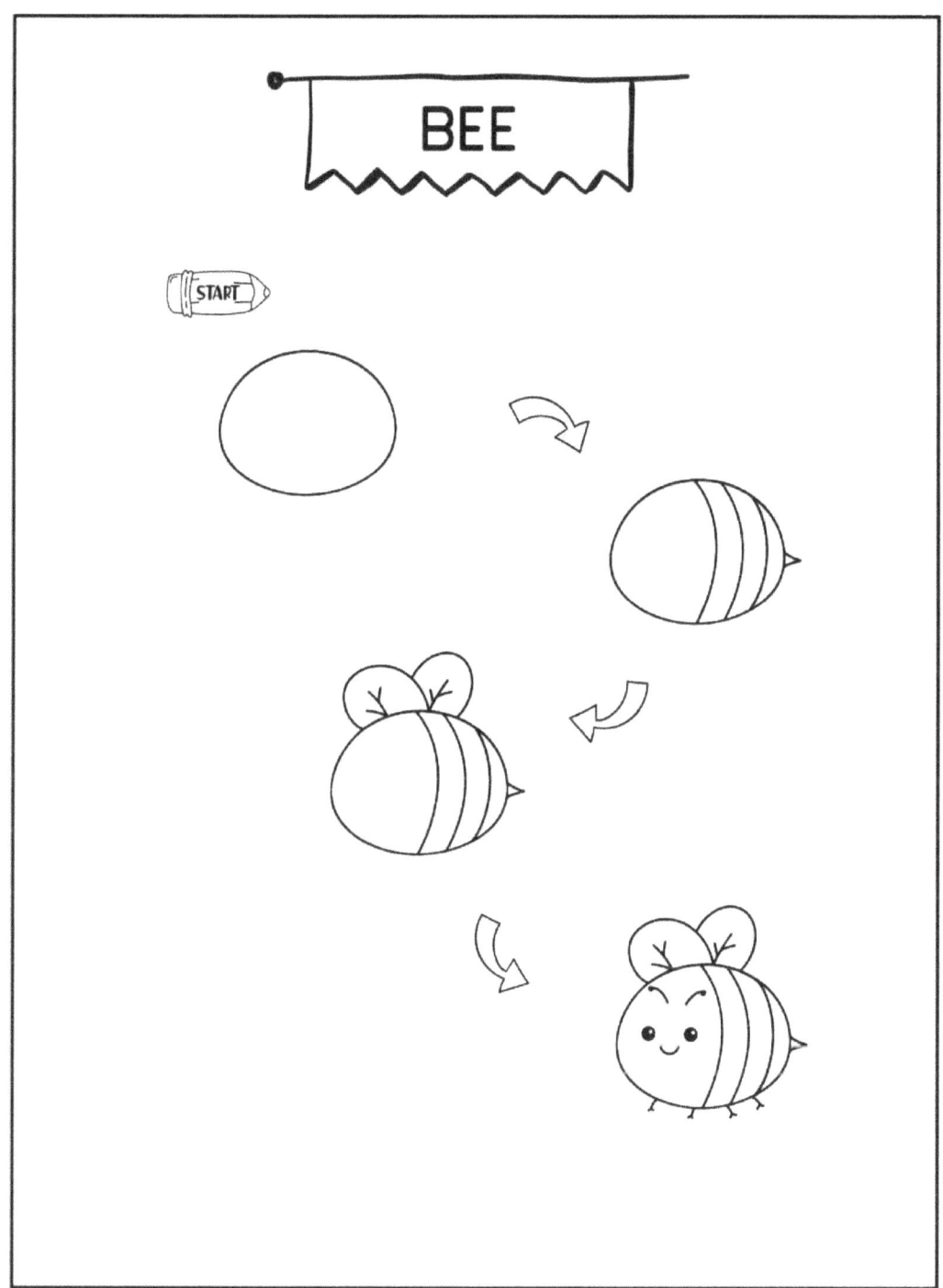

BEE

START

STAPLER

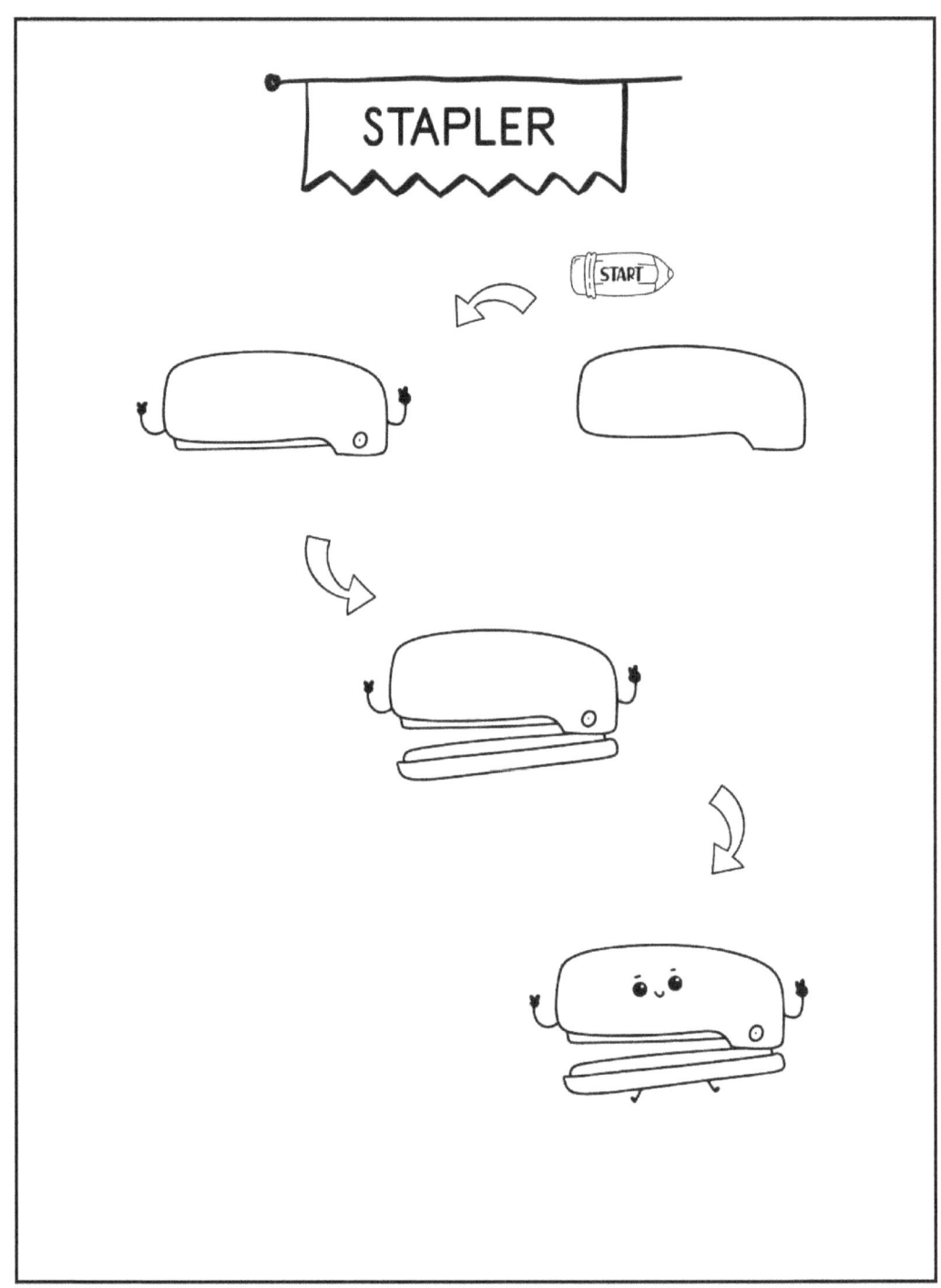

GUITAR

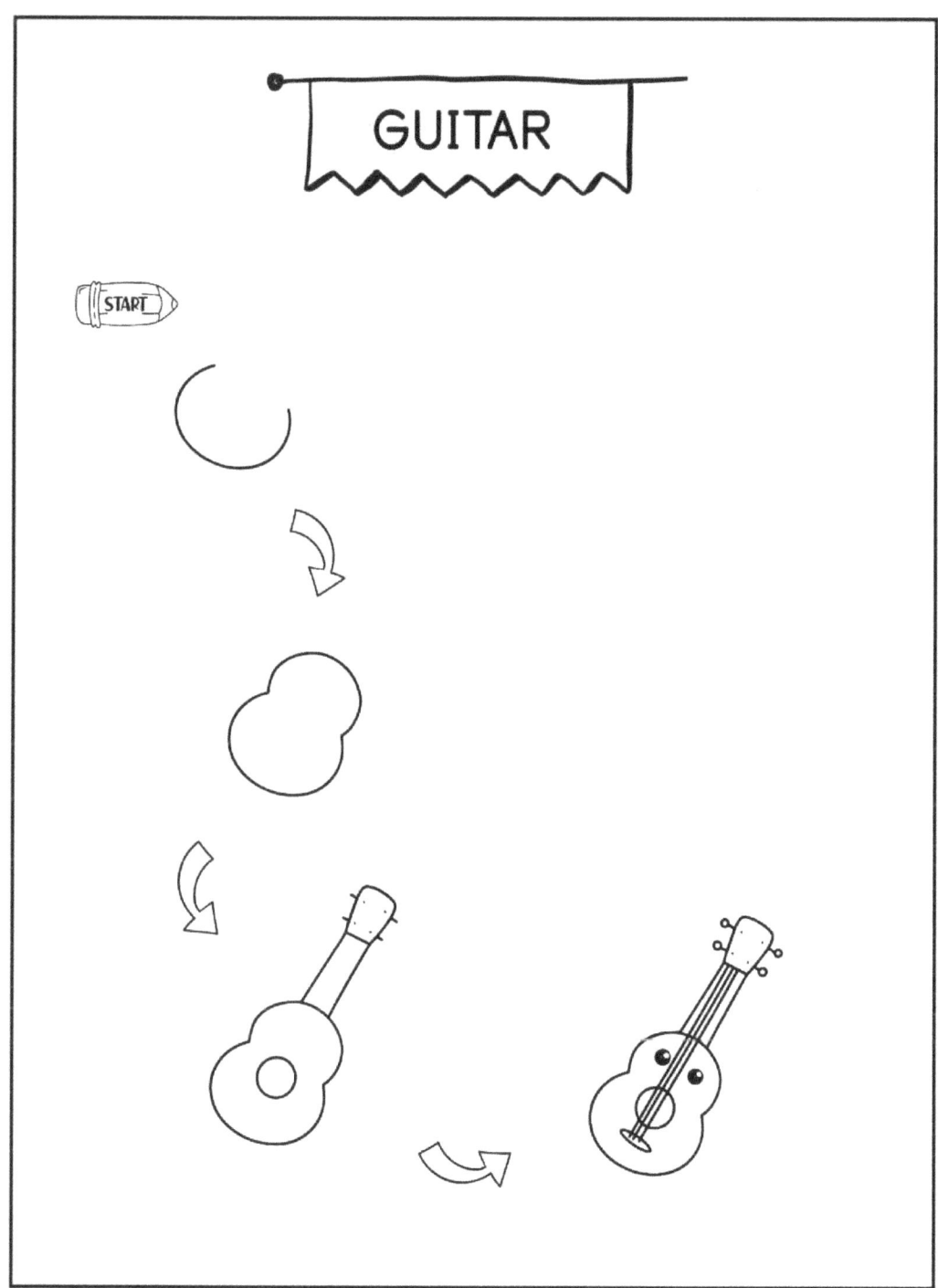

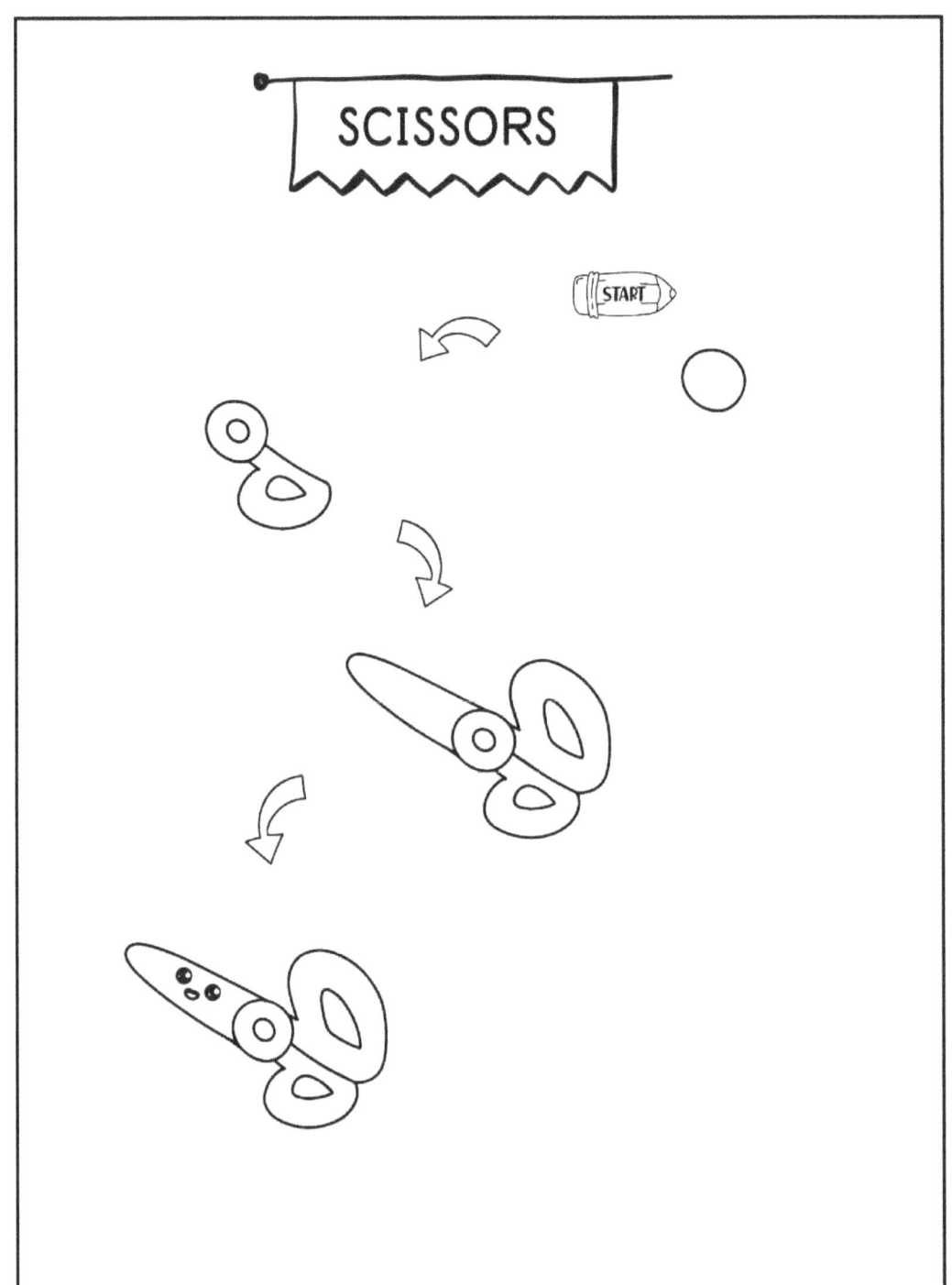

FRENCH FRIES

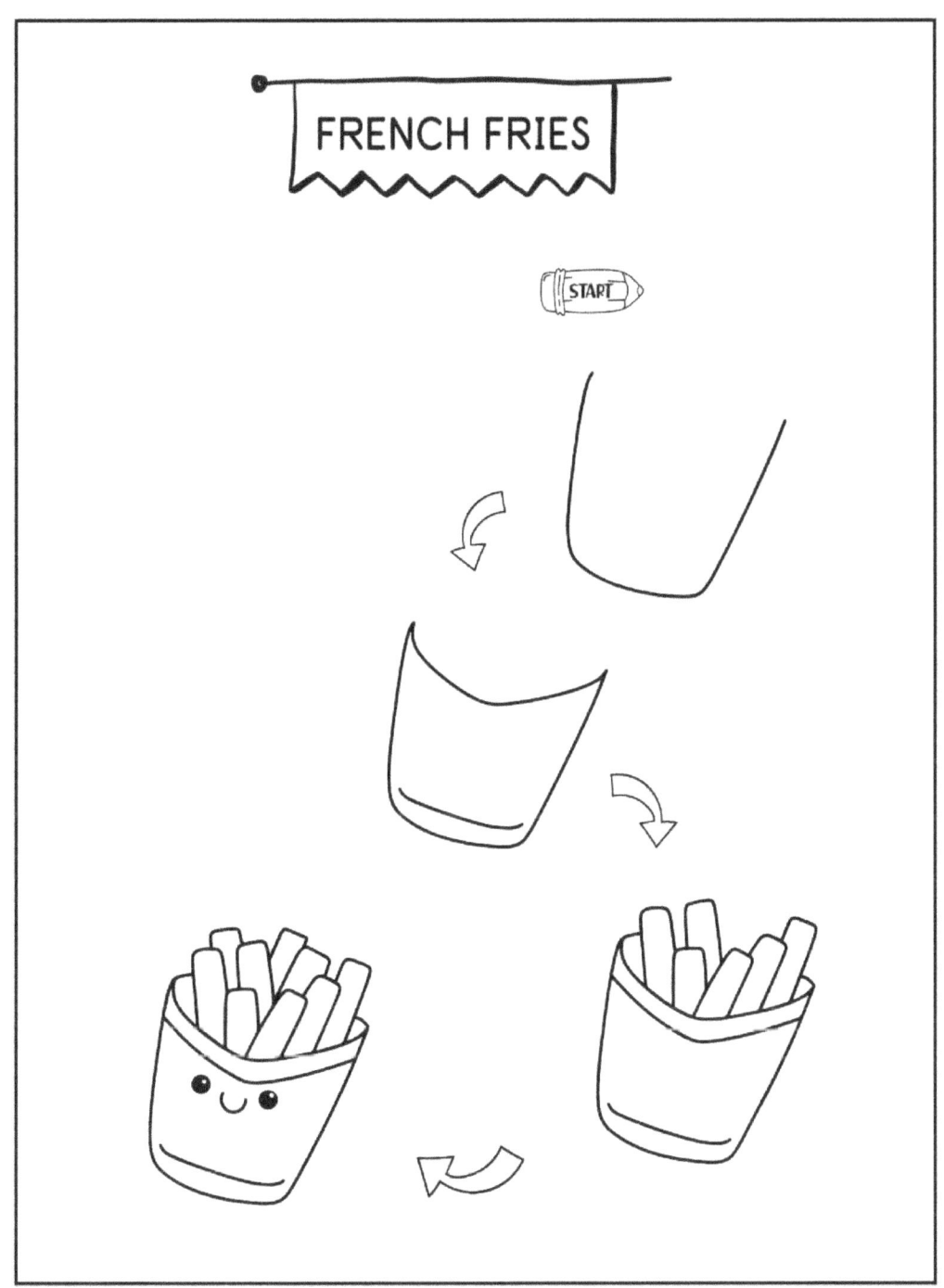

BURGER

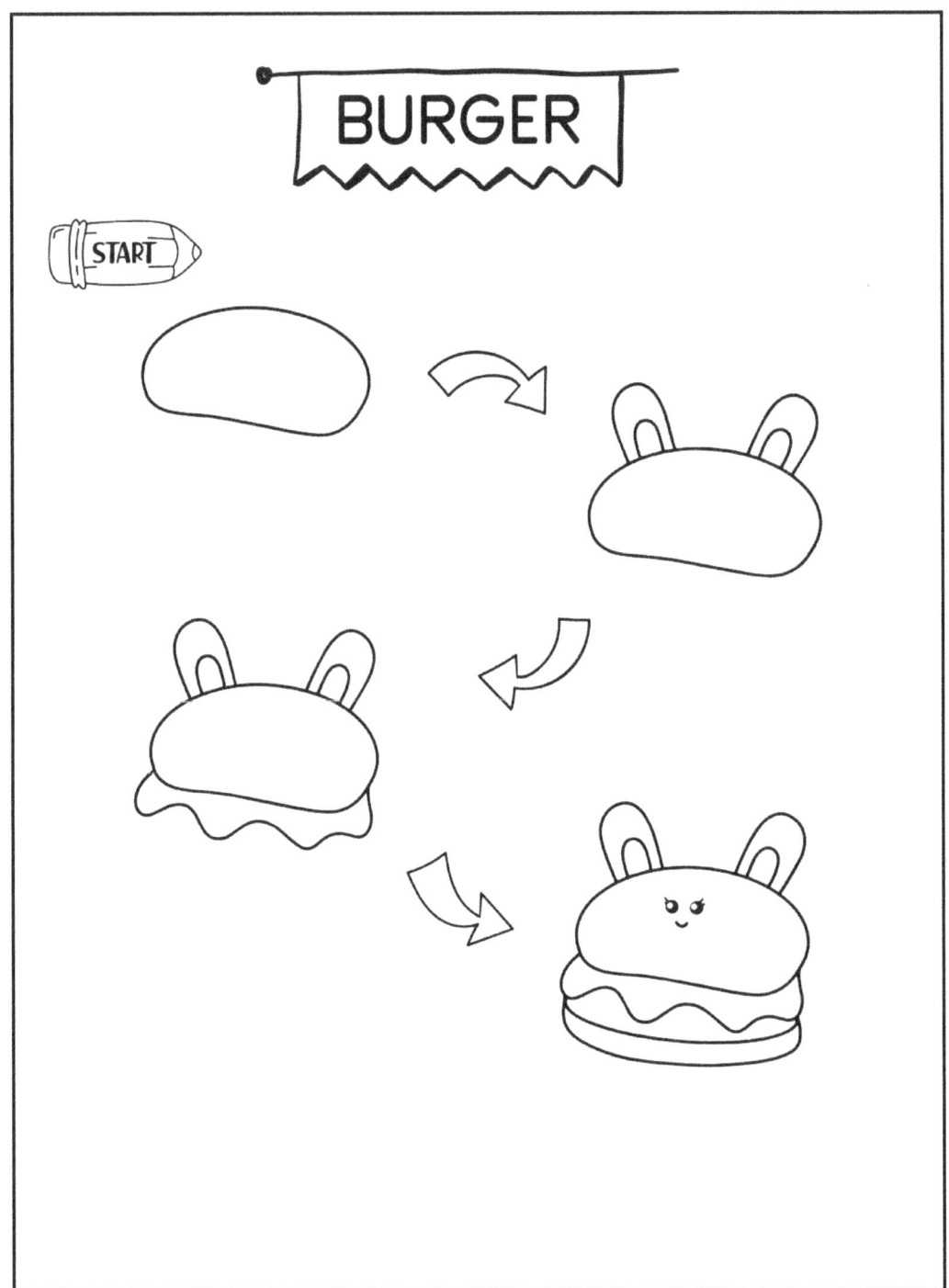

HAIR DRYER

START

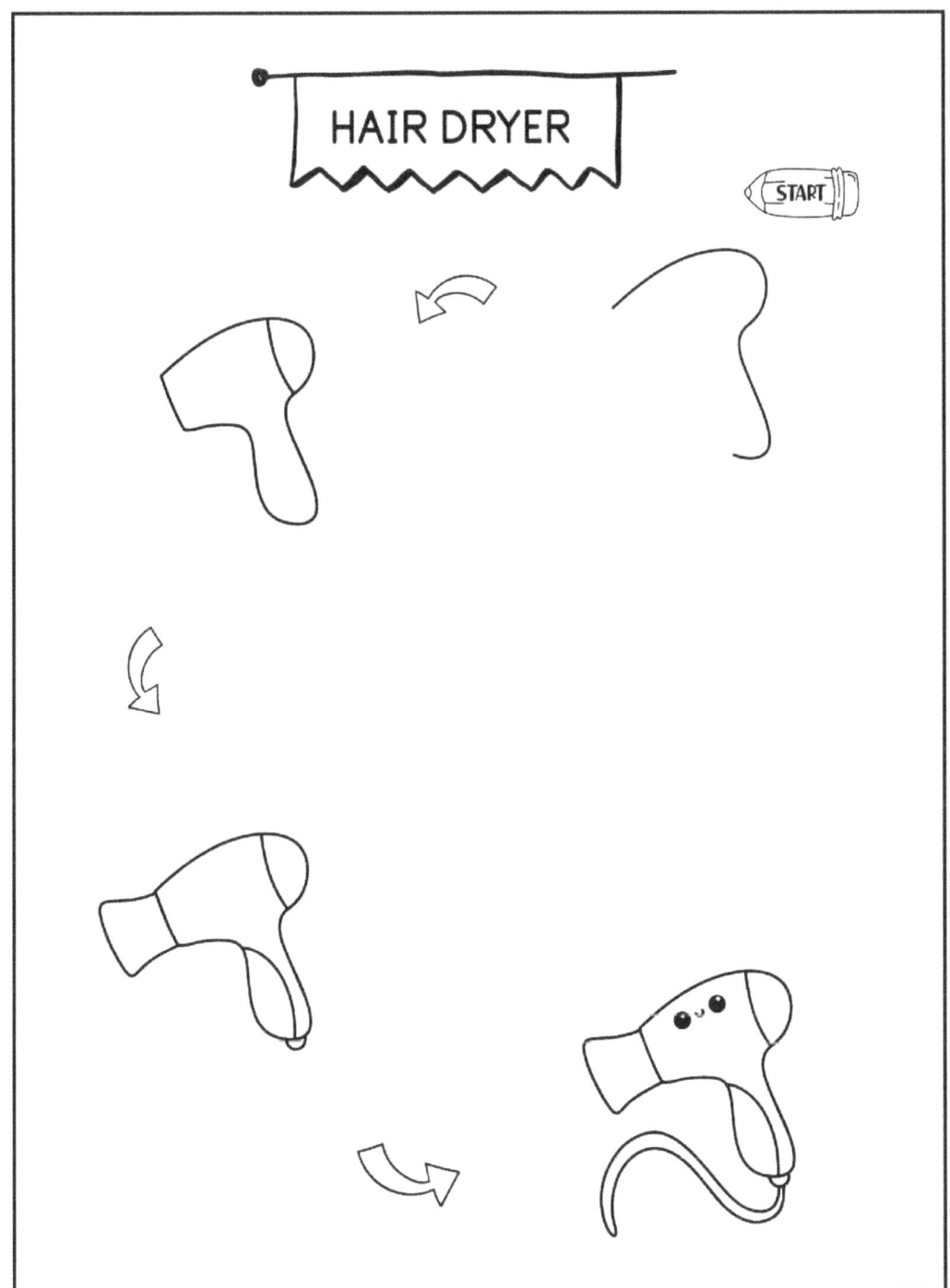

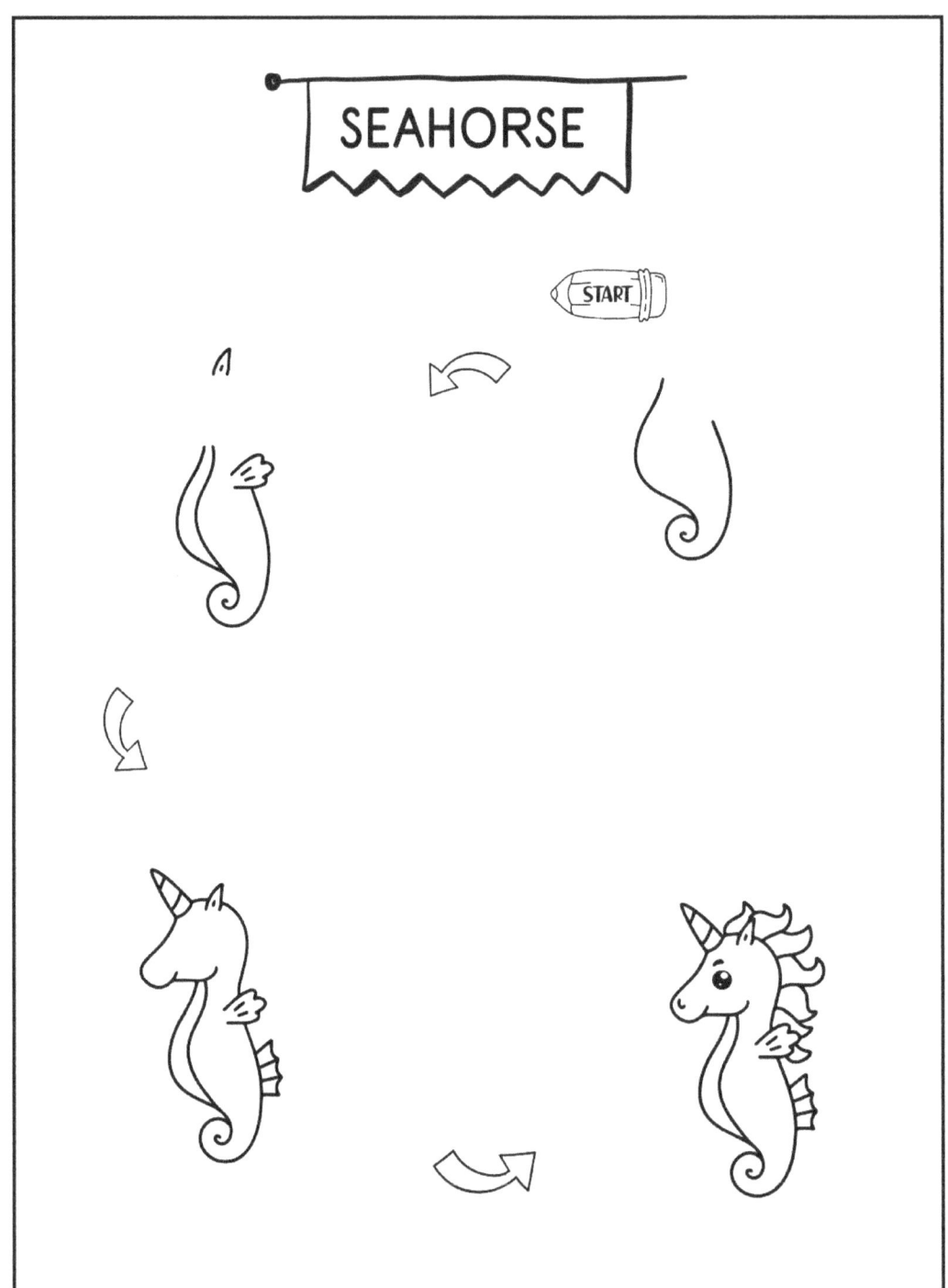

SEAHORSE

START

BACKPACK

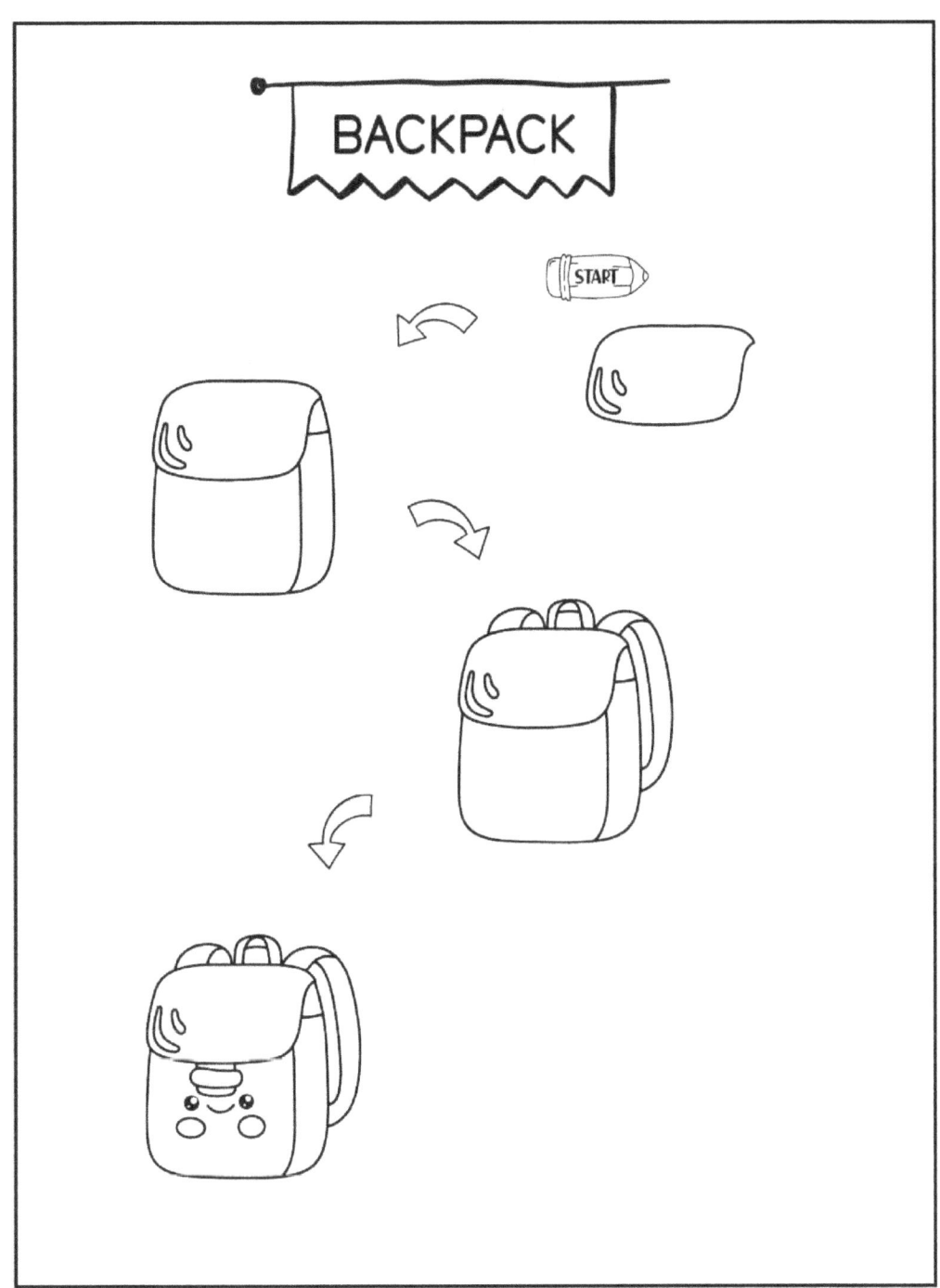

LLAMA

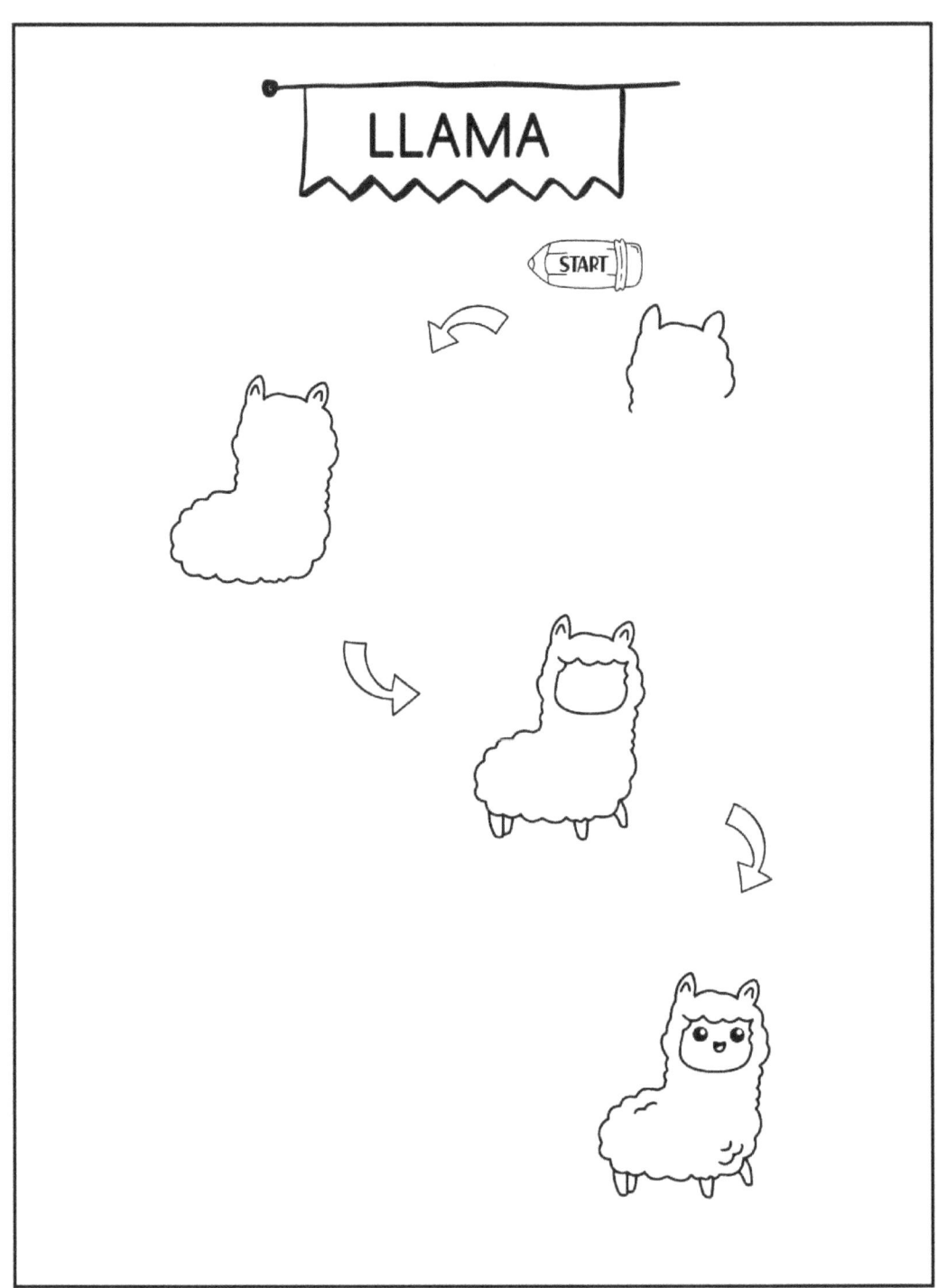

BATHTUB

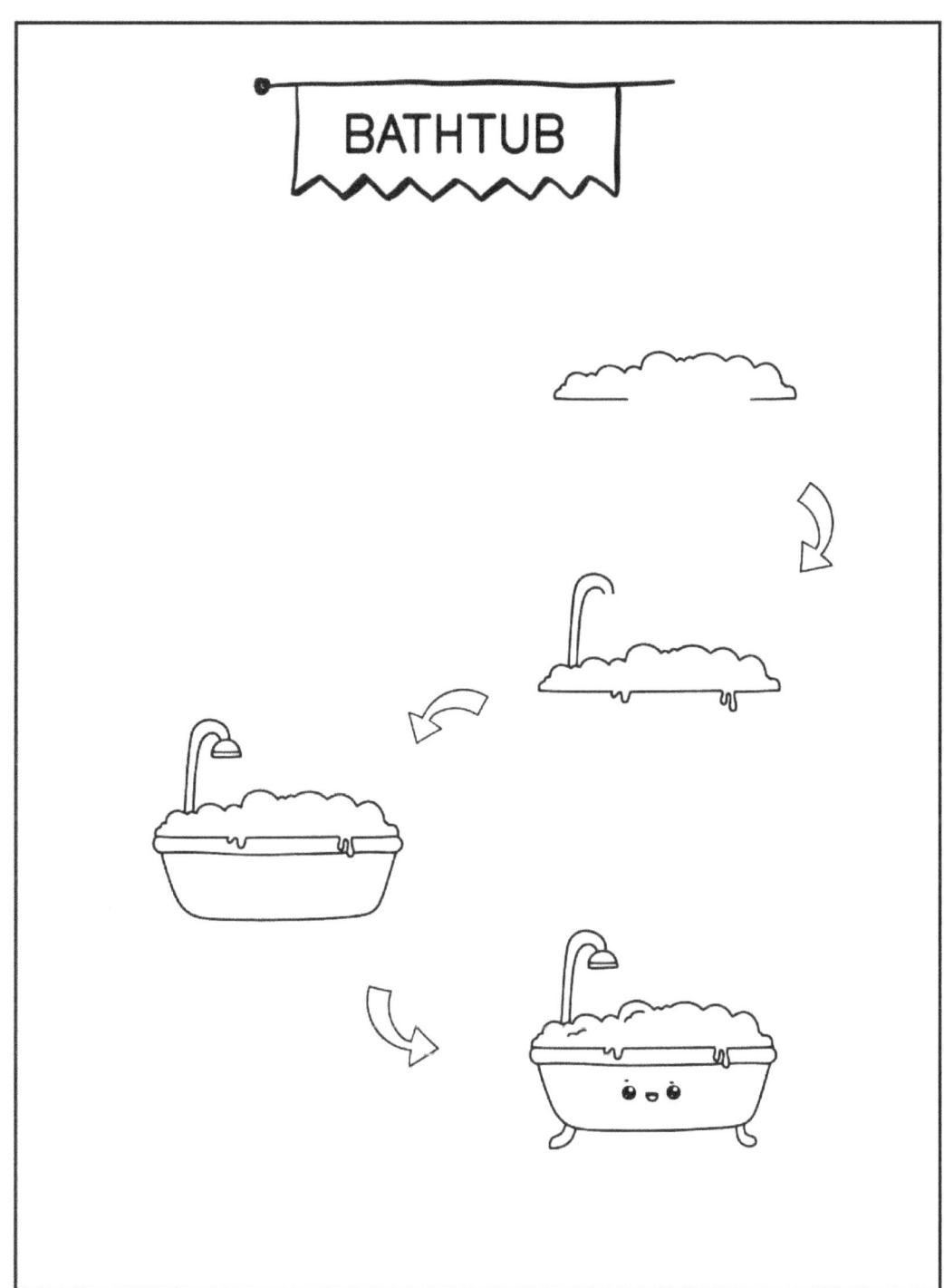

CANDLE

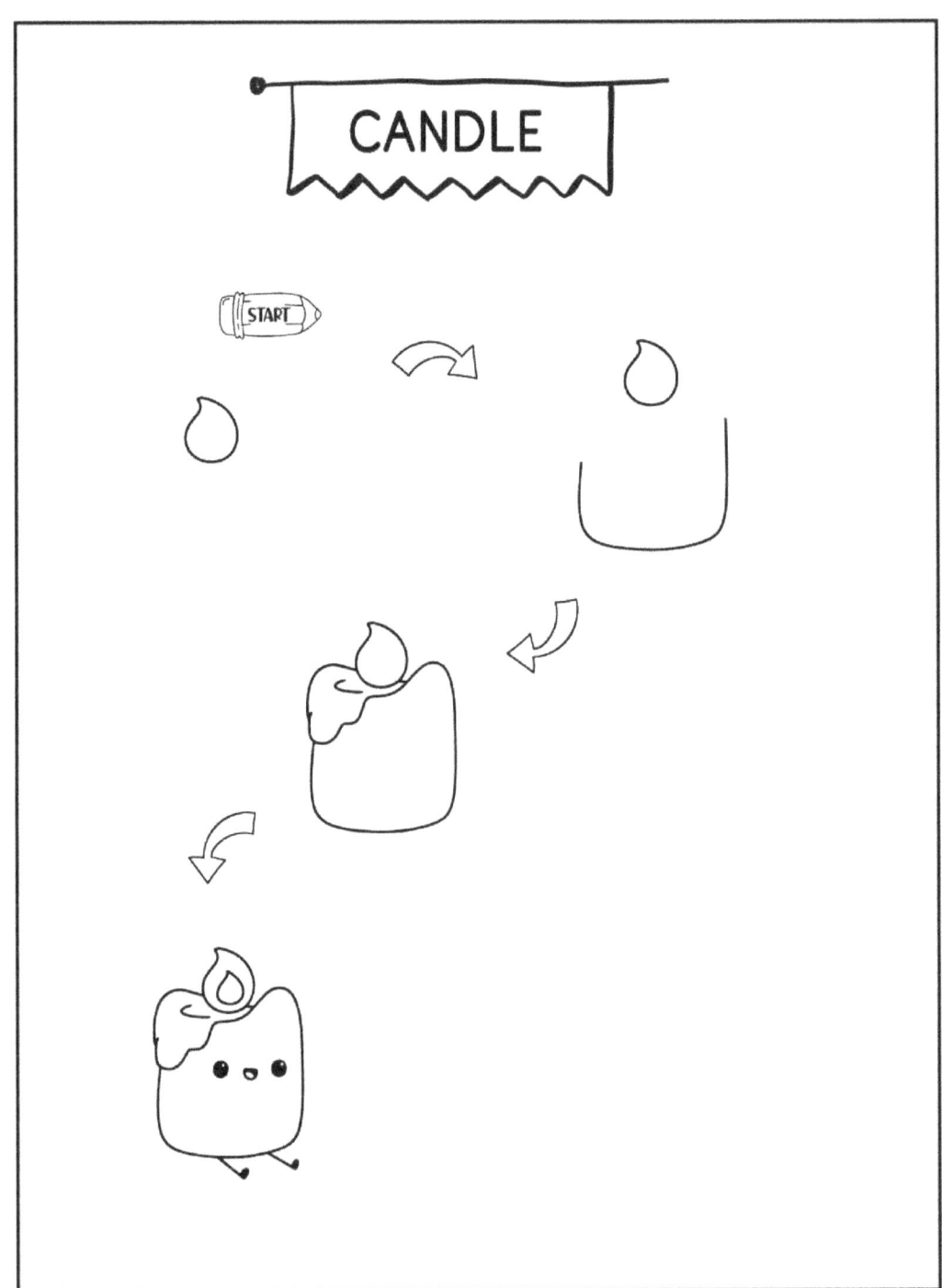

MUSHROOM

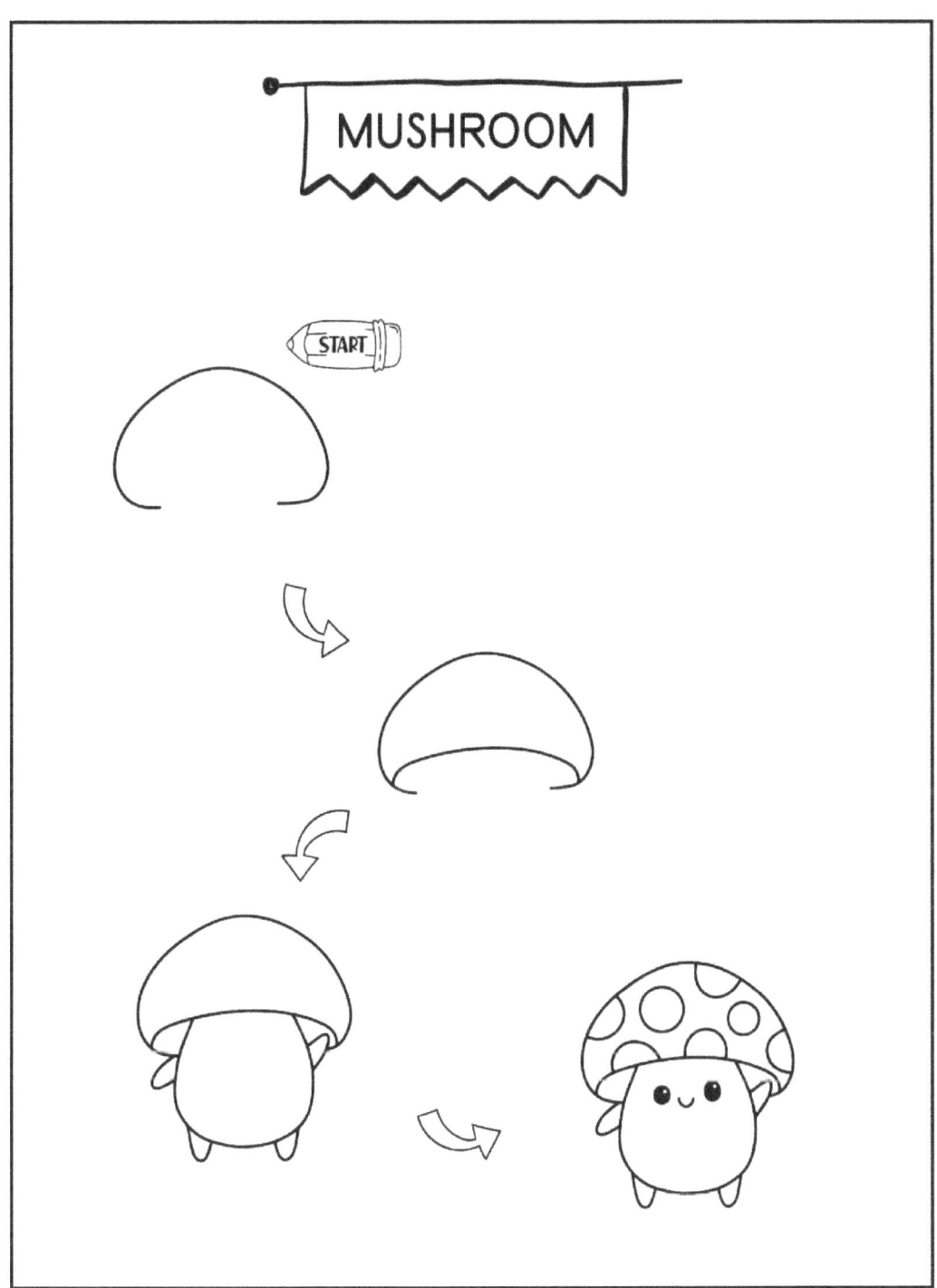

SLOTH

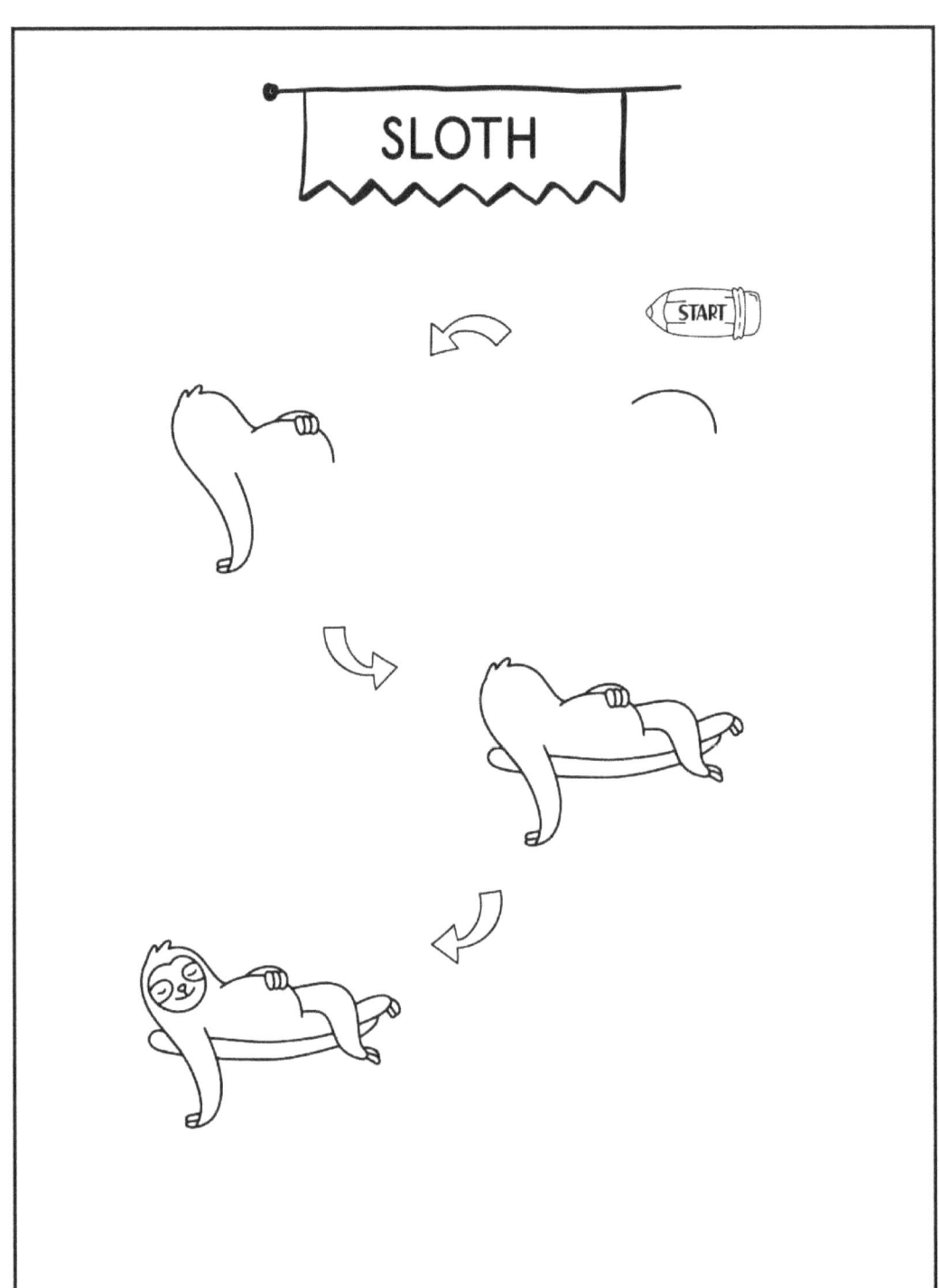

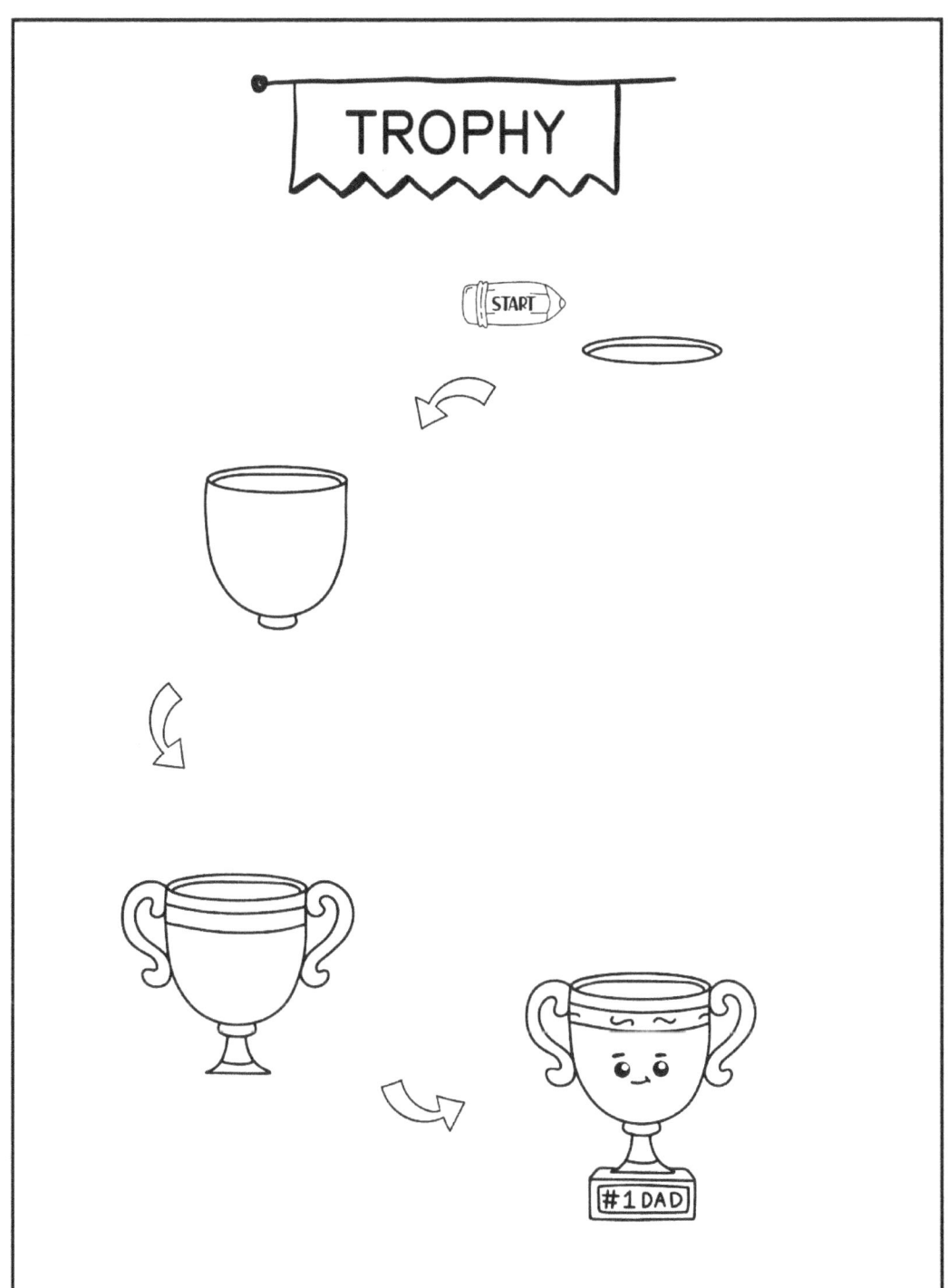

PINEAPPLE

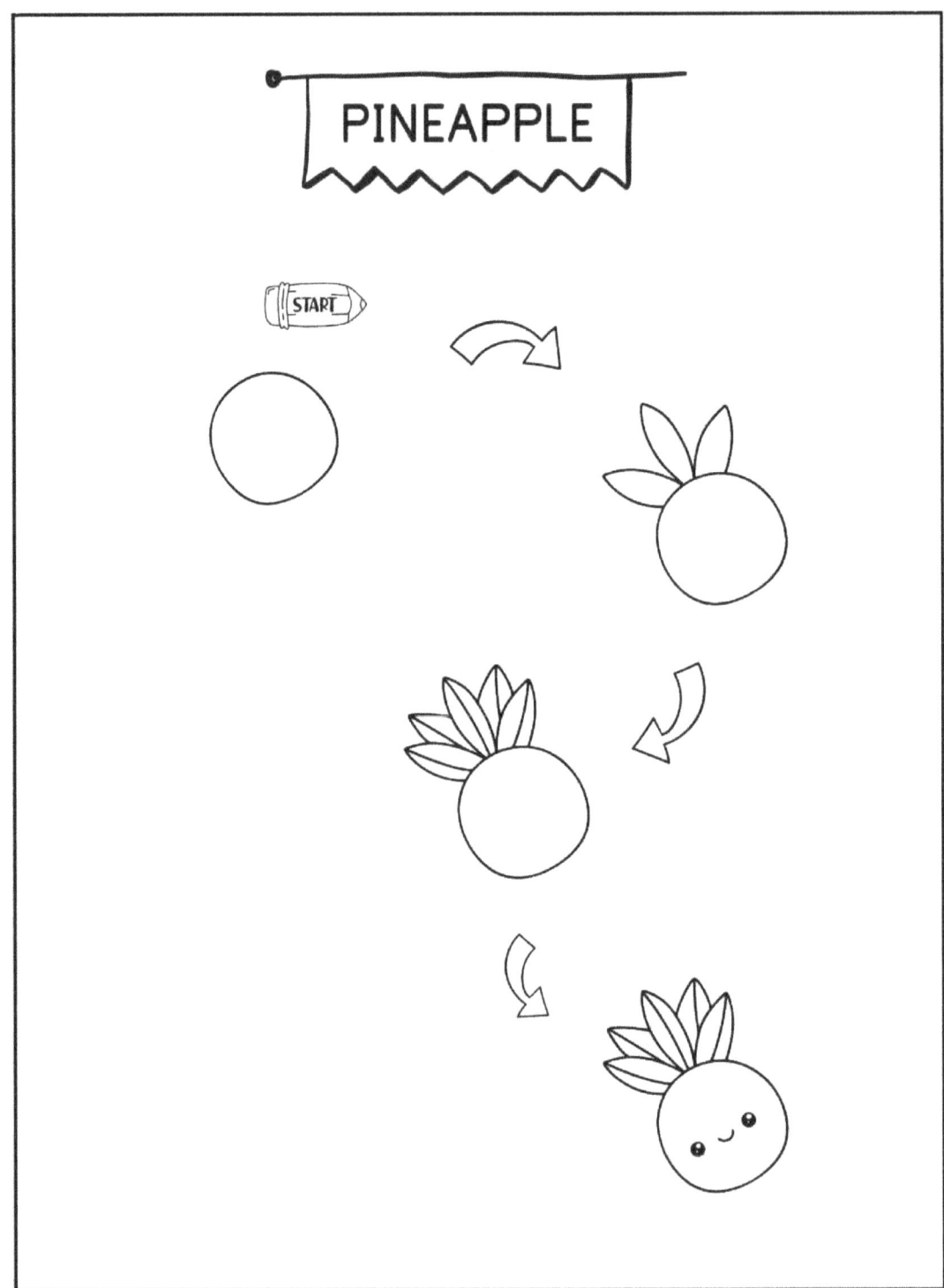

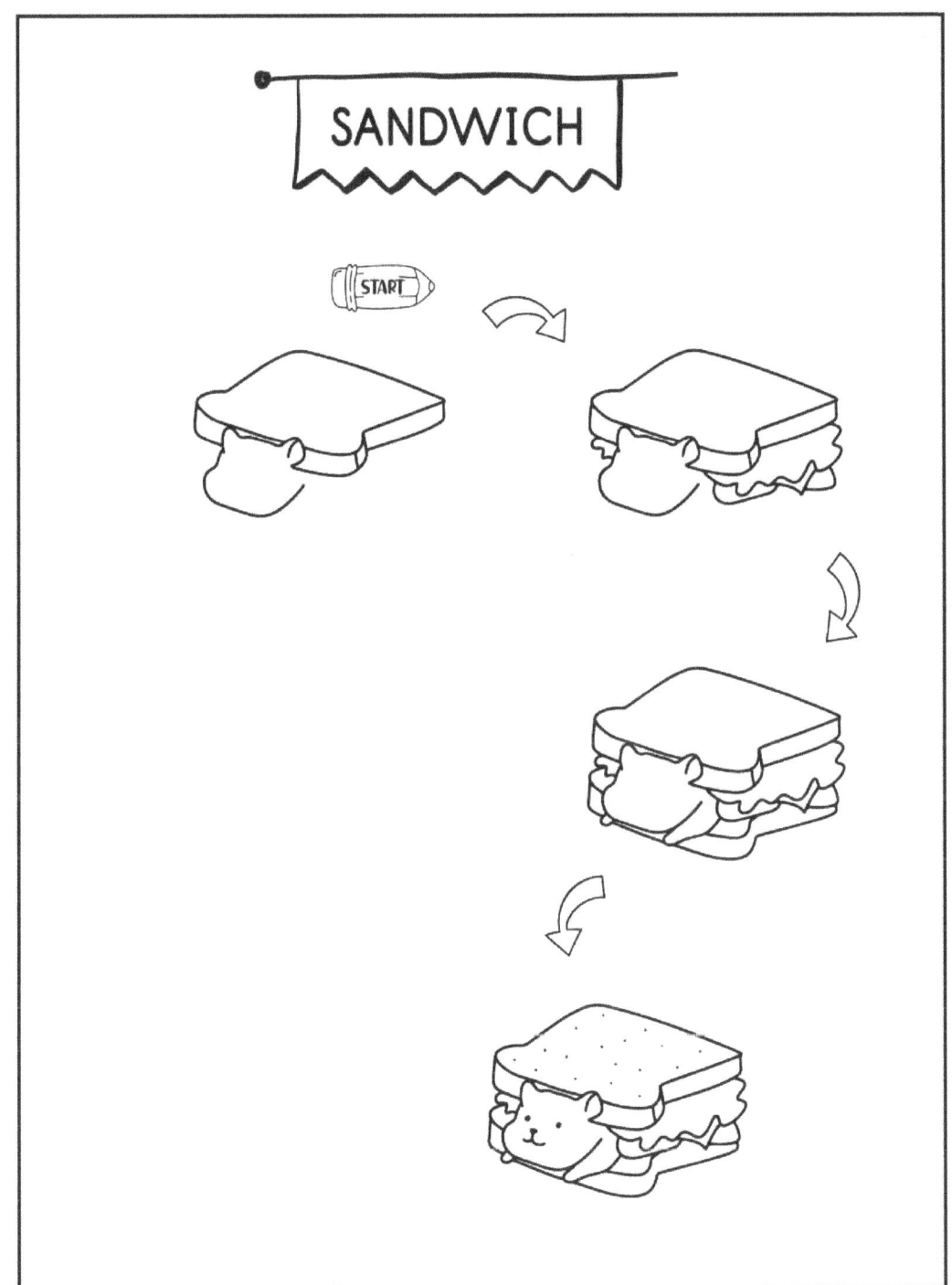

MERMAID TAIL

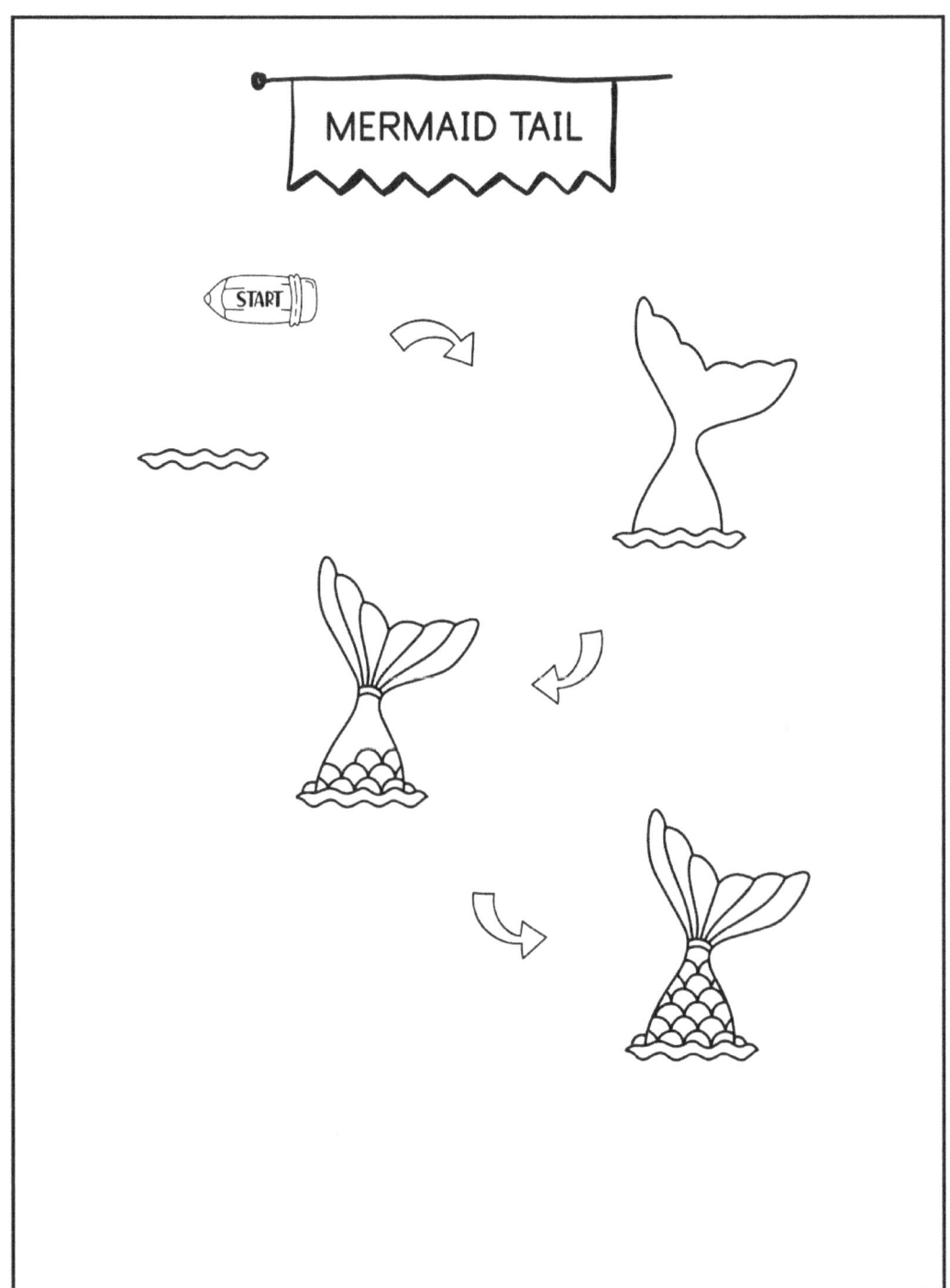

CUPCAKE

MUG

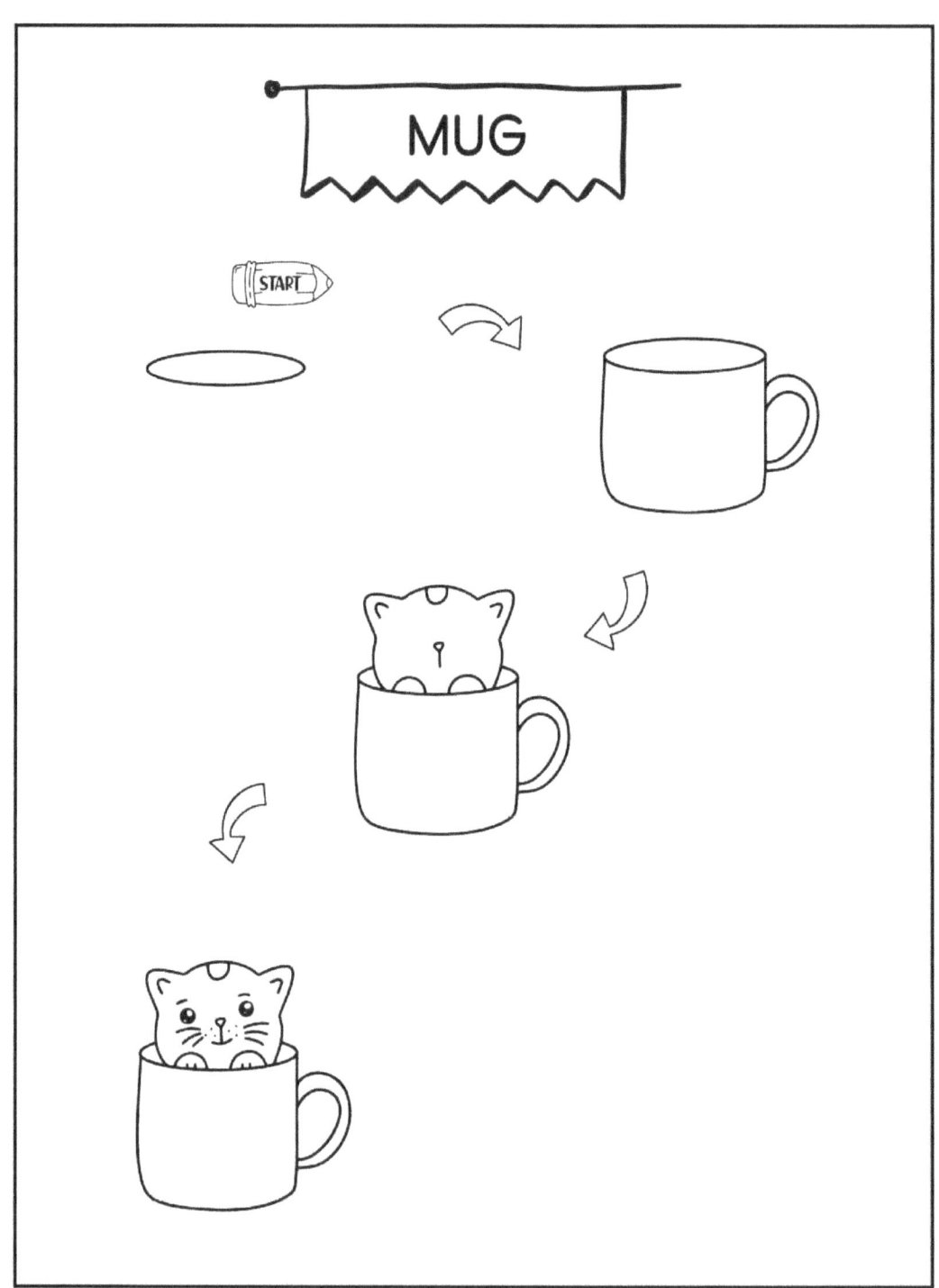

TURNIP

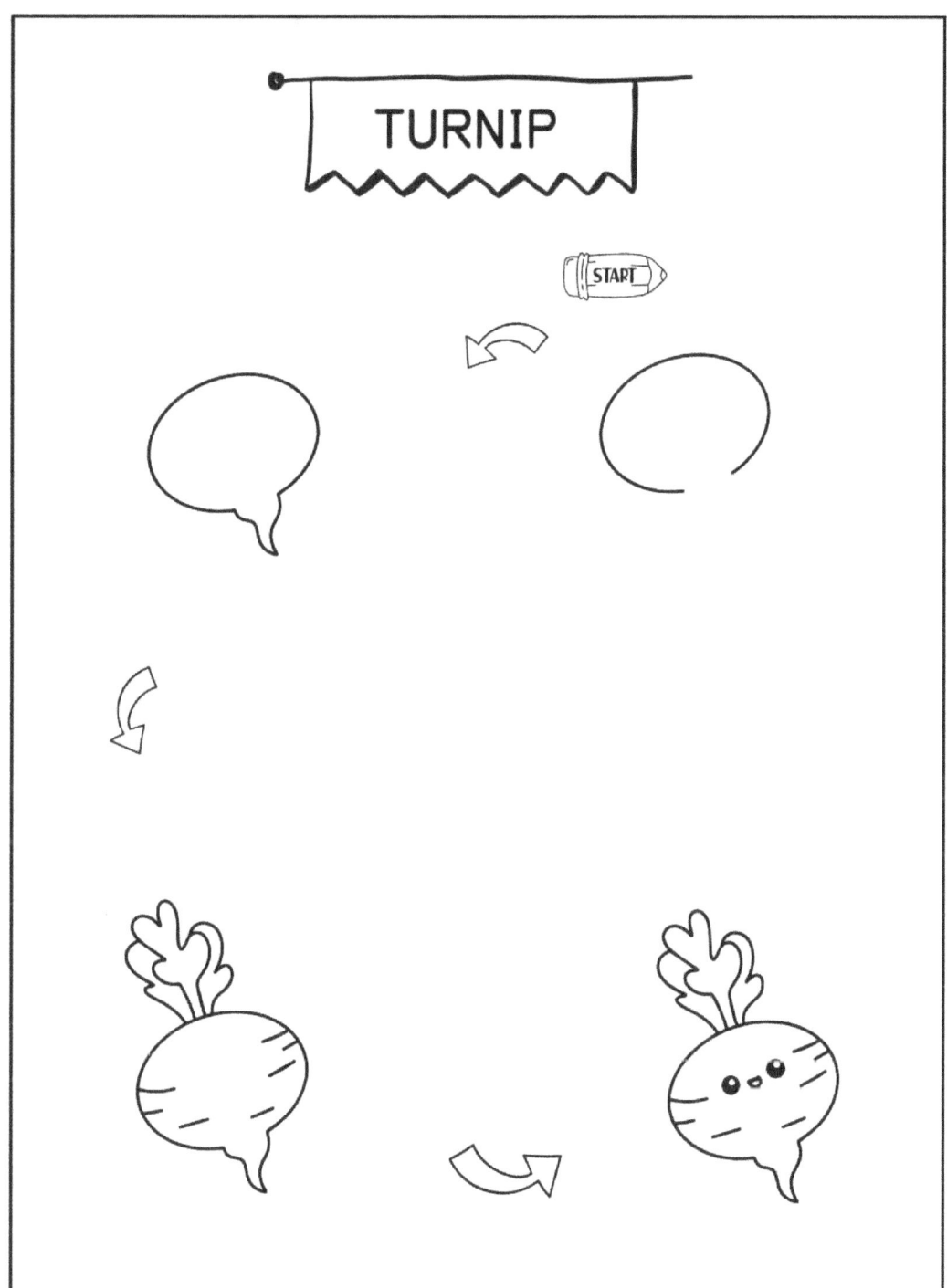

PIZZA

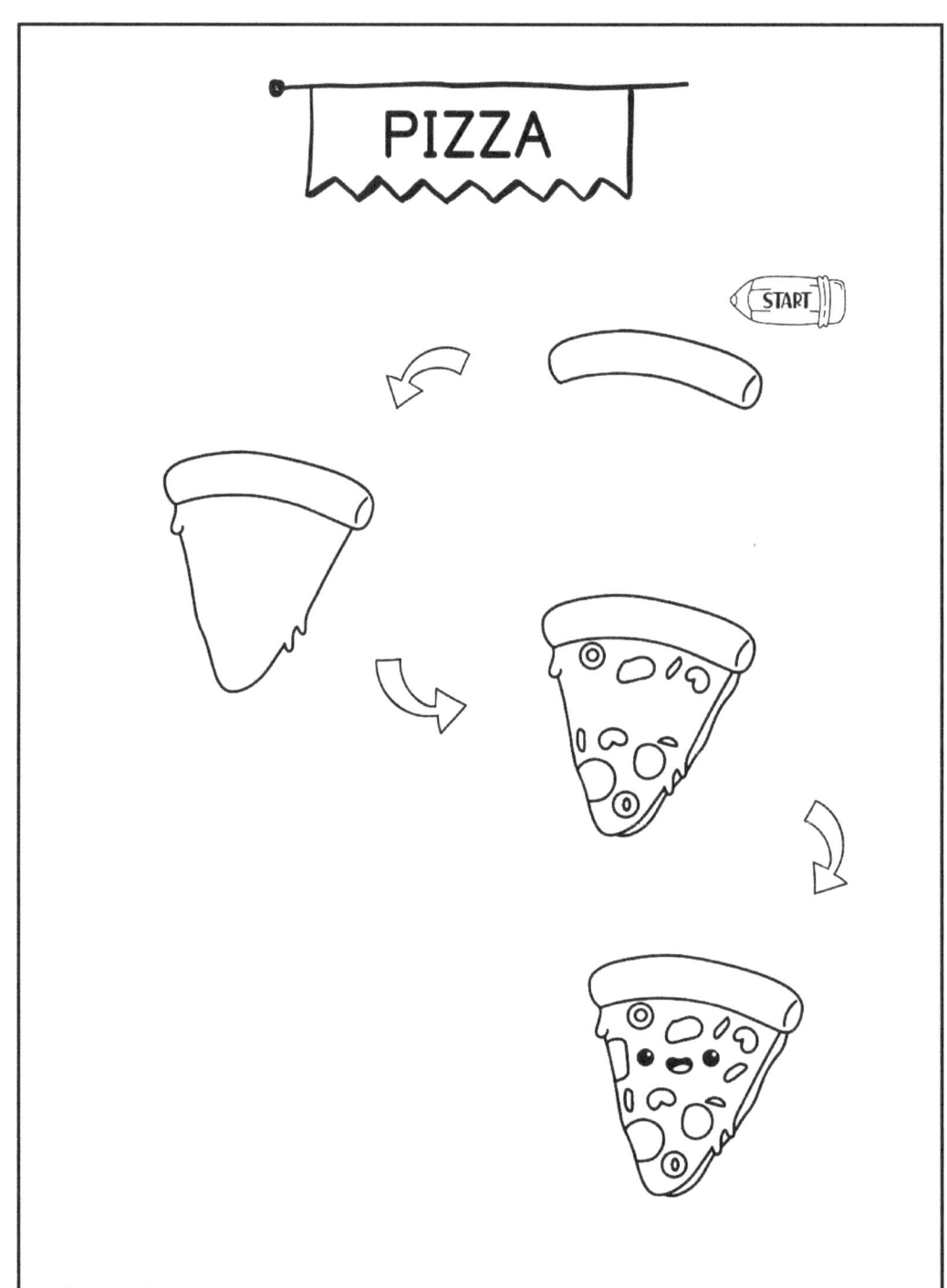

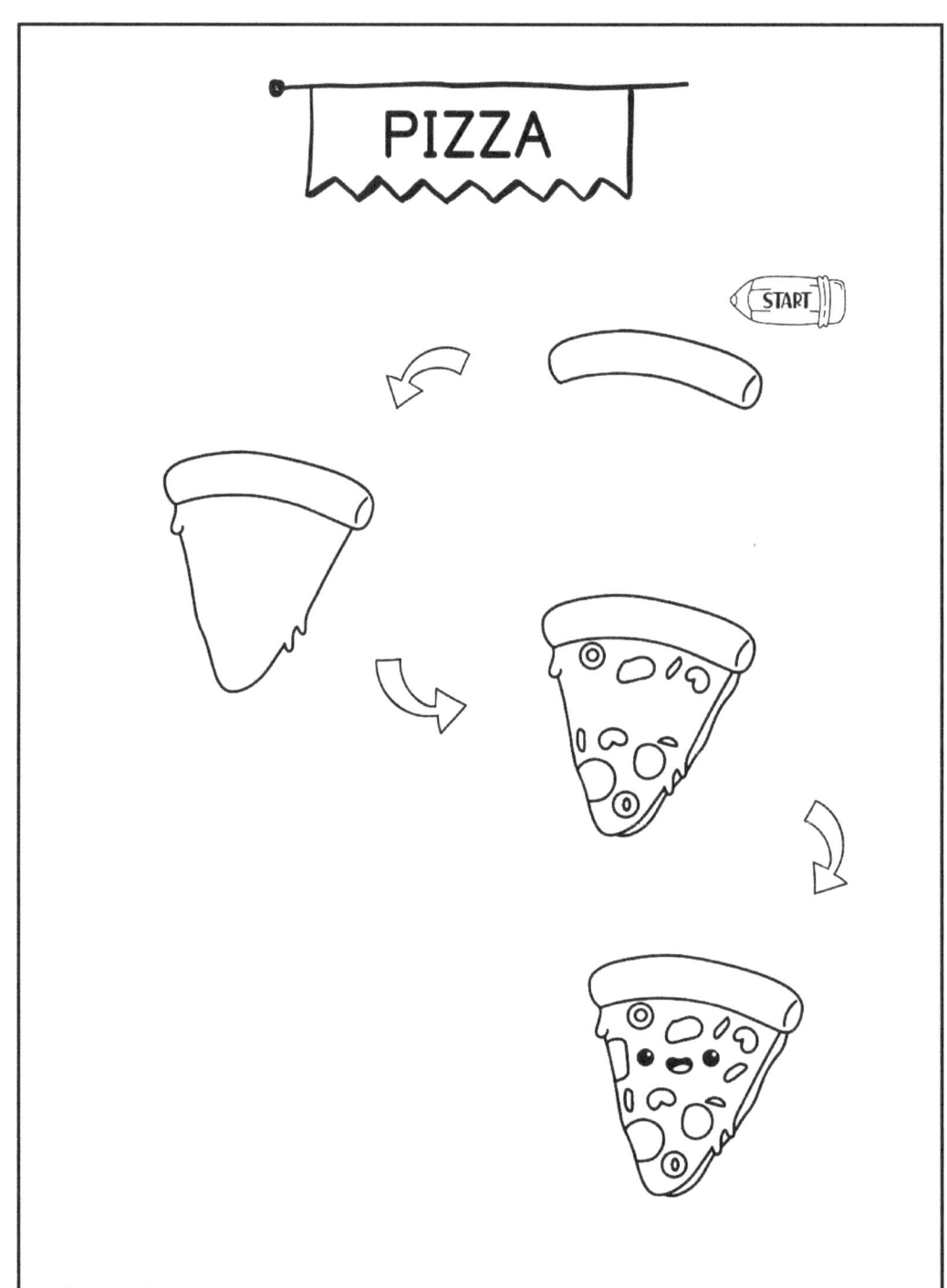

92

BREAD

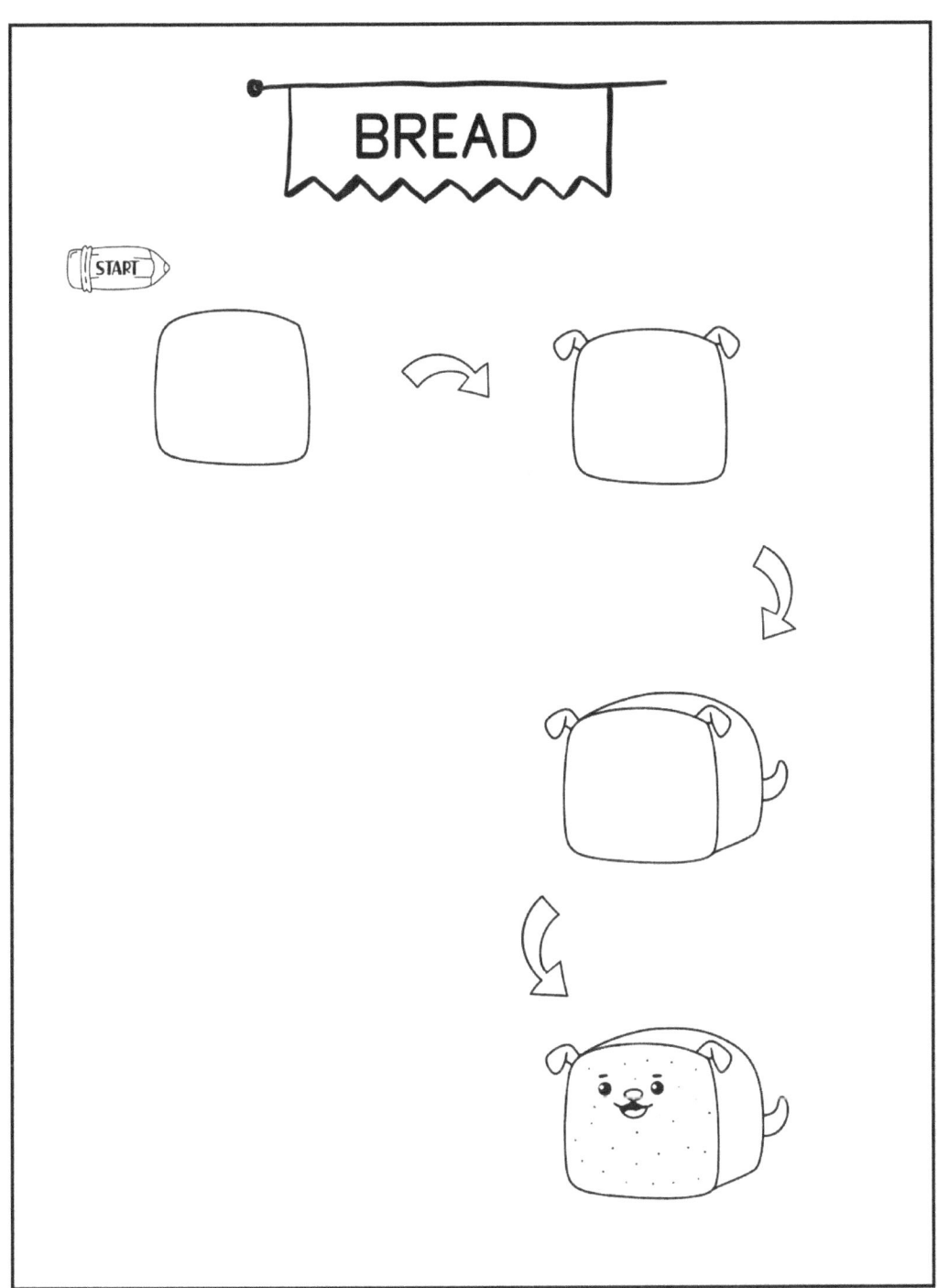

CINNABON

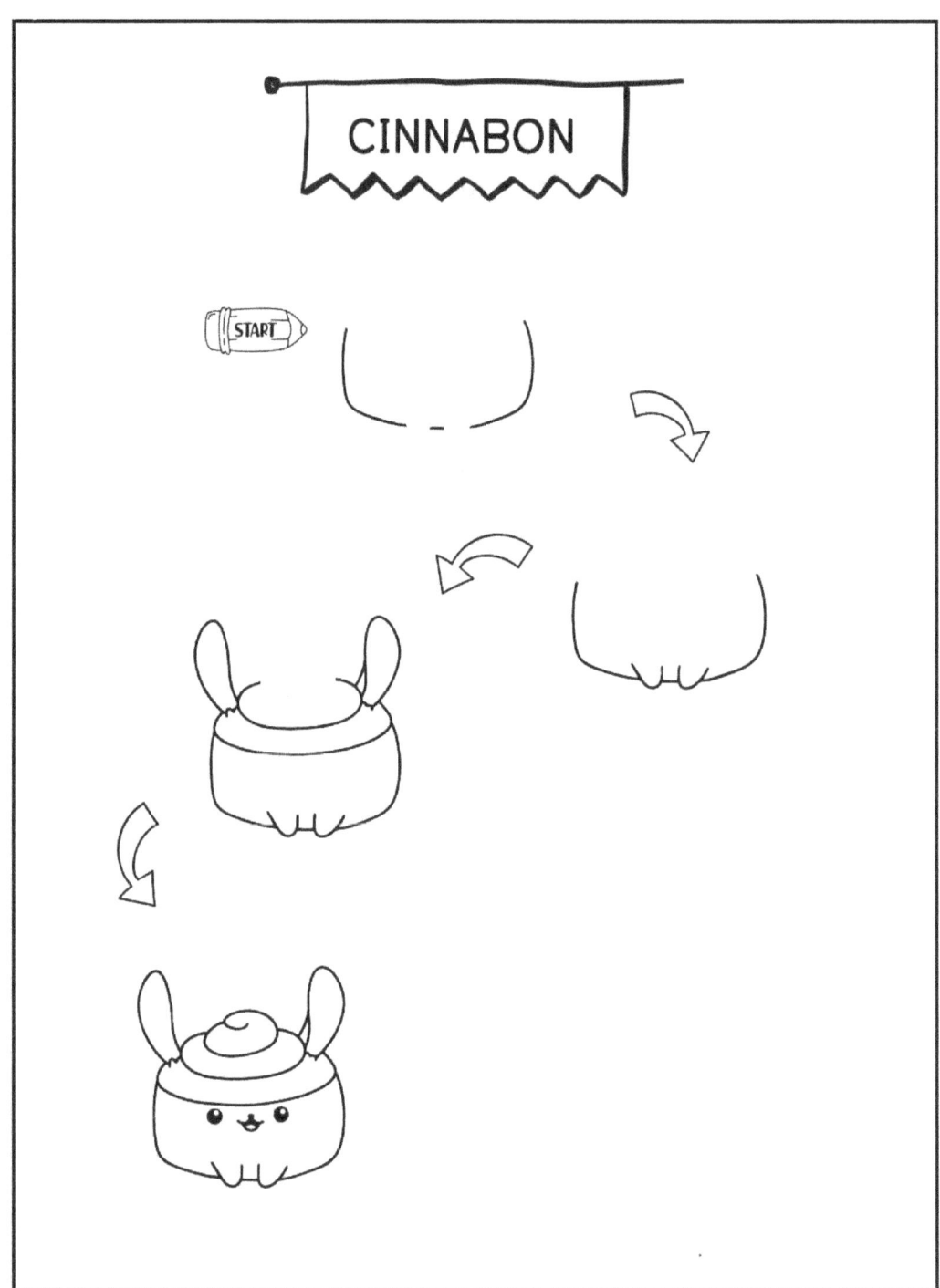

WALLET

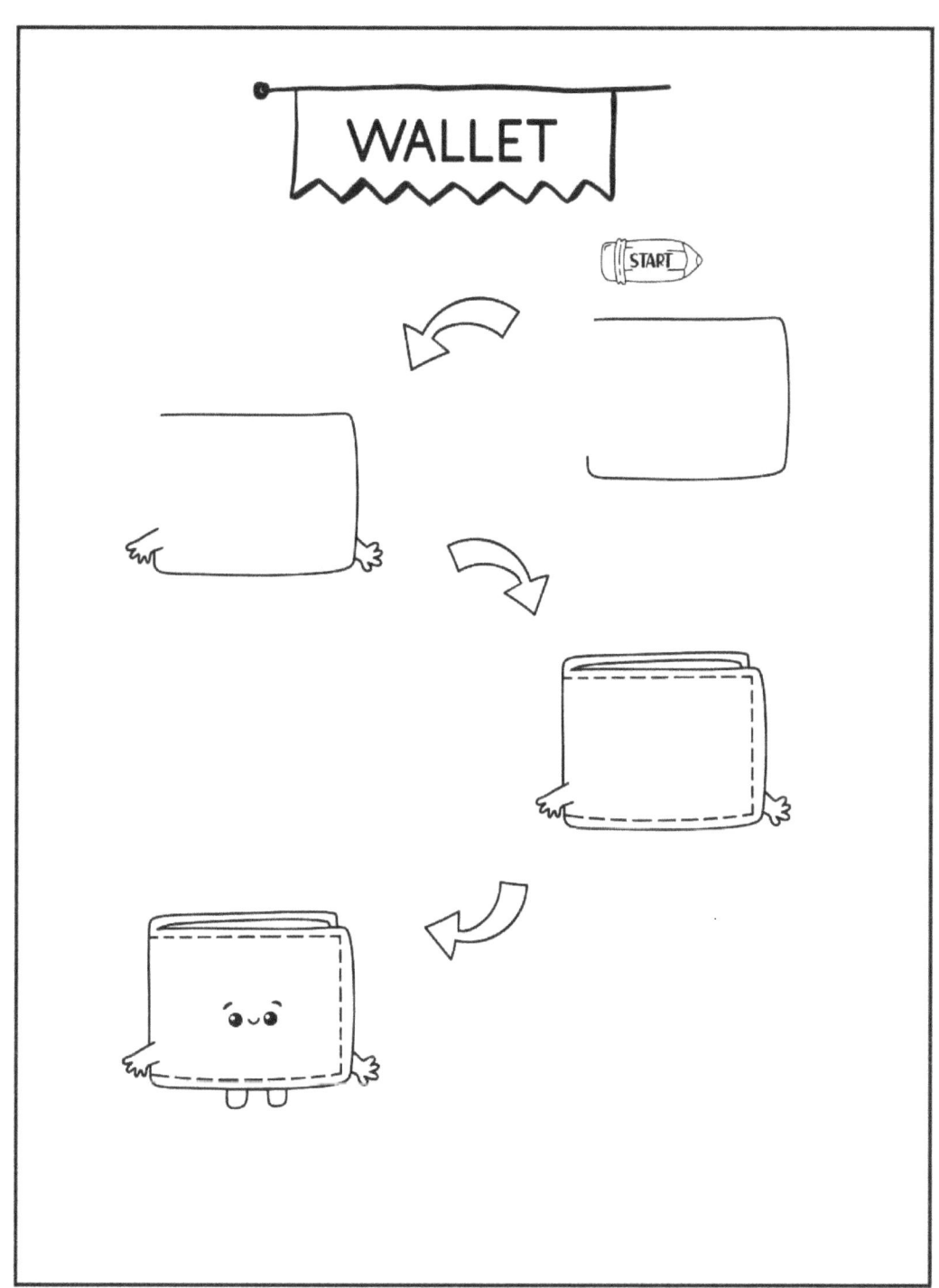

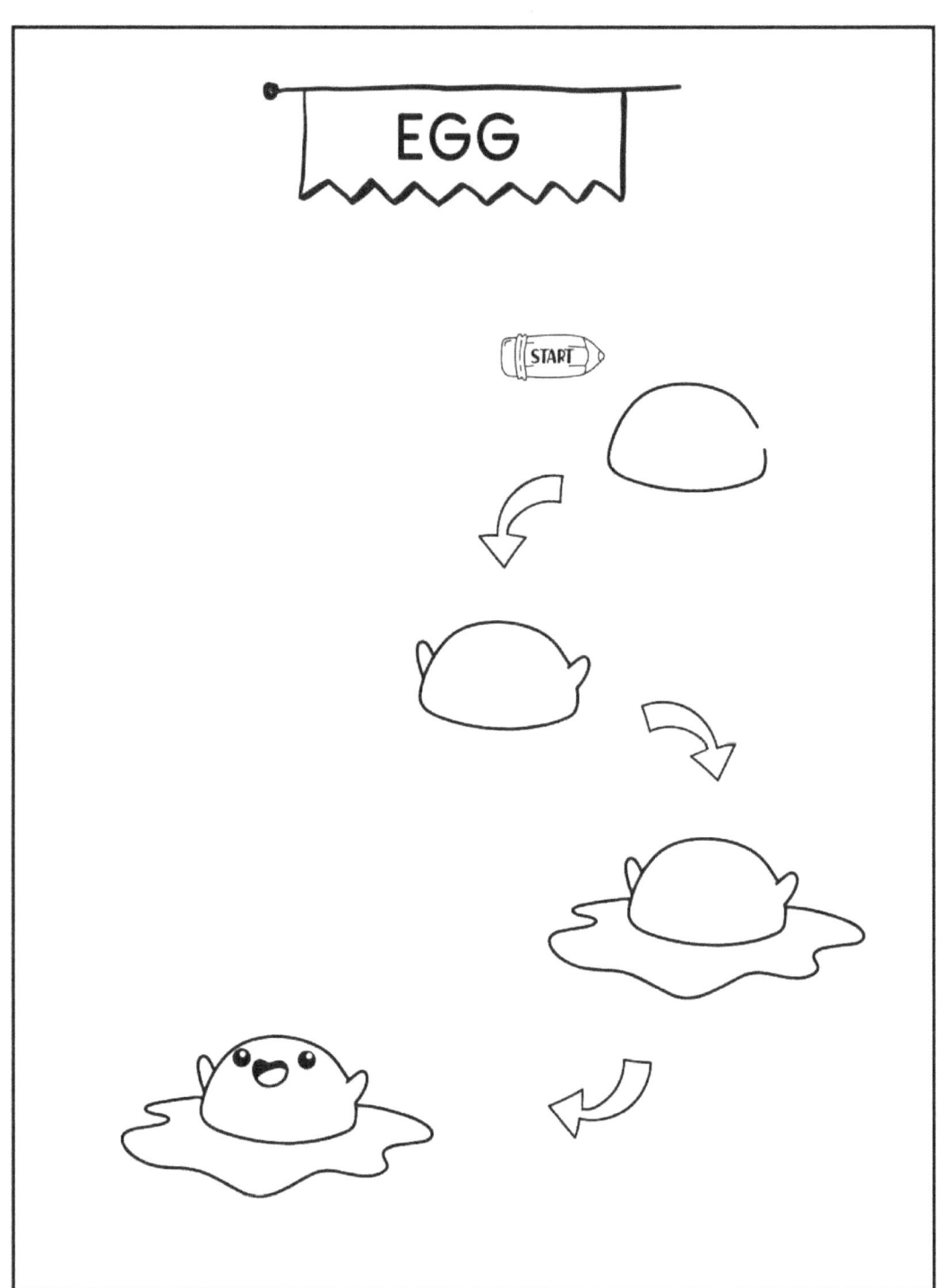

EGG

PEACH

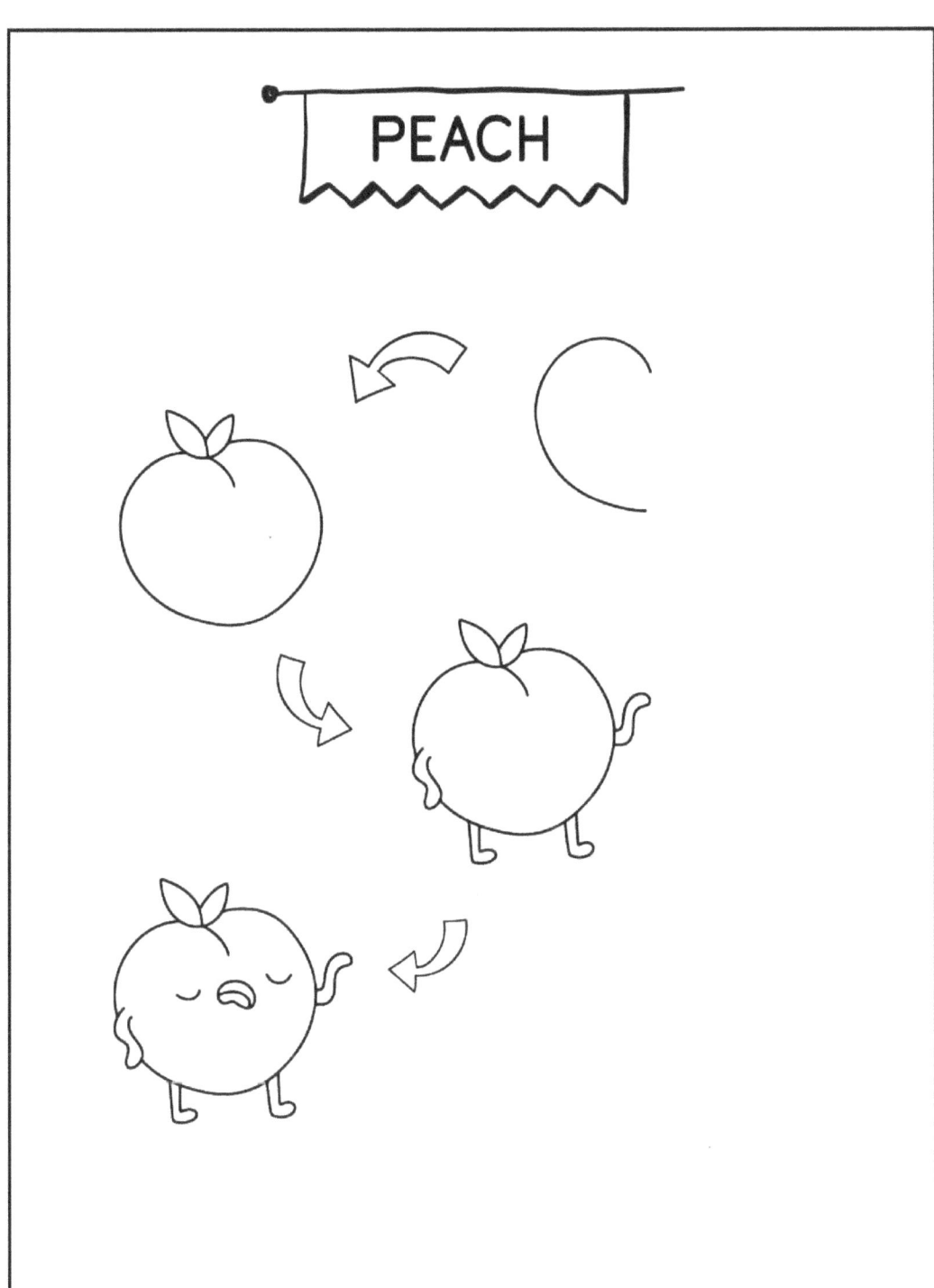

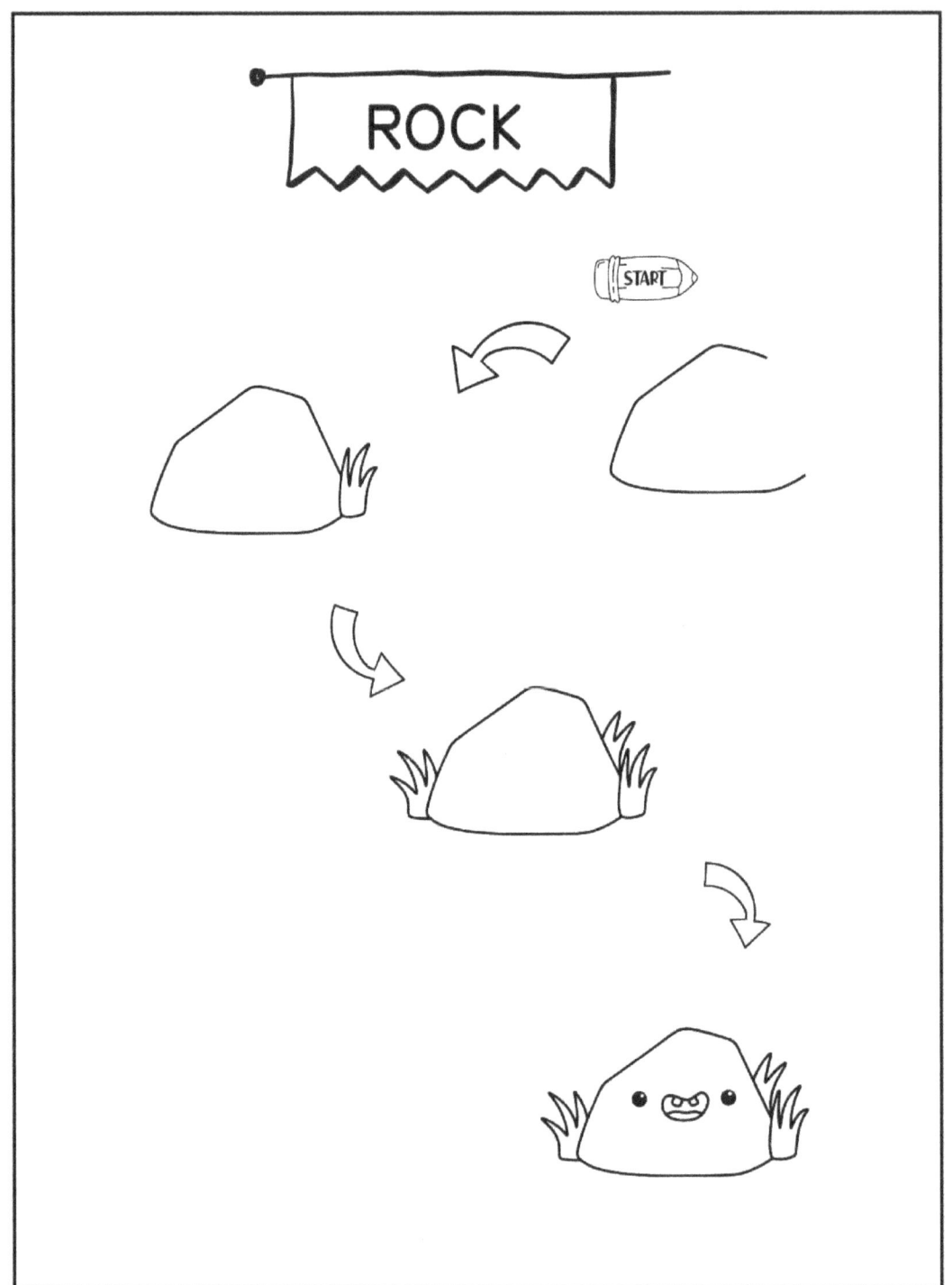

CAT

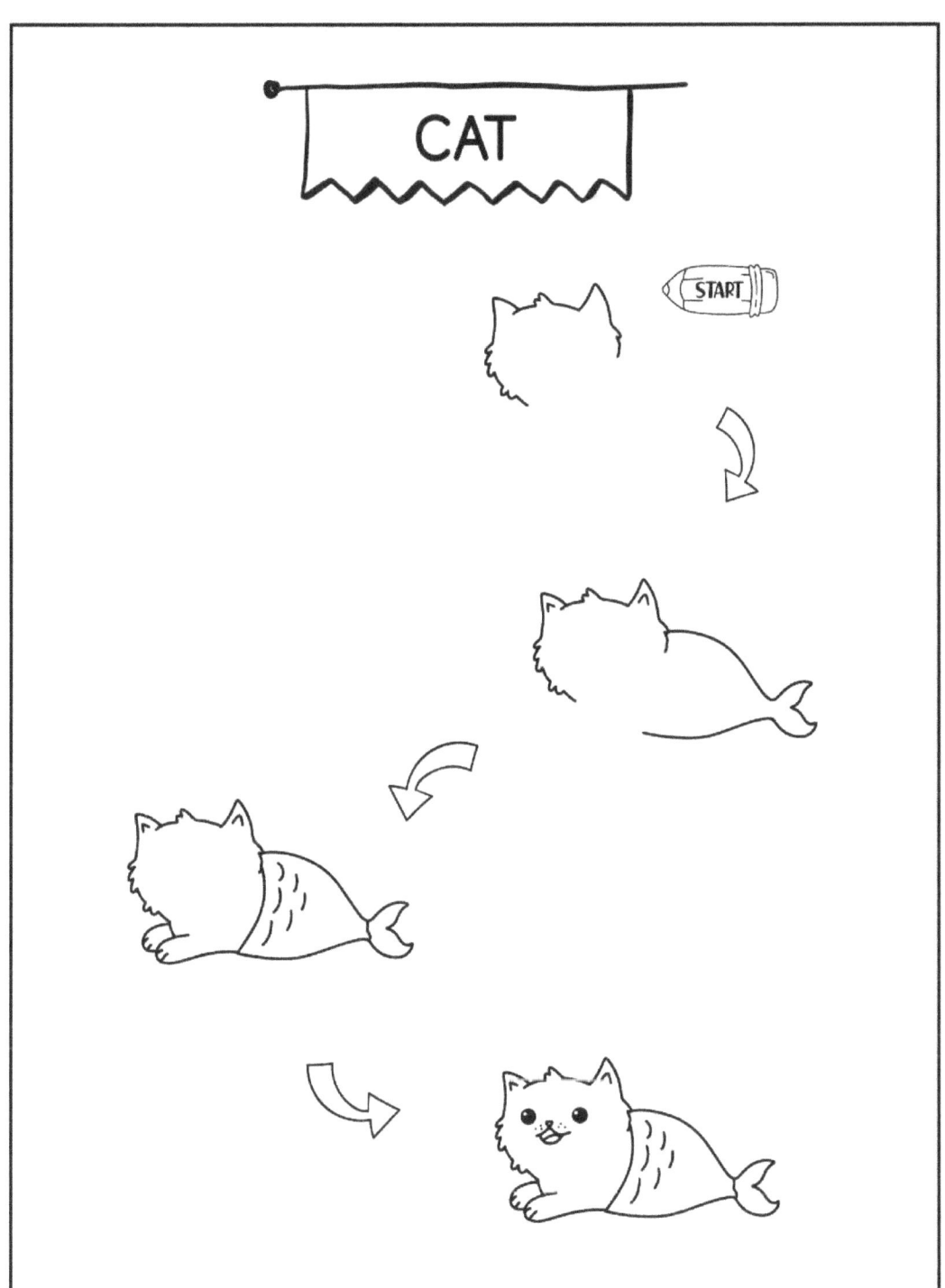

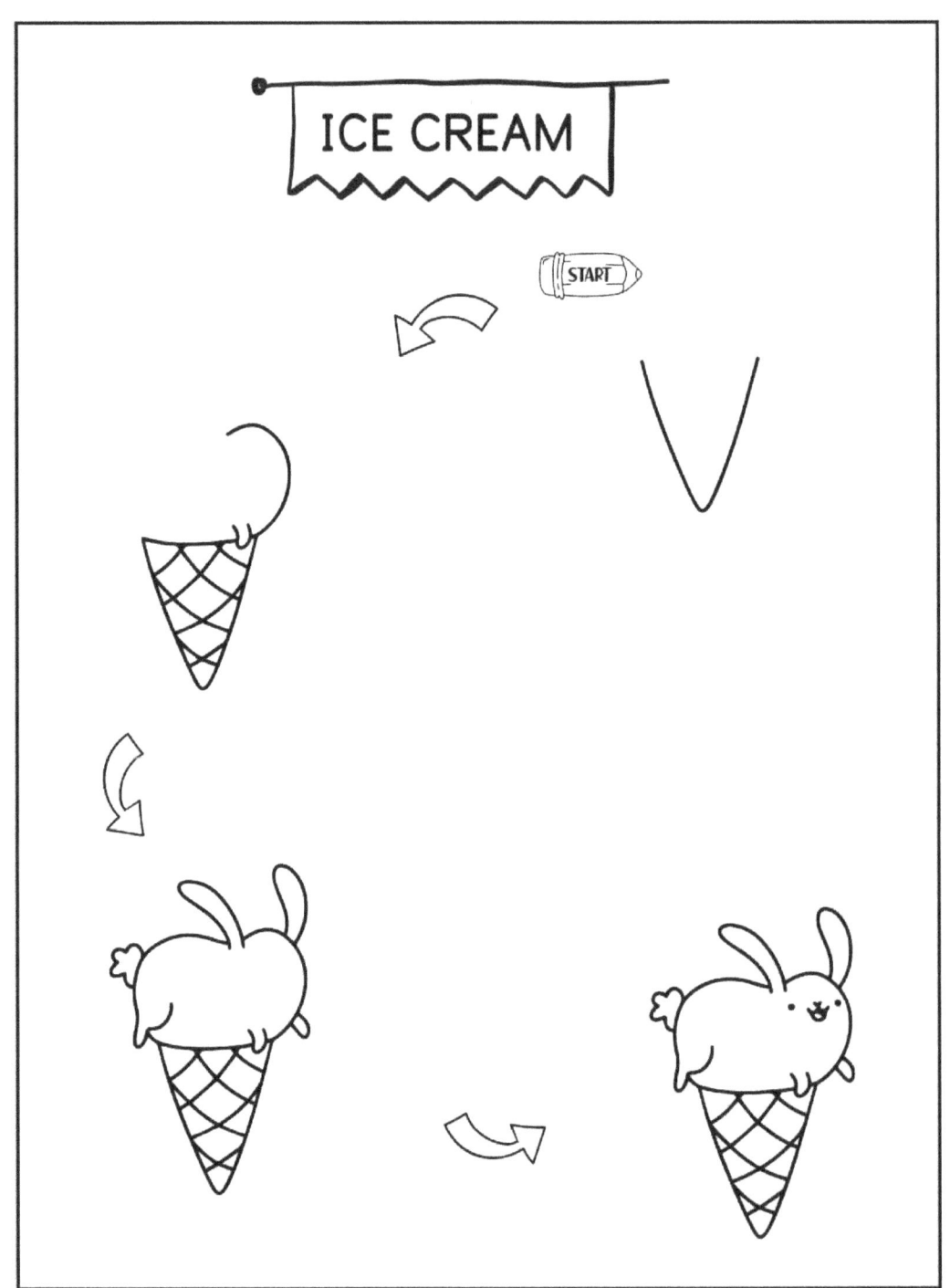

ICE CREAM

START

CORN

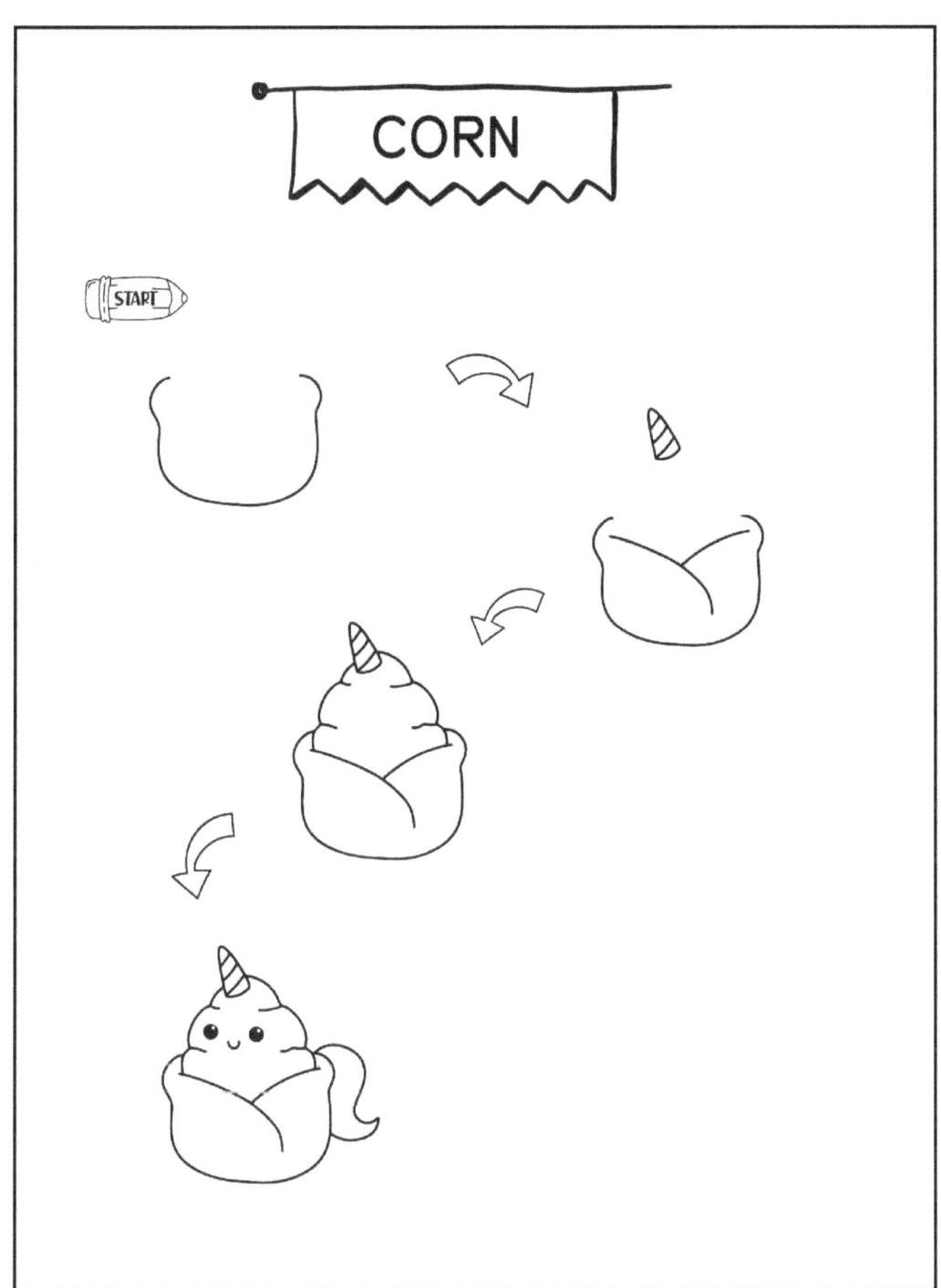

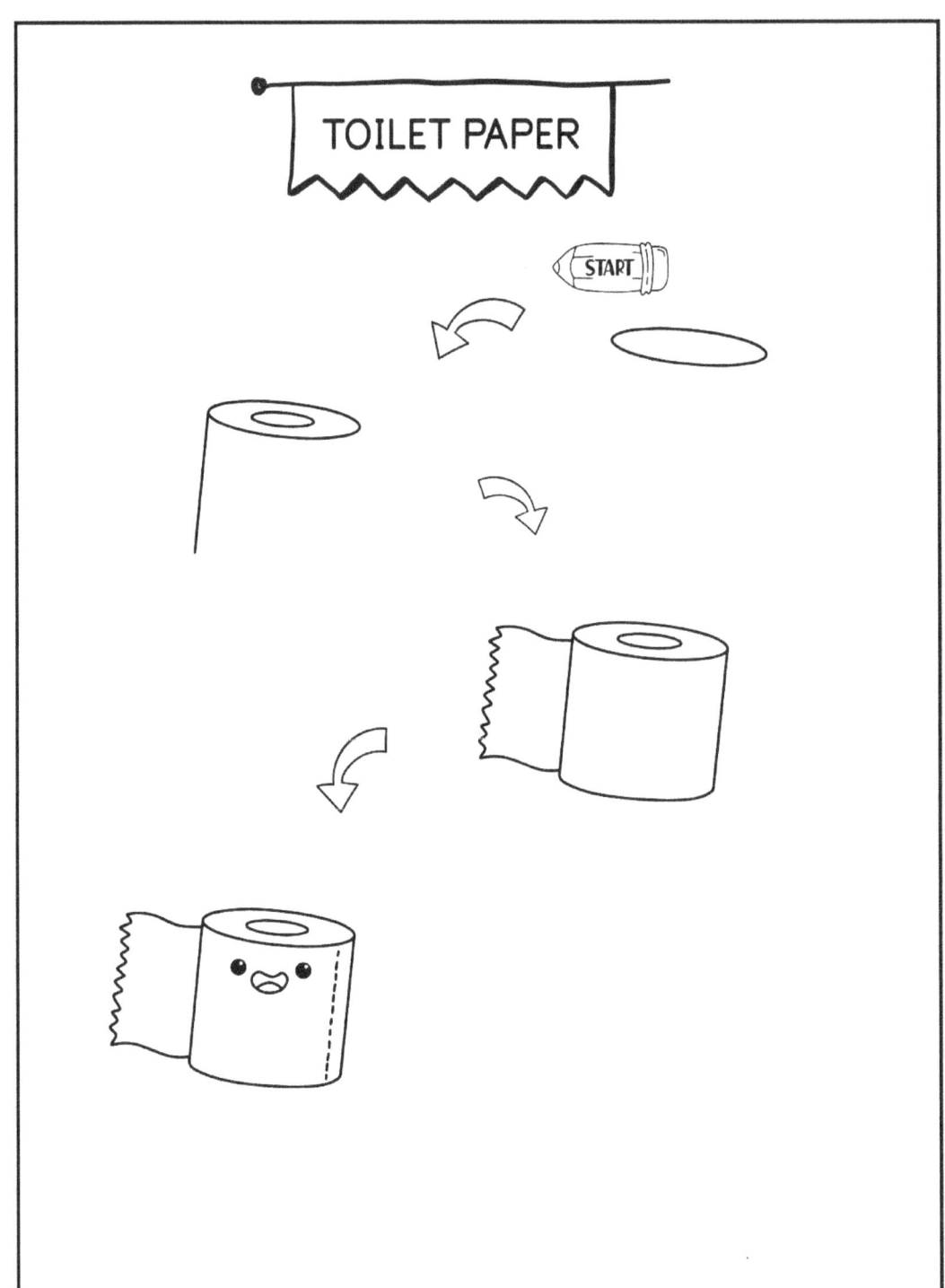

PEAR

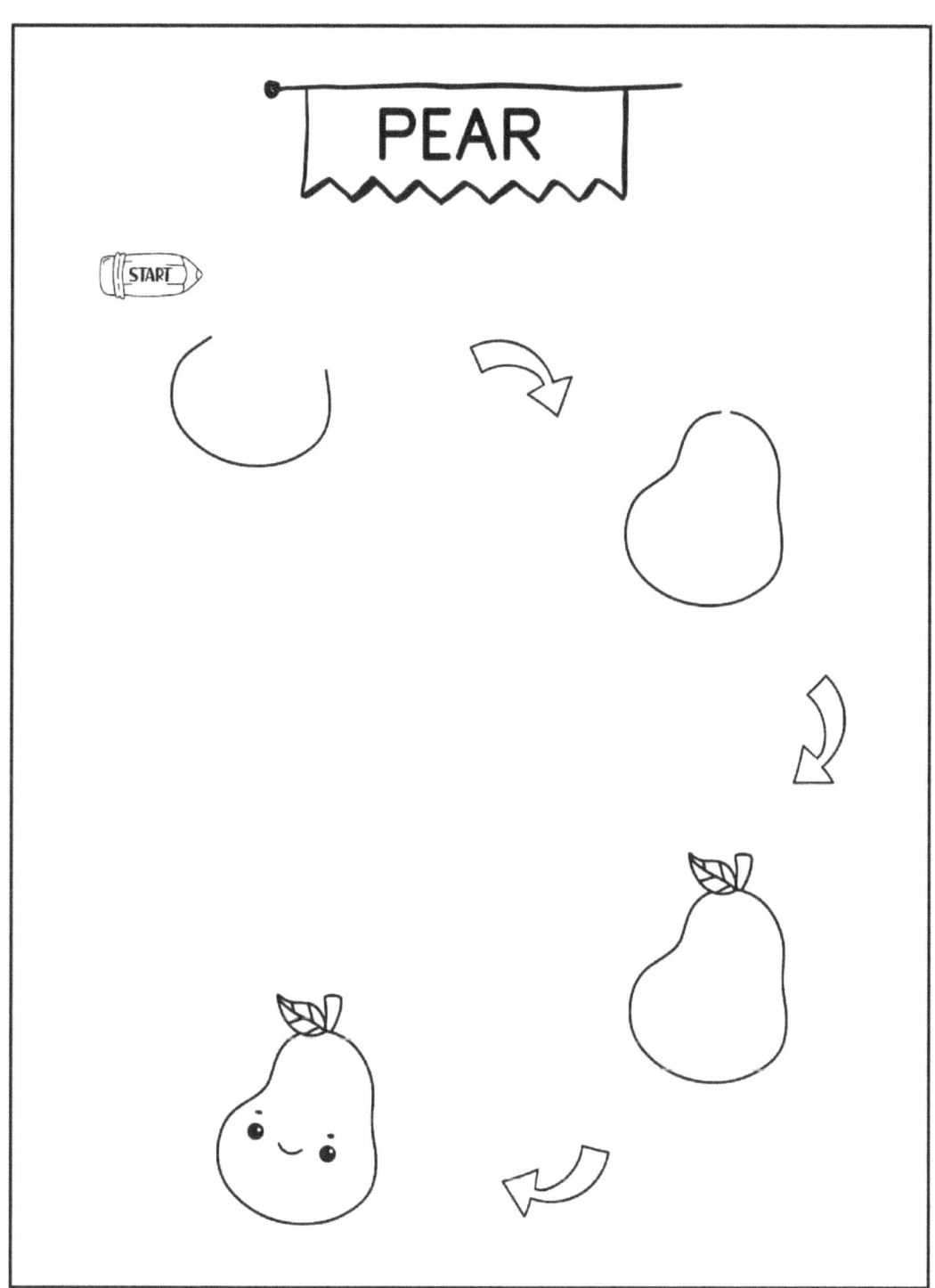

SQUID

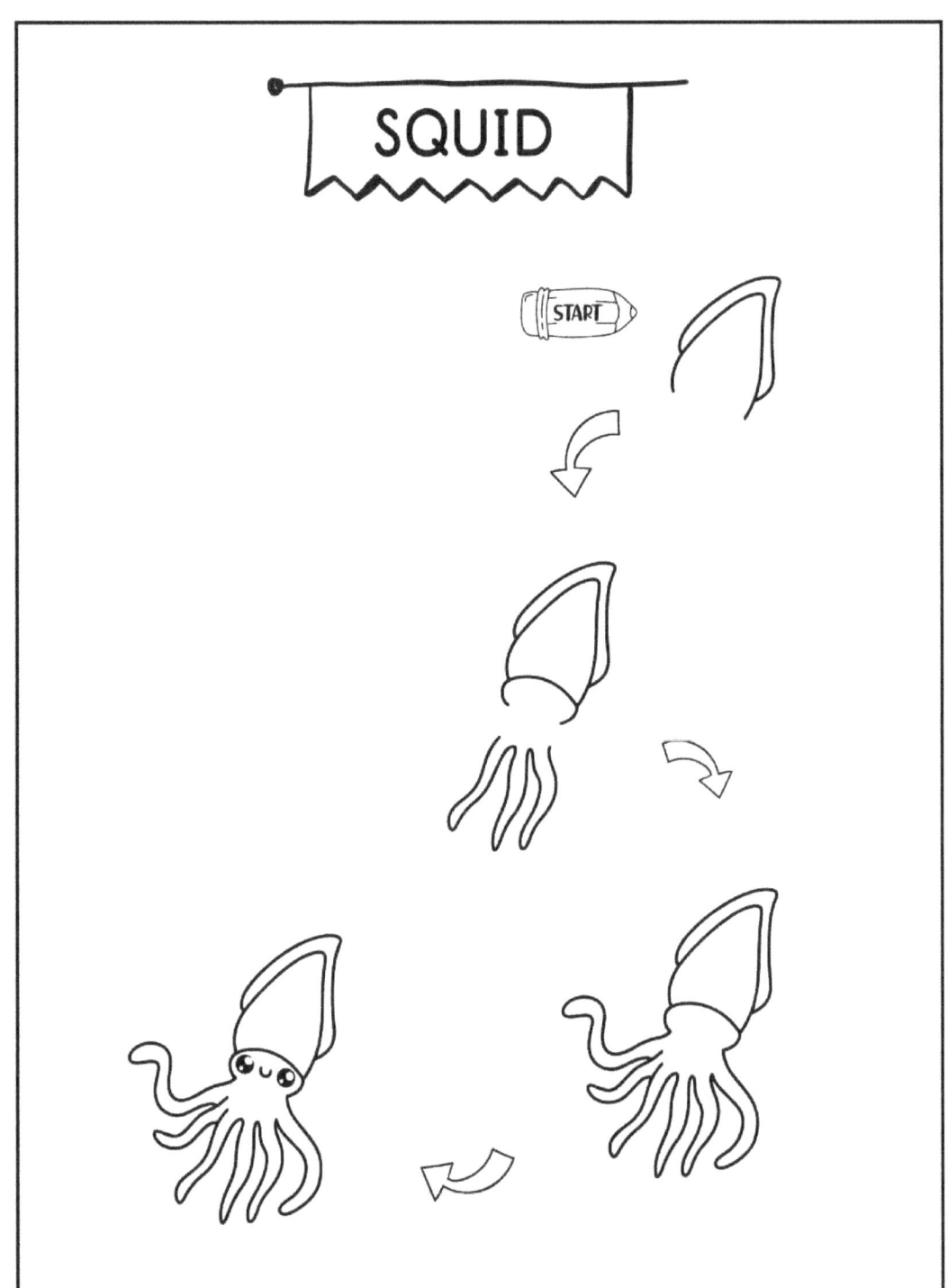

TURTLES

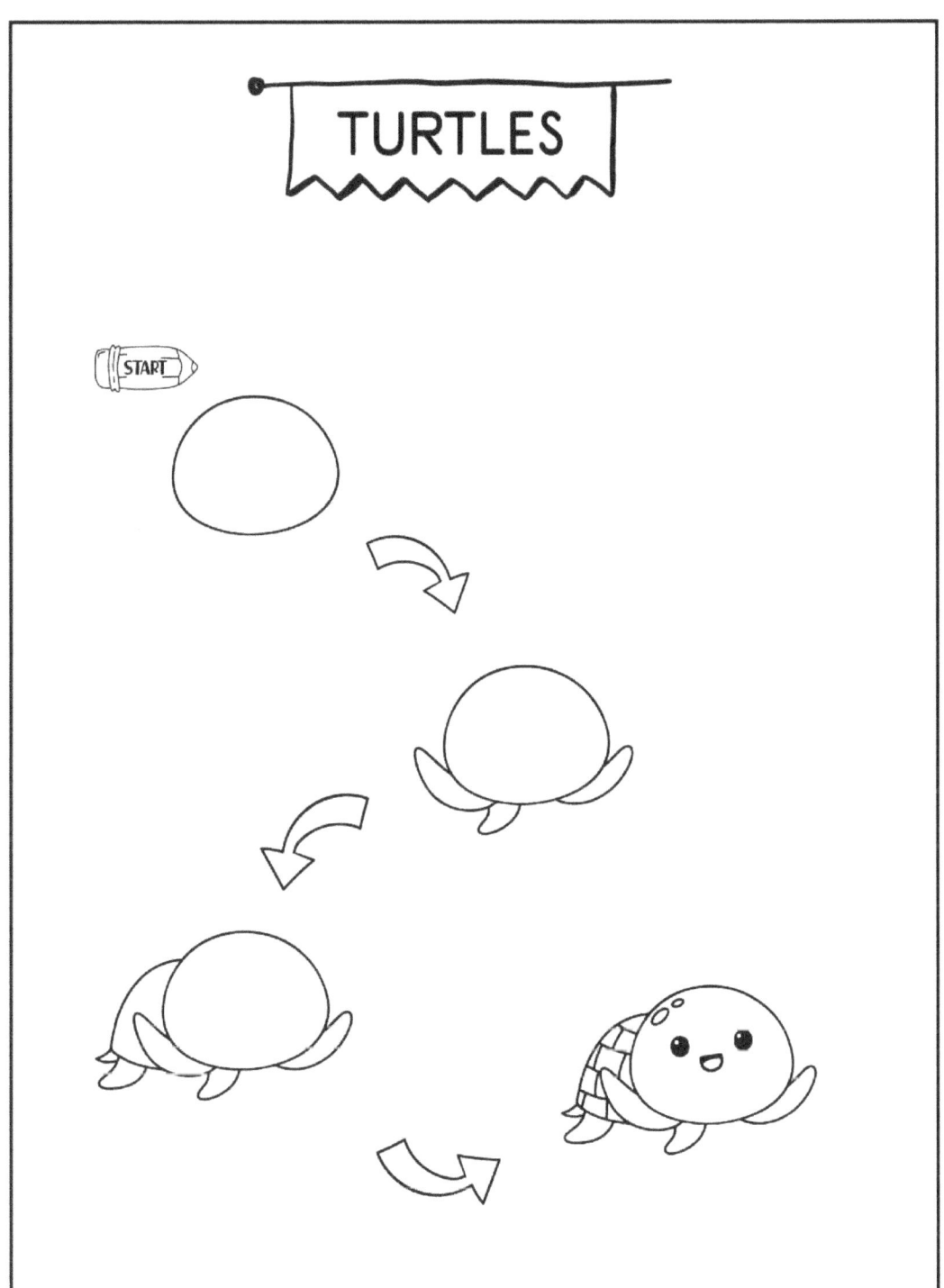

CHOCOLATE

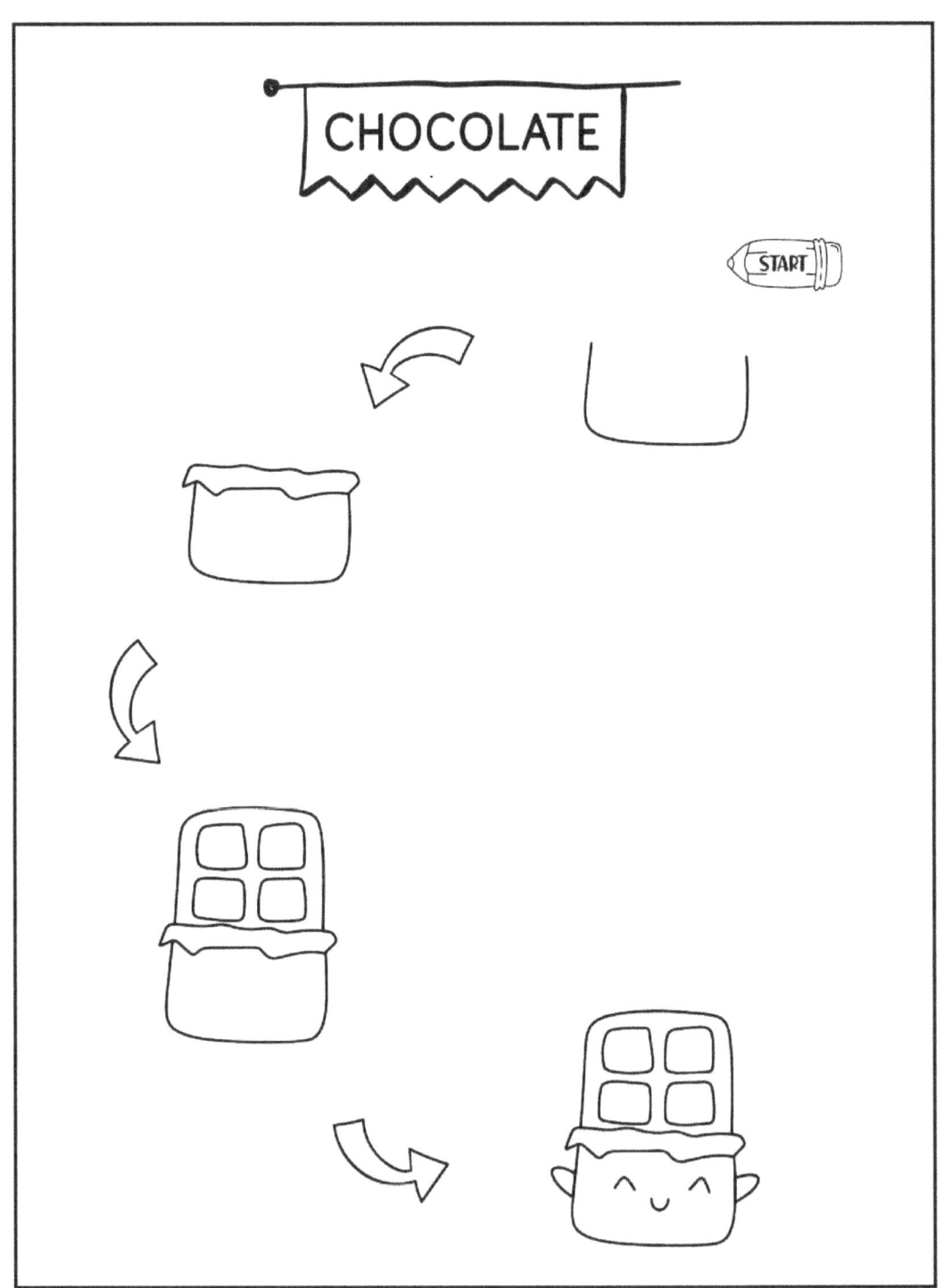

JUICE

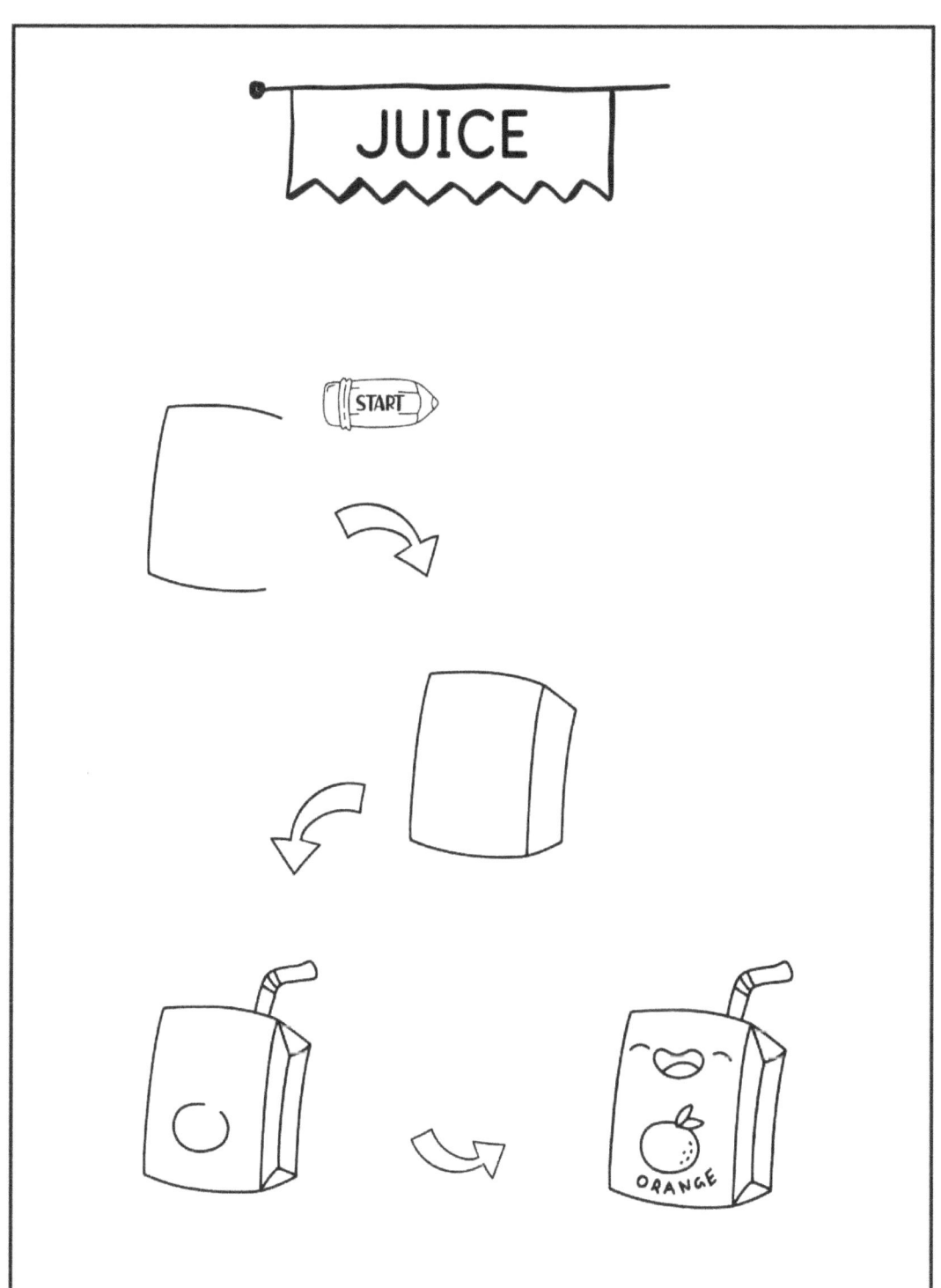

GHOST

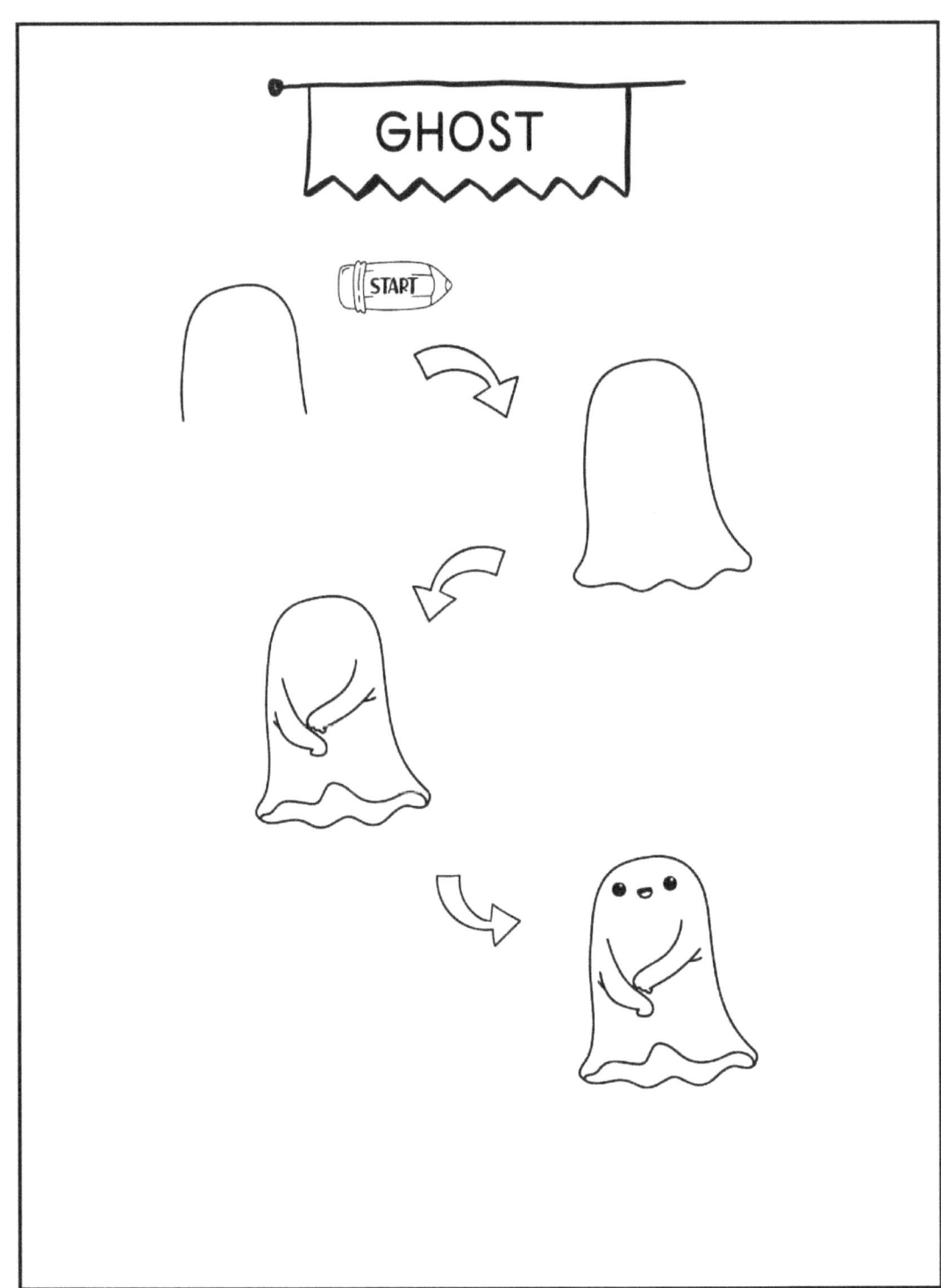

SNAIL

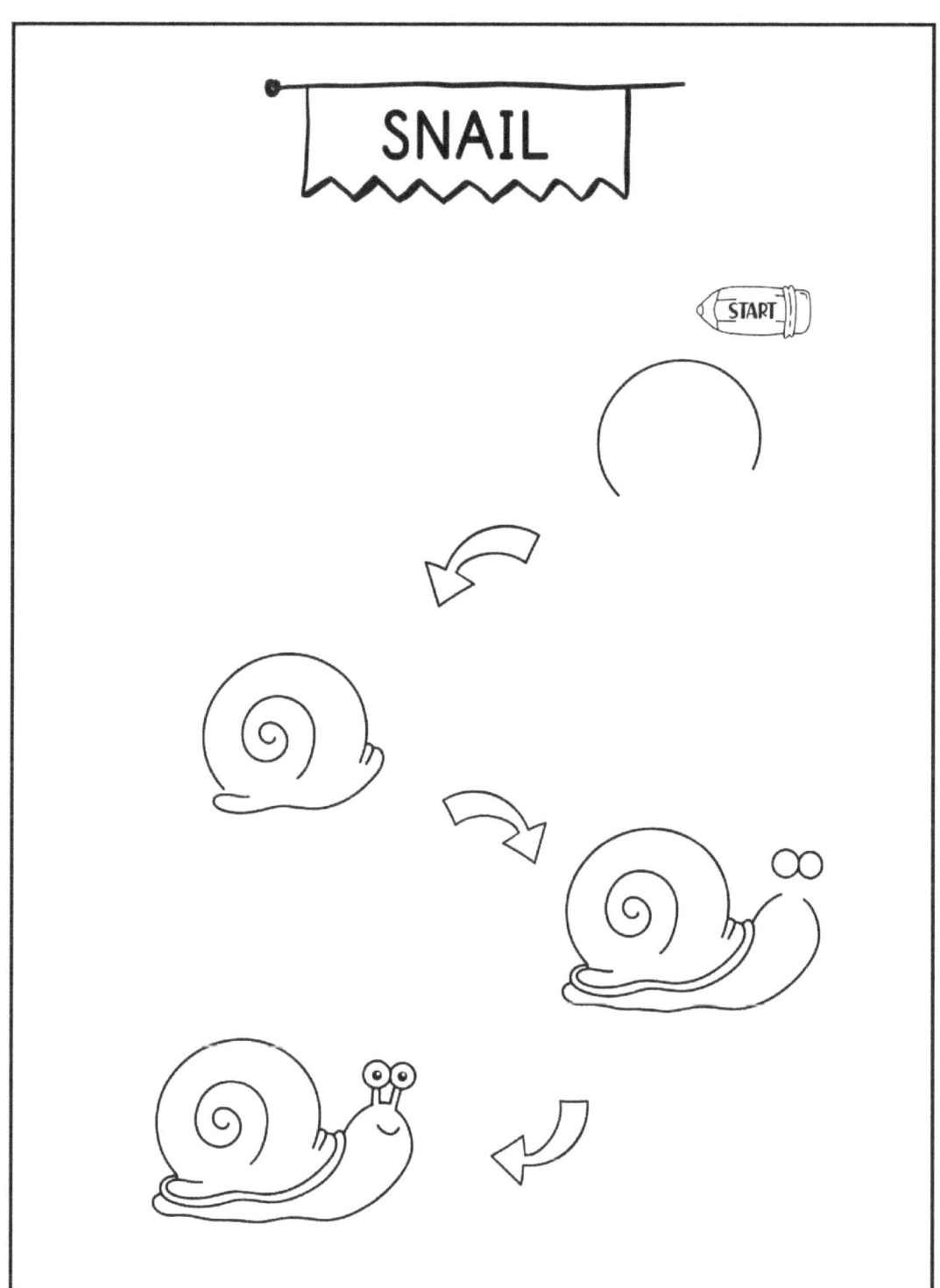

FLOWER

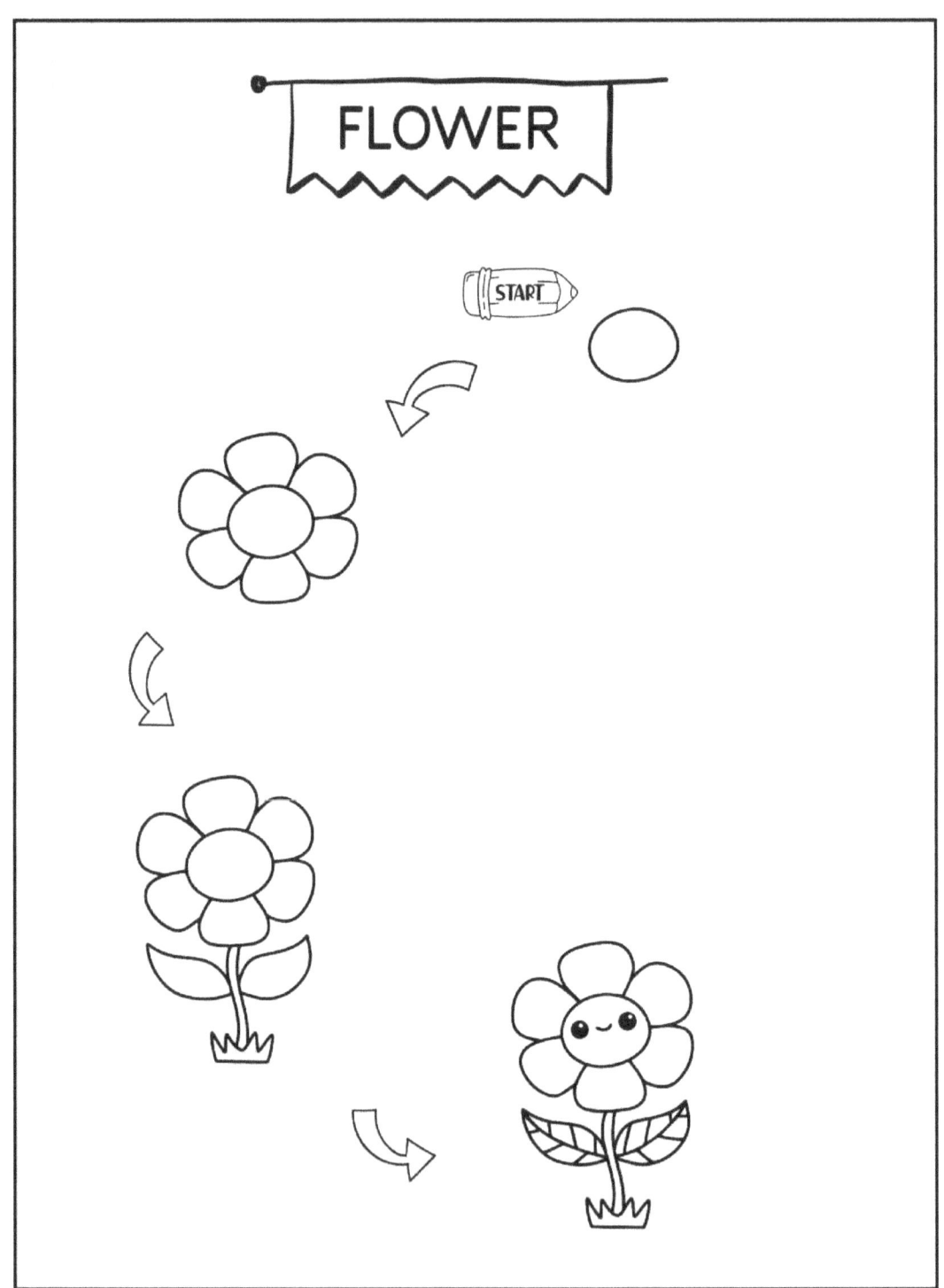

BIRD

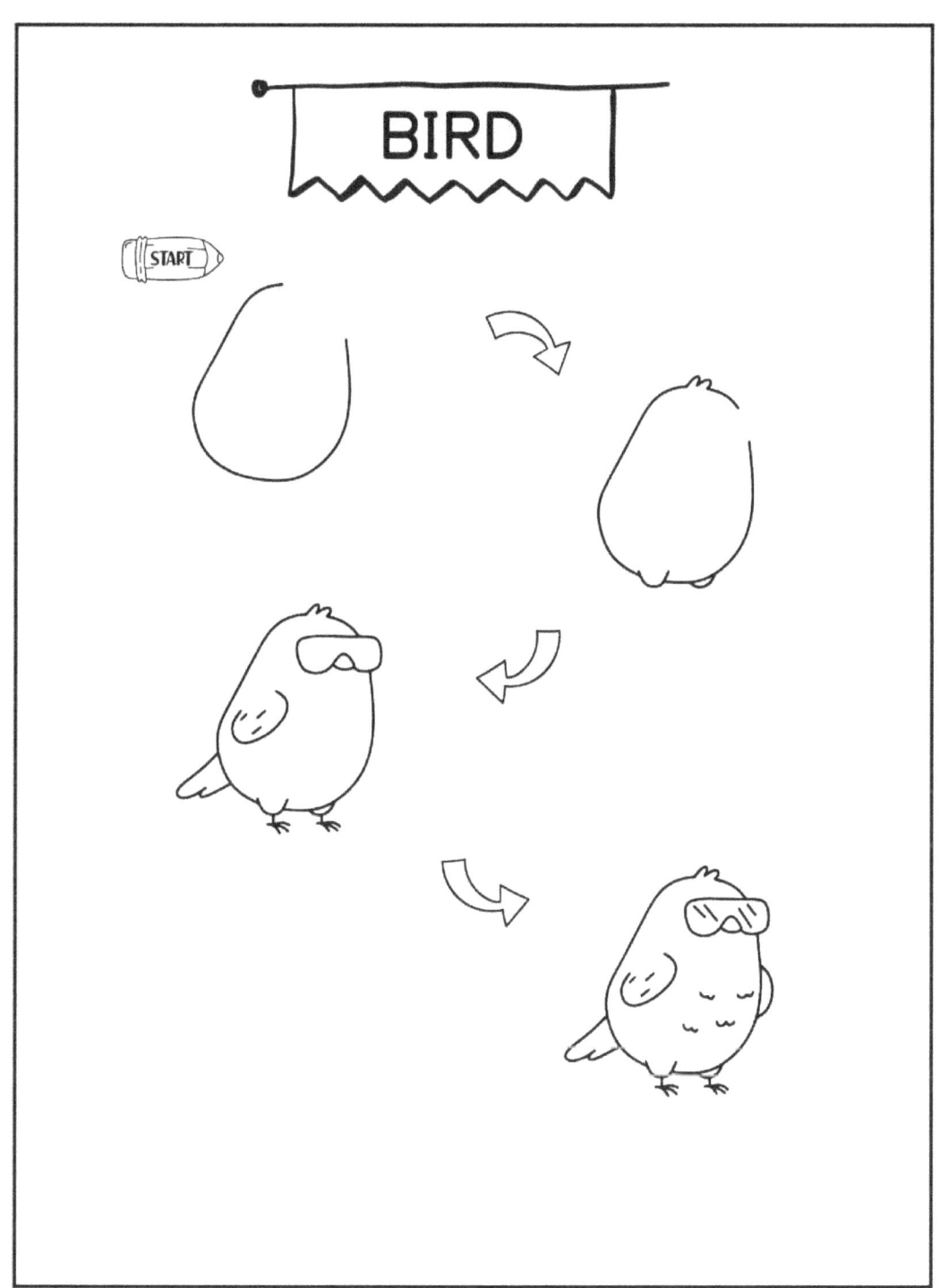

START

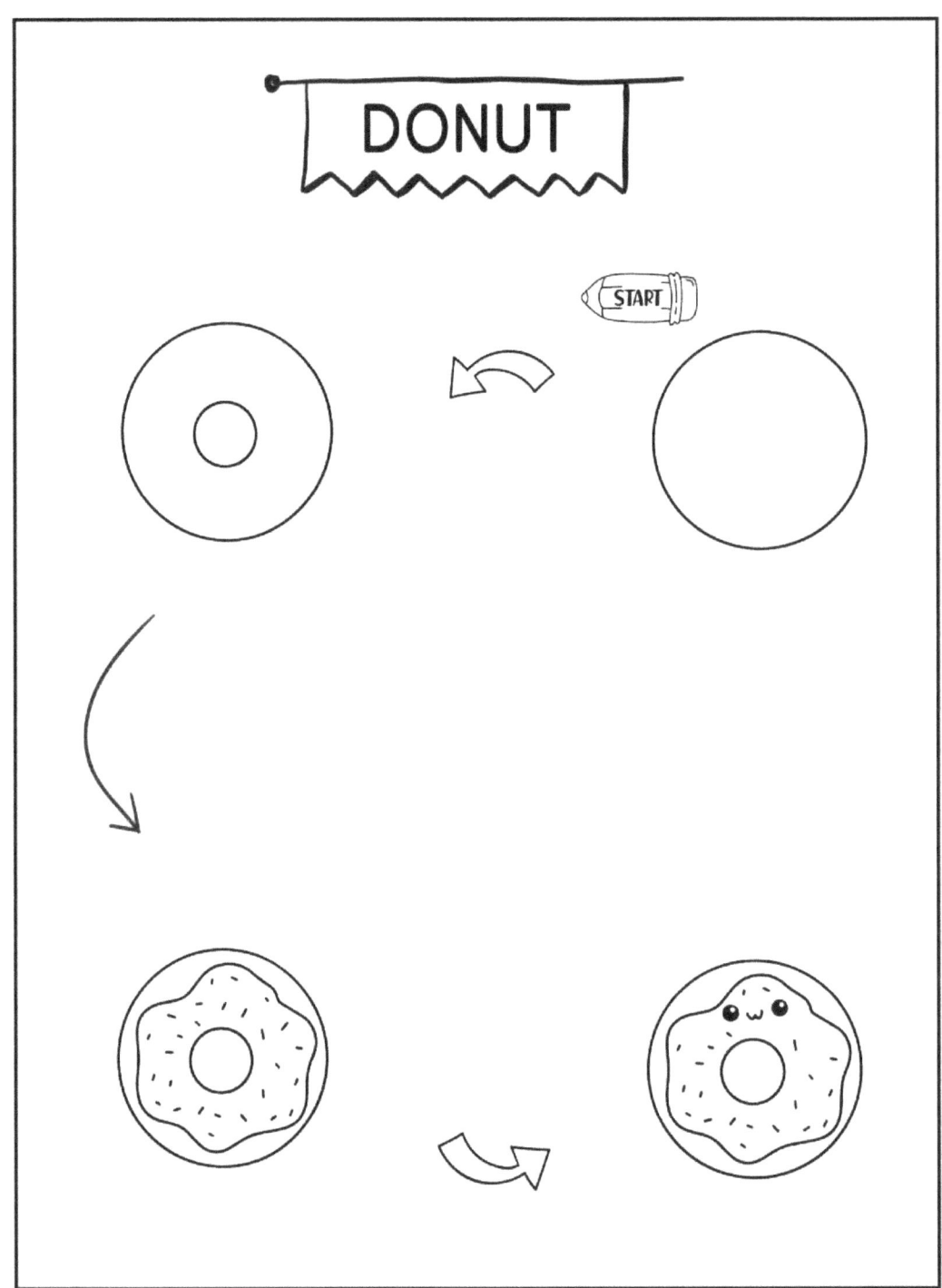

CLOUD

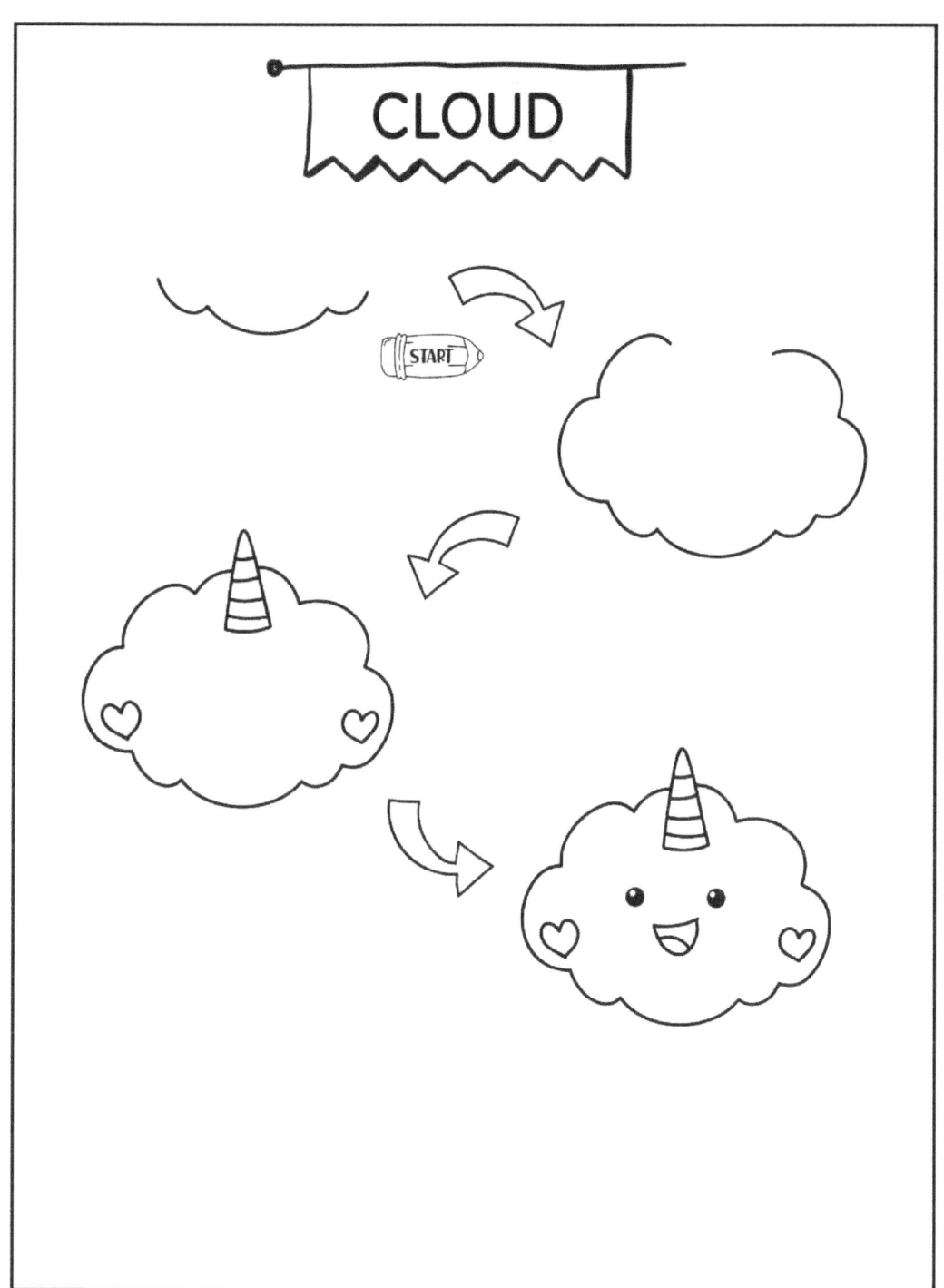

PENGUIN

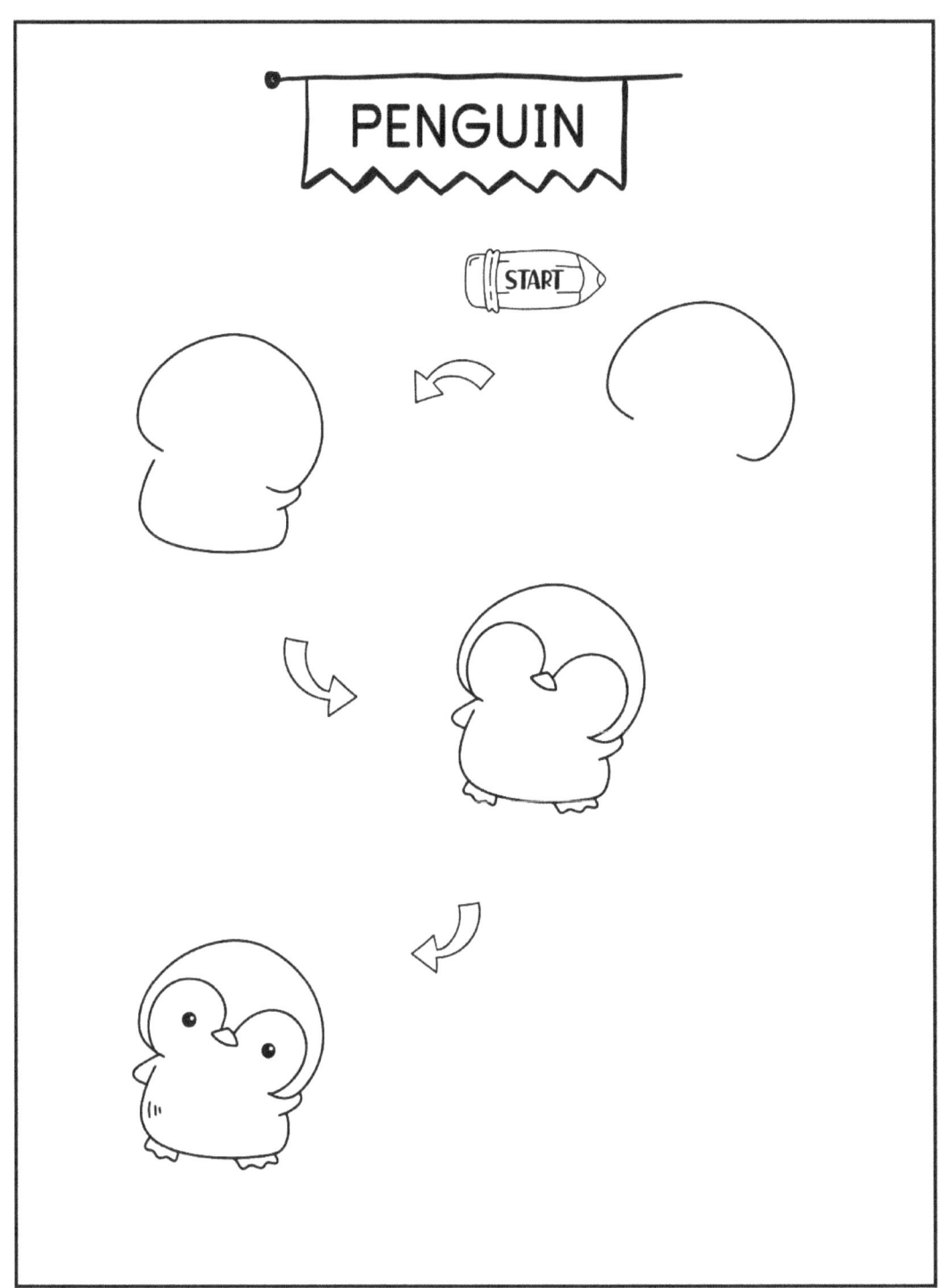

START

114

ABOUT THE AUTHOR

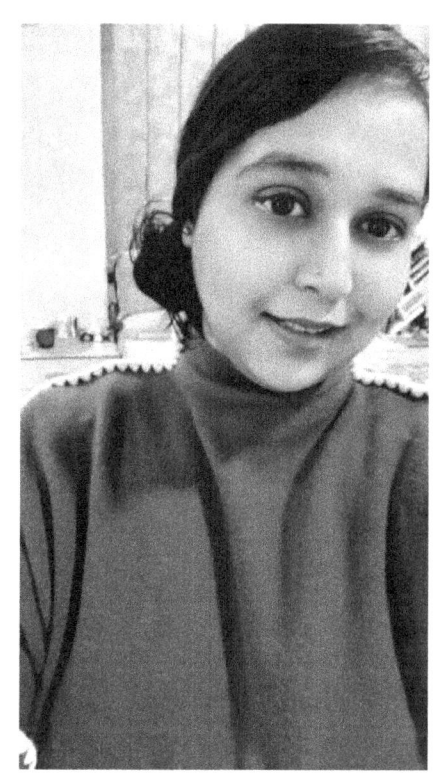

Sanjoli Mahajan, the creative mind behind Doodles by SM, is an artist, content creator, and stationery enthusiast who believes that a little creativity can go a long way. Known for turning everyday moments into charming illustrations, their signature style blends simplicity with cuteness, making art accessible and joyful for everyone.

With a growing community on Instagram and YouTube, Sanjoli shares relaxing doodles, ASMR coloring videos, and inspiring content that encourages people to express themselves—one tiny doodle at a time. How to Create 101 Fun Things is their debut book, born from a love of sketchbooks, soft lines, and the magic of turning blank pages into smiles.

When she is not doodling, she enjoys sipping coffee and spreading positivity through art

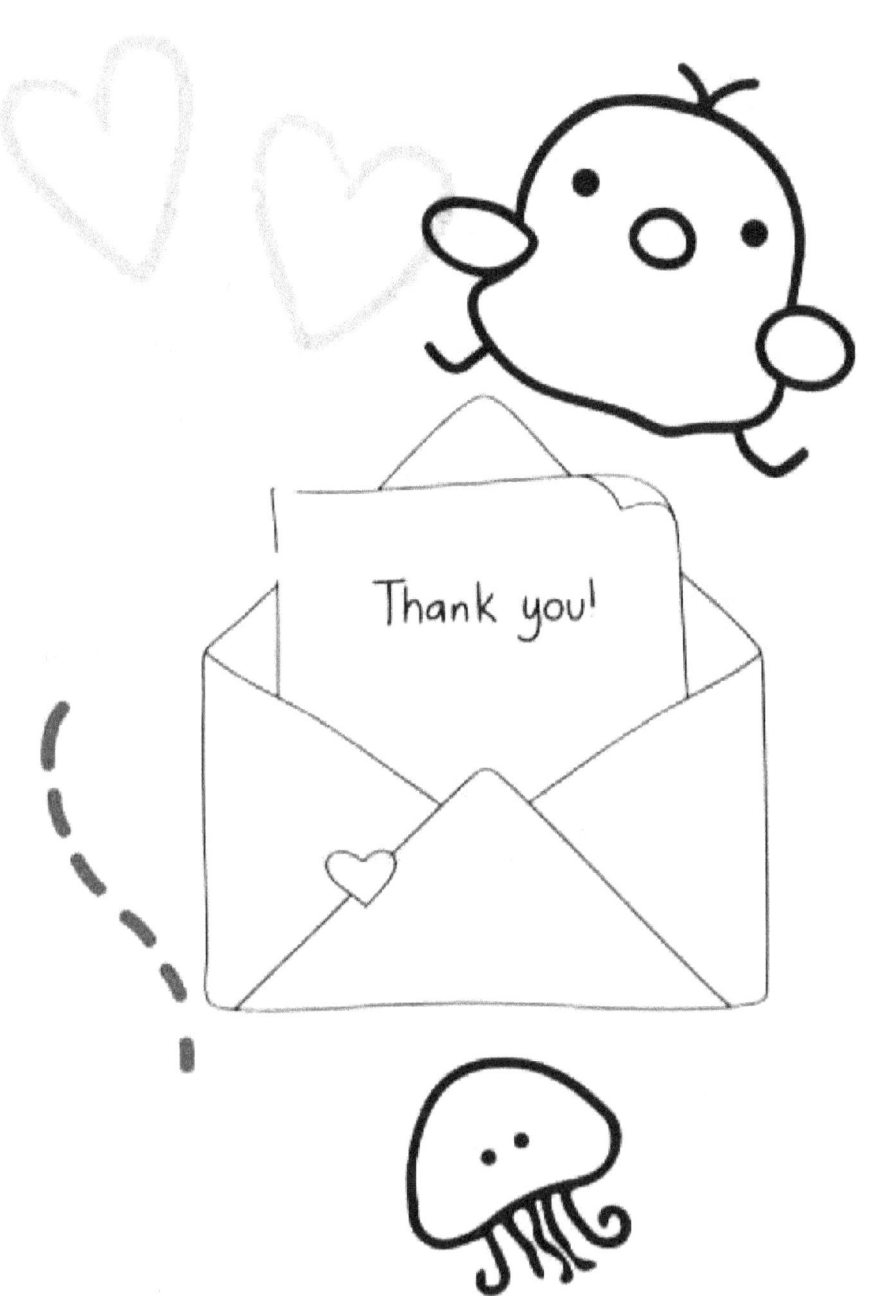